THE AIR LOOM GANG

ALSO BY MIKE JAY

AS AUTHOR:

EMPERORS OF DREAMS
BLUE TIDE

AS EDITOR:

ARTIFICIAL PARADISES
1900
UNDERWORLD OF THE EAST

THE
AIR LOOM
⸎ GANG ⸎

THE STRANGE AND TRUE
STORY OF
JAMES TILLY MATTHEWS
AND HIS VISIONARY MADNESS

MIKE JAY

Four Walls Eight Windows
New York

Copyright © 2003 by Mike Jay

Published in the United States by
Four Walls Eight Windows
39 West 14th Street
New York, NY 10011

http://www.4w8w.com

First edition April 2004.

This edition is published by arrangement with Transworld Publishers, a division of the
Random House Group Ltd. All rights reserved.

The right of Mike Jay to be identified as the author of this work has been asserted in accordance
with sections 77 and 78 of the Copyright Designs and Patents Act 1998.

Library of Congress Cataloging-in-Publication Data

Jay, Mike, 1959 Dec. 14–
The Air Loom gang : the strange and true story of James Tilly
Matthews and his visionary madness / Mike Jay. — 1st ed.
p. cm.
Includes bibliographical references and index.
ISBN: 1-56858-297-8
1. Matthews, James Tilly—Mental health. 2. Mentally
ill—England—Biography. 3. Mental illness—England—Case
studies. 4. Bethlem Royal Hospital (London, England)—History.
5. Haslam, John, 1764–1844. I. Title.

RC464.M379J39   2004
616.89'0092—dc22
[B]
2003069141

10 9 8 7 6 5 4 3 2 1

Printed in the United States

A TALE OF THE
MADNESS OF POLITICS
AND THE
POLITICS OF MADNESS

4/30/04   24.00

CONTENTS

ACKNOWLEDGEMENTS

I'D LIKE TO THANK MANY PEOPLE FOR THEIR TIME, HELP, THOUGHTS
and encouragement on this project, including Edward Bramah,
Tim Burns, Grant Carlin, Tony Creedon, Ben Goldacre,
Nicholas Goodrick-Clarke, Marie-Andrée Guyot at the Archives
des Affaires Etrangères in Paris, Greg Hollingshead, Andrew
Lott at London Metropolitan Archive, David Mander at
Hackney Borough Archives, Antonio Melechi, Sharon
Messenger, Frances Morgan, Liz Parrett, Mark Pilkington, Bob
Rickard, Paul Sieveking, Susanna Thomas at Cardiff Local
Studies Library, Trevor Turner and Peter Lamborn Wilson.

I'd also like to offer special thanks to the following people:
my agent Andrew Lownie and editor Simon Thorogood for
their enthusiasm and persistence in making this book a reality;
Colin Gale and Patricia Alleridge at the Bethlem Royal
Hospital Archive, impeccable custodians of the James Tilly
Matthews legacy; Robert Howard at the Institute of Psychiatry
for his great generosity both with his professional insights
and his own extensive research on Matthews and Haslam; and
Louise Burton and Michael Neve, for their patience
and encouragement from beginning to end.

Finally, I'm extremely sorry that my thanks to Roy Porter
must be offered posthumously. Roy was more responsible than

anyone for rescuing the James Tilly Matthews case from obscurity, and he published many of its essential texts in a superb critical edition. He retained an enduring affection for the story, and made typically valuable contributions to it in several of his later works.

LIST OF ILLUSTRATIONS

1

THE AIR LOOM

'In some apartment near London Wall, there is a gang
of villains profoundly skilled in Pneumatic Chemistry . . .'
John Haslam, *Illustrations of Madness*, 1810

ON 30 DECEMBER 1796, ONE MAN WAS ON A UNIQUE MISSION – AND
in unique and unprecedented jeopardy. His mission was taking
him through the packed thoroughfares of London, the world's
only city of a million inhabitants, to the House of Commons,
the most public place in Britain where truth, once spoken,
could not be ignored. The jeopardy, by contrast, emanated
from the most private place in London: an underground cellar
concealed somewhere beneath the paving, cobbles and pipes of
the central streets whose existence was, as far as he knew, a
secret to everyone but him.

The House of Commons at that time was not Augustus Pugin
and Charles Barry's Victorian gothic icon of today but, in the
words of a disappointed German visitor in 1782, 'rather a
mean-looking building, that not a little resembles a chapel'.
This is because it was a chapel, a plain, stone, single-celled
building with a steeply sloping roof, a Tudor adjunct to the
Palace of Westminster which had been co-opted as the House

The House of Commons in the eighteenth century

of Commons chamber over two centuries earlier and still served its new secular ministers. It stood in a courtyard, surrounded by the palace's other buildings – the Law Courts, the House of Lords – and backing on to the Thames, where Westminster Steps teemed with river traffic, a mêlée of barges and passengers, goods and traders.

He approached the House seemingly unnoticed, yet he was well aware that it would nonetheless require a powerful effort of will for him to reach it. There was no-one pursuing him, and no-one to block his way. But neither of these was necessary to engender the jeopardy he faced, which was generated by something new both to science and to history: a machine which operated invisibly, from a distance, and with irresistible force.

He knew that, in the darkness of its basement cellar, the machine was in operation. Although the cellar was dank and airless, the windmill sails that powered the device were turning slowly, filling it with its mysterious charge. Its rows of hooped brass barrels hissed quietly, conspiratorially, as their chambers began to fill with pressurized gases. Its wooden levers creaked as the warp of its central loom was tensed by magnetic currents.

He entered the House of Commons. Inside, its origins as a chapel were unmistakable: a single vaulted space, with ante-chapel and chapel separated by a screen into lobby and debating chamber. The Speaker, in a huge wig with two knotted tresses, sat on a raised dais behind the former altar with the gilt sceptre lying upon it, backlit by three arched windows. The members' benches, covered with green cloth, were the old stalls, crammed in a steep rake into an area little larger than a tennis court. Above them, the only modern improvement: Christopher Wren's gallery, more raked seats set into the walls fifteen feet up, where visitors could take their chances on finding a space between the members who over-flowed into these higher perches.

In the cellar, the machine was building towards full power.

Its gases and fluids agitated ever more intensely, producing a muffled cacophony of swishing and crashing sounds like ocean turbulence in a subterranean cavern. The smell was foul beyond belief, noxious gases and corrosive acids ripped apart and recombined in the magnetic flux. 'Factitious airs' – gases that had never existed naturally – hissed ominously into life, jets of pressure forcing them through tube valves, sending them out like sightless eels into their new world. A pair of gloved hands worked in silence, modulating the keys on the machine like organ stops, focusing an invisible force out through the cellar's solid stone walls and down the London streets, where it passed without resistance through houses and crowds, infallibly seeking out its target.

As he climbed the steep, crowded stairs to the public gallery, the man began to feel a turbulence in the air around him, and a probing pressure around his mouth, sucking at his breath. He could taste copper in his saliva. He knew what this meant: the bellows on the machine's controls were being delicately primed, feeling for the rhythm of his breathing and attempting to synchronize with it. Each time he filled his lungs he felt a little more of the magnetic fluid seeping into them, into his bloodstream and brain. Each breath dulled his mind a little, like a shadow passing over the sun.

But he also knew what to do. He opened his mouth and held his breath for as long as he could, then took in a sharp, unexpected draught of air. The lever of the bellows, at its lowest arc, was raised immediately, but the magnetic fluid seeped out too slowly to reach him. The machine, he had discovered, could be temporarily fooled in this way. He expelled the breath from his lungs sharply, sucked it in again immediately and held his mouth wide open, like a suffocating fish. He could hear a faint, frustrated hissing around him as it searched again for his rhythm. The people on the stairs looked at him oddly, so he clutched his chest in a pantomime of asthmatic attack.

He reached the public gallery and jostled his way into

earshot and towards a seat. Both House and gallery were packed. A random visit would likely have found members stretched out on benches, cracking nuts, eating oranges, sleeping or gossiping. But today there were nearly three hundred MPs in attendance for a debate that would surely be crucial to the nation's political future.

Since the execution of Louis XVI on 21 January 1793, Revolutionary France and Britain had been locked in a costly and exhausting war. Over the last four years, France had changed more than Britain had in the whole of the last century. The Revolution had made it a pariah state, and its monarchist neighbours had quickly begun manoeuvring to invade and partition it. In 1793 it had taken the offensive, blazing into war under the leadership of Jacques-Pierre Brissot and his Girondin faction, who were now long forgotten, purged and guillotined. By then, every sign of the old France was being deliberately expunged. The calendar had been changed: 1792 was now Year One. The monarchy had been dismembered, both figuratively and literally. 'Terror' had been proclaimed the order of the day, the old tiers of authority bloodily demolished, all power handed over to a suspicious, brutalized and implacable people. Then the architects of this new dispensation, Robespierre and the Jacobins, had themselves been purged and guillotined. Now, France had invaded Italy under a young General Bonaparte. Who was Britain actually at war with? And who had the power to end it?

The political earthquake across the Channel had rocked Britain, too. The fall of the Bastille in 1789 had been warmly welcomed by many, rather like the collapse of the Berlin Wall two centuries later: the French people had liberated themselves from a corrupt tyranny which had clung to power for too long. Londoners had donned red revolutionary bonnets, and greeted each other as 'citizen' in the streets. Poets such as William Wordsworth had rushed to the scene and proclaimed the glories of the new dawn. With its monarchy still intact but its despotic wings clipped, France seemed to have achieved the sort of enlightened, civilized transition into modernity the Glorious Revolution had brought to England almost exactly a century earlier.

But within months the Revolution had moved on into darker, more turbulent and uncharted waters, and the mainstream of British opinion had abruptly withdrawn its warm welcome. The Republic had ushered in a new politics, with a new language of 'left' and 'right'. Those in the French revolutionary assemblies who wished to consolidate its more moderate reforms took to sitting on the right of the president's chair; those pressing towards total revolution took up positions on the left. It was the left who had won, allying themselves with the Paris mob who resisted with protest and violence any attempt to allow those in power to maintain their unequal advantages.

The victory of the French left had been counterbalanced by a British lurch to the right. The Whigs, broadly in favour of further democratic reform and perhaps an eventual republic, had been split by the defection of one of their leading lights, Edmund Burke, to the monarchist cause. Burke's book, *Reflections on the Revolution in France*, had laid out for the first time the philosophical foundations of the new 'right-wing' politics. All convulsive, violent, revolutionary change was bad; God, King, aristocracy, tradition and private property were the *sine qua non* of a functional state. The Revolution was bound to end in tears.

Burke's *Reflections* was published in 1790, within a year of the fall of the Bastille. It immediately drew sharp responses from the left, including the towering bestseller of the age, Thomas Paine's *The Rights of Man*, a polemic against Burke's appeal to hidebound tradition and a clarion-call to trust the people to forge a new republican democracy. Burke was mocked as yesterday's man, the voice of the past, a crabby, superstitious reactionary who saw sinister conspiracies where others saw common sense and equal rights. But just a few months later, events seemed to be proving Burke's analysis horribly accurate. The French Revolution had developed an unstoppable, ghoulish momentum. With all tradition swept away, violence bred more violence, bloody purges of whole classes of society. Equality was no longer a noble principle but a cold-blooded justification for the execution of one set of leaders after another. When the King himself was guillotined, it was clear this was no Glorious Revolution along enlightened British lines; rather, it was a flashback to the barbarism and mutually assured destruction of the English Civil War.

Now the Tories, the King's party, took firm control of British politics. The defection of Burke and his allies had turned the Whigs into a weakened rump. As well as left and right, another new language took centre stage: Terror and terrorism. The Prime Minister, William Pitt, introduced a raft of draconian anti-Terror legislation. The hard-won right of habeas corpus was reined in, allowing suspected revolutionaries to be interned without trial. A Treasonable Practices Bill banned political agitation of all sorts, including the 'corresponding societies', networks of campaigners for liberty and democracy that had bloomed in recent years, inspired by Paine's *Rights of Man*. These 'gagging bills' were directed against the threat not just from France but also from Ireland, where the fall of the Bastille had occasioned much public rejoicing and boosted the cause of Irish independence. The Society of United Irishmen was declared a terrorist organization, turning Irish republicanism into a revolutionary cause for the first time. The Post Office began secretly to open mail from France, Ireland and the corresponding societies. Lurid and uncorroborated stories of Jacobin atrocities were leaked daily from the Foreign Office to the newspapers. Spies were despatched to infiltrate groups suspected of republican sympathies.

There were many who felt that this crackdown was a cynical power-grab. Britain, after all, was no corrupt and decadent monarchy as France had been, and the alarm that revolution might spread across the Channel was not so much a genuine threat as an excuse to stifle dissent and create 'a nation of self-appointed policemen'. The leading Whig, Charles James Fox, fought the new gagging bills bitterly, warning Pitt that 'you may prevent men from complaining but you cannot prevent them from feeling'. But the Jacobin menace had the effect of polarizing British opinion. From 1793 onwards, all democratic or republican views ran the risk of being labelled 'Jacobin' and prosecuted for treason, with its grim medieval sentence of public hanging, drawing and quartering. Thomas Paine was declared a traitor, burned in effigy by 'Church and King' mobs and forced to flee the country for his life.

Despite the alarm at the savagery across the Channel, it had recently emerged that a plan for peace with the French leaders had been hatched. On Boxing Day, King George III had revealed that secret peace negotiations had been running in parallel with the military conflict. The message he had to communicate, though, was that these negotiations were over. His secretary had announced that 'it is with the utmost concern that His Majesty acquaints the House of Commons that his earnest endeavours to effect the restoration of peace with France have been unhappily frustrated'. Along with this announcement, the secretary had delivered a package of letters detailing the secret negotiations, and 'the said papers were ordered to lie upon the table, to be perused by the members of the House'. They had been there for the last four days, and now they were to be debated.

The papers comprised exchanges between the British government and the Directory of the Republic of France, and comments upon them by the Cabinet. They revealed that in March 1796 the British ambassador to Switzerland had sounded out the French Directory on the possibility of ending the war, and had been told that France 'ardently desires a just, honourable and solid peace'. Much diplomatic shuffling had ensued: the confidential briefing of neutral powers, and the eventual appointment of a German dignitary, Count Wedel Jarlsberg, for negotiations with France. But the Count had been kept waiting in Paris for three days, the Directory refusing to meet him. Another flurry of communiqués; yes, France still desired peace. This time Lord Malmesbury was appointed directly by the government to negotiate. The French, in turn, appointed their Foreign Minister, Charles Delacroix.

Malmesbury and Delacroix had finally met in October. Malmesbury's opening gambit was couched in magnanimous terms: it asked for no restitution or financial compensation, simply an acknowledgement that France's 'conquests on the continent of Europe', notably the Netherlands, were 'essentially implicated' with British interests and needed to be discussed as part of the peace proposal. But to the French this was incendiary arrogance, a request not for peace but for surrender. Delacroix replied that 'the Executive Directory sees with pain' that Britain had no interest in seeking a just peace, but was simply pursuing war by other means. Malmesbury was outraged: these were 'offensive and injurious insinuations', 'only calculated to throw new obstacles in the way' of honest negotiation. After six months of diplomatic slow dancing, the first exchange was an explosion of mistrust and self-righteous fury.

More demands had flown from both sides. French troops out of Italy; a French peace with Germany and Russia; Britain to surrender its conquests in the West Indies and Newfoundland; all territorial claims to be restored to *status ante bellum*, before the war. In the commentary letters between Malmesbury and the Leader of the Lords, Lord Grenville, the gloss was spelled out: the French had simply been fishing for military intelligence under the guise of wanting peace. Every time the British had made an offer, Delacroix had moved the goalposts. He had asked if the British were prepared to surrender their colonies, and then 'affected to treat any restoration of territories as quite impractical'.

The man in the gallery watched as the Speaker called for silence for the Debate on the King's Message Respecting the Rupture of the Negotiation with France to begin. He opened the floor to the Prime Minister, William Pitt. Pitt, instantly recognizable with his milky aristocratic features – weak chin, thin nose, fair curls – rose to speak. From his opening sentence, which effortlessly built hanging clause upon hanging clause, it was clear that he would, as usual, be on his feet for some considerable time. 'I am perfectly aware, Sir, that in rising upon the present occasion, that the motion which I shall have the honour to propose to the House in consequence of His Majesty's most gracious message, and founded upon the papers on which it was accompanied, involves many great and important considerations . . .'

The man in the gallery knew Pitt. He had met with him in private session, though there was no question that Pitt would now deny it. But he also knew that this was not really Pitt speaking. As the Prime Minister's chest rose and fell with magisterial rhythm, he sensed the bellows breathing from afar. Pitt was under the control of the machine.

Many had suspected that the political disasters of the past few years had a hidden cause. The bloodiness of French mob rule was something unnatural, irrational, something which had never been seen before. How had they been so clinically manipulated against their own civilized interests? How had the Terror erupted from such humane and enlightened beginnings? Burke and the religious right had suspected all manner of conspiracies: the Jacobin clubs were fronts for some deeper organization, dedicated and invisible puppetmasters behind the scenes, the Freemasons or the Bavarian Illuminati. But the man in the gallery knew that the strings were being manipulated not by men alone, but by the Air Loom.

The Air Loom had been constructed by the Jacobins in Paris

around the time of their *coup d'état* in 1793. Just as they had corrupted republican ideals to their despotic ends, so had they corrupted republican science. The secret of its power was pneumatic chemistry, the chemistry of invisible elements recently christened 'gases', a science that had been developed by some of the greatest geniuses of the Revolution. Its prophets had been explicit that the new science would eventually provide the means for the people to seize power from the old elite; Burke had railed against it, comparing the revolutionary spirit to the scientists' 'wild gas', unnatural and uncontrollable. And, as the world turned, the pneumatic chemists had paid a heavy price. The great British pioneer Joseph Priestley, a leading republican sympathizer, had recently had his laboratory in Birmingham razed to the ground by loyalist mobs as the police stood by and watched. His French counterpart Antoine Lavoisier had suffered worse: his passion for enlightened reform had secured him a post in the early republican administration, but he had been denounced in the Jacobin press by the jealous failed scientist Jean-Paul Marat, and had been purged and guillotined. The judge had pronounced that 'the Republic has no need of scientists'; the truth was that they had their machine, and needed his science no longer.

The Air Loom's power was pneumatic, but its effects were accomplished by harnessing the mysterious magnetism which ran through all living things, a technique popularized in pre-Revolutionary France by the Viennese doctor Franz Anton Mesmer. Mesmerism could cure disease, twist and constrict the body, and control the speech and brain, all without the subject even being aware of it. The Air Loom used its pneumatic force to expand these powers far beyond those of even the most skilled human mesmerist. Man had made a machine that could turn men themselves into machines.

It was the Air Loom that was now filling the Prime Minister's lungs with magnetic airs and his mouth with

William Pitt the Sleepwalker (James Gillray)

sonorous, pre-scripted verbiage. Pitt's eyes were waxy; his frame sagged like dead meat inside his clothes. Others had noticed this: the cartoonist James Gillray had recently lampooned Pitt as a sleepwalker, with nightshirt and candle, mesmerized by the war with France. But only one man knew that he was really mesmerized by a machine. The Prime Minister was a pneumatic puppet, programmed to maintain the line that war with France was inevitable and irreversible.

Pitt spoke for nearly three hours. He proposed that MPs should 'return His Majesty the thanks of the House for his most gracious message'. He attributed the breakdown in negotiations to 'the pride, the ambition, the obstinacy, and the arrogant pretensions of the enemy'. He discoursed at length about the Netherlands, Santo Domingo, the Treaty of Utrecht. He concluded, eventually, that 'the calamities of war can be imputed only to the unjust and exorbitant views of His Majesty's enemies'.

When the Prime Minister sat down, finally deflated, Thomas Erskine rose to lead the Whig opposition. Politicians and public sat forward eagerly. Pitt's message, even for those who knew nothing of the Air Loom, had been entirely predictable: war was a patriotic necessity. But Erskine promised something a great deal more incendiary. A wild-eyed and passionate Scot, he was not only a parliamentary reformer but a personal enemy of Pitt and, in the words of his Tory opponents, 'outrageously French'. He had long favoured a peaceful entente between France and Britain; he had even defended the traitorous republican Tom Paine. How far would he take the opposition's case? Would he go further than disputing the Foreign Office's story? Would he personally criticize the King?

No-one was listening more eagerly than the man in the gallery.

It was clear from his opening sentence that Erskine wasn't about to disappoint. He took issue immediately not only with Pitt's position, but with the King's account of the actions that had prompted it. Instead of 'binding the House to an engagement to His Majesty to prosecute the war with vigour', he suggested that we should have the courage to tell a less partisan and more honest story. And that this story should begin with an examination of how the war actually started.

The man in the gallery gasped, then held his mouth open, starving himself of breath. He felt the Air Loom's current pass over him, sweep down and seek out Erskine. As he released his breath cautiously, he heard the faintest of sighs echo around the speaker. It had found him.

Erskine, unaware, continued to speak the unspeakable. There had been peace negotiations before, in 1793, just after the war had begun. But 'at that time the correspondence between Lord Grenville and the French ambassador was concealed from the House'. It was presumptuous to present these recent diplomatic exchanges to the House and expect this gesture to be taken as proof of His Majesty's transparency and honesty, especially since the documents did little but lay the blame at the door of the French Directory. What about the government's own cynical intrigues, which had been instrumental in starting the war in the first place?

The man in the gallery knew it was only a matter of time. This was the heart of the story, in which he himself had played a leading role. There had been no need for war; he himself had carried Britain's terms of peace to the Republican Assembly in Paris, and they had accepted them. But Pitt's government had betrayed him, and the nation. The fiction of a just war with France could not survive the truth about the man's diplomatic mission. Here lay the act of sabotage which had truly engineered the war four years ago, until this moment a treasonable secret.

But neither could Erskine survive the power of the machine. The sails were thrumming in the cellar now, blasting out the rays which focused on the speaker like sunbeams through a lens. Erskine continued nonetheless. Pitt's main bone of contention was the Netherlands, but, he reminded the House, at the time when Britain declared war not even Belgium was yet in French possession . . .

An almost invisible turbulence rippled the air around him. Erskine's hands went to his neck; his breath froze in his throat. In the cellar, the gloved hands were twisting a brass cylinder, constricting the muscle fibres at the base of Erskine's tongue. He stood motionless and silent, the House gazing on un-comprehendingly. As the mechanism tightened, he staggered, and fell heavily back into his seat. He gasped, unable to fill the vacuum that ruled his throat. He could offer neither apology nor explanation. *Hansard*, in a short and mysterious paren-thesis, would merely record that

[Here Mr. Erskine suddenly stopped, and, after a pause, sat down under evident symptoms of indisposition.]

In the crowded floor and gallery, there was only one man who understood what was going on. He even knew its name: this trick was called 'fluid locking'.

Gradually, a hubbub of whispers. A consensus quickly developed that Erskine had fallen suddenly ill. In his place, quieting the growing commotion, rose the Whig veteran Charles James Fox. Fox was Pitt's great sparring partner: he had welcomed the storming of the Bastille as 'by far the greatest and best thing that has ever happened in the history of the world', and they had thundered at each other ever since across the bitter divide stoked by the Revolution, the new chasm between left and right. He was also Pitt's physical opposite: burly frame, coarse features, blue-stubbled chin, bushy eye-brows. Where Pitt usually dressed in court clothes, complete with lace and sword – either having just visited the King or encouraging members to assume that he had – Fox was well known as the scruffiest man in the House, his blue frock coat and buff waistcoat shiny and threadbare with age. Famously

THE AIR LOOM GANG

dissolute, a heavy gambler and a hard drinker, his passion for reform and republicanism had long since cast him as either hero or traitor: champion of the rights of man, or collaborator in the holocaust of Terror across the Channel.

Fox apologized in advance for his lack of preparation, having been so unexpectedly called to the box; he commiserated with the House for having had to sit through three hours of Pitt's 'bellicose rhetoric', and then proceeded to speak for three and a half. He began by concurring with Erskine: if we had not been seduced by our partisan loyalty to the monarchy, we should have sued for peace years ago. Britain had been fighting 'a war of passion and prejudice, not of policy and self-defence'.

The man in the gallery felt the Air Loom hanging back, its rays dancing around Fox like a swaying snake, ever ready to strike. But, throughout the hours that followed, Fox made not a single mention of the secret peace mission of 1793. Did he know nothing? Or did he know too much? He was permitted to attack the King, and to propose that he should not be congratulated for the fumbled peace negotiations. He was even allowed to conclude that 'we cannot help lamenting to Your Majesty the rashness and injustice of Your Majesty's ministers'.

Fox finally resumed his seat, and the debate continued with further statements from the Cabinet. Members of Parliament began to mill around and vacate the benches, knowing from long experience that the main parade had now gone by. Lord Grenville, the Leader of the Lords, gave his brief statement, regretting the rupture but insisting it was not the government's fault.

But the moment for which the man in the gallery was waiting had not yet arrived. It did so when Lord Liverpool stood to make his statement. It was Liverpool whom the man knew best; Liverpool with whom he had conducted the most secret negotiations; Liverpool for whom he had risked his life, and who had finally presented him with the cold face of betrayal.

And it was Liverpool who was now trying to inflame the war with France for his most monstrous ends.

Robert Banks Jenkinson, Lord Liverpool, was not a man who aroused passions in many of the other spectators. His smooth rise to government by the age of twenty-one had been widely predicted; his father, now Earl of Liverpool, had been in Pitt's Cabinet and he himself had been groomed as a statesman from an early age. His speeches were mocked for their mimicry of Pitt's style, and his traditional causes – opposing the abolition of slavery, pushing new bills against sedition and treason – were selected with an eye for the mainstream of his party which would eventually see him reach the rank of Prime Minister. On the French question, he was clearest of all. He had been an eye-witness to the fall of the Bastille, and a diehard anti-republican from that moment on; he had defended British aggression against Dunkirk and Toulon in 1794, and had even urged later that year that the British army should march on Paris.

Liverpool's statement contained no surprises. What Britain had offered to France, he asserted, was a fair equivalent to what we had asked them to give up. There were not the slightest grounds for the Directory to have terminated negoti-ations so abruptly. Having already heard three hours of this from Pitt, there were few who were paying close attention to their dull echo. Which is perhaps why the machine now became so sharply aware of the man in the gallery.

As he stared down at Lord Liverpool, the man felt a new rhythm to his own breathing. The bellows were taking control of his chest, like an incoming tide. He had lost concentration; the rays had found him. The air inside his lungs was reaching into his vitals, moulding itself into spectral fingers, twisting his guts into spasm. Liverpool continued, untroubled by the machine's attention, for he was already doing its bidding. It was clear from the King's Message, he insisted, that the French, 'far from desiring peace, were determined that the negotiations should never arrive at that stage . . .'

A flash of panic brought the man in the gallery to his senses. There was a babble of ghostly voices audible now inside his own head, a distant hubbub, but soon one of the voices would be selected to become the commanding force which had held Pitt in its thrall. This was the moment at which, in the full force of the Air Loom's rays, he could see reflected dimly in his head the dripping walls of the cellar, the machine itself, and the gang of seven who controlled it. Into focus came the sharp, pock-marked face of the operator, whom he knew only as the Glove Woman. Behind her, inspecting her work, loomed the gang's leader, Bill the King. His attendance was a sign that this was an important operation. Bill was growing impatient with the Glove Woman; in a couple of years, for the attempted assassination of George III at the theatre, he would take the controls himself. Behind the Air Loom, as ever, sat Jack the Schoolmaster, a sly smile on his face, taking detailed notes with one hand and pushing his wig back from his forehead with the other. The rest of the gang were lost in the shadows, but he could hear Sir Archy's coarse guffaws, and The Middle Man muttering his mantra: 'Yes, he is the talisman.'

As the man's breath rose and fell in sympathy with the machine, he realized that these were the last few moments that his voice would be his own. He knew from experience that, once he could see the gang, they had him trapped in their sights. He was ensnared, past any hope of escape. A rasping intake of breath, a grimace, a spasm, then a single word exploded from the gallery.

'TREASON!'

Only one word but, as he knew, more effective than the most eloquent speech. This was the one word guaranteed to bring the business of the House to a standstill; it had been the grounds for so many duels that the Speaker had recently had to protest against the trend. Even today, any man convicted of treason is forbidden ever to stand for election, sit or vote in either House again.

Stewards rushed into the public gallery to confront the man who had spoken. They found a traumatized-looking individual, agitated, shabbily dressed. He was arrested and escorted to Bow Street Magistrates Court.

After this brief commotion, the business of the House was resumed. The Whig motion to censure the King and his ministers for the Rupture of Negotiations with France was crushed by 212 votes to 37. Charles James Fox was so distraught by the result that he came close to abandoning politics. The last serious attempt to find an entente with the new Republic had lost political ground which it would never be able to recover. The war would grind on for six more years before a drained and bankrupt Britain finally sued for peace.

The peacemakers had lost, and the Air Loom had won.

2

BEDLAM

---

*'They called me mad, and I called them mad,
and damn them, they outvoted me.'*
Nathaniel Lee, admitted to Bedlam in 1684

AT BOW STREET MAGISTRATES COURT THE FOLLOWING FACTS WERE established. The man's name was James Tilly Matthews. He was a pauper of the south London parish of Camberwell. He had a wife and young family. He appeared to be of unsound mind.

He was transferred to a secure workhouse at Tothill Fields – modern King's Cross – and an examination was made of his state of mind, and why he had 'cried out Treason in the House'. He explained that he had been involved in a top-secret diplomatic mission to turn the politics of Europe on its head by negotiating peace between England and France, and that he had been dealing at the highest level with both governments. He had had secret meetings with Pitt, with Lord Liverpool, and with the French foreign ministers Brissot and Le Brun. He had been backwards and forwards between England and France four times, but had never received any reward for his labours, not even his travelling expenses.

Over the following years the facts of Matthews' case, his madness or his sanity, would be investigated in more detail than that of any suspected lunatic in history. Arguments for both sides would be rehearsed by doctors and lawyers, judges and governors, family and friends and other witnesses, who would produce a torrent of affidavits and contradictory testimonies as to his state of mind. But this initial claim after his arrest, that he had been involved with the British and French governments on a secret, high-level political peace mission, would only ever be discussed as evidence of his mental condition. None of them would ever consider that it might have been true.

Every word of it was. Matthews' shout of treason in the House was no random outburst of lunacy, but the last act in an astonishing adventure, one which might indeed have changed the history of Europe. But, by this point, there was no-one left to confirm the truth of his story. Most of the witnesses were dead, and those who had survived were quite definitely not talking.

But the medical diagnosis was understandable in the light of Matthews' further claims, which placed him – implausibly, to say the least – centre stage in the political intrigues following the French Revolution. The Committee of Public Safety, which enforced martial law under the Jacobins, had apparently been set up for the specific purpose of intercepting Matthews' letters. In Britain, the Traitorous Correspondence Bill had been passed for the same purpose. In Flanders, the Duke of York had commanded his army to make 'various marches and countermarches to beset him', all with the sole intention of handing Matthews over to the enemy as a spy. But the Duke of York, marching his men up the hill and down again, was by no means the prime mover in the plot. It was, in fact, the King of Prussia who, according to Matthews, was 'at the bottom of a deep scheme by which the Duke of York was to have been made King of France'. The Duke and the King had even 'formed a plan of destroying General Washington & to have divided America into two monarchies'.

Not only did James Tilly Matthews know of these plots, the politicians knew he knew. According to the doctors who examined him after his arrest, the reason he gave for his outburst was that 'when he called out Treason in the House of Commons they durst not arrest him lest he should discover the author of the plot'. The information he held was, he believed, too sensitive to risk letting him reveal what he knew. But, unfortunately for Matthews, the laws on lunacy intervened before any member of Parliament was forced to risk exposure. The Act of 1714 allowed for dangerous lunatics to be restrained and confined on the opinion of a medical practitioner, and this *force majeure* intervened before Lord Liverpool or any other politician was obliged to give an account of himself.

After their initial assessment of his condition, the Bow Street magistrates recommended that the patient was a lunatic whose liberty was a danger to the public safety, and who should consequently be committed to an asylum.

As a pauper, the obvious destination for James Tilly Matthews was the leading charitable asylum in London, the Bethlem Hospital, already long known in popular slang as Bedlam. It had accepted dangerous and insane paupers as 'objects of charity' ever since its founding, and was proud of the claim that it had never turned anyone away. All it asked when patients were admitted was that their parish entered into a bond of a hundred pounds to cover their clothing, their removal when discharged or their burial when dead. The parish of Camberwell was approached by the Bow Street magistrates 'to enter into the usual Bond' for Matthews, and they concurred.

The formalities of admission were relatively few. The standard form, *Procedures for the Admission of Patients into Bethlem Hospital*, required responses to only four questions:

1. Patient's name and age
2. How long distracted? – Whether ever so before? – Whether strong enough to undergo a course of physic?
3. Whether melancholy, raving or mischievous?
4. The Patient's present legal settlement? – How many church-wardens and overseers are there in the parish?

Once these were answered, a certificate was signed and sealed by the churchwardens of the parish in the presence of two witnesses, and sent for the attention of the Bethlem Governors Subcommittee, which met every Saturday morning. The week after its approval the patient could be admitted. And thus it was that on 28 January 1797, less than a month after the episode in the House of Commons, James Tilly Matthews entered Bedlam.

There's little doubt that the same judgement would be made today: Matthews was mad. These days we would phrase it more carefully – 'suffering from acute mental illness' – but that begs rather too many questions at this stage. Let us persist with the term 'mad', not in any derogatory sense but merely in the interests of historical accuracy and plain speaking. It was the term current at the time, and is still perfectly well understood.

As well as the diagnosis, the procedure for dealing with Matthews would also be surprisingly similar. Creating a disturbance in the public gallery of the House of Commons would lead to arrest and, if the police determined that the subject was sufficiently dangerous, detention under Section 136 of the 1983 Mental Health Act and a twenty-four-hour arraignment under medical care where his condition would be assessed by a psychiatrist. The psychiatrist would attempt to calm him down, using anti-anxiety and anti-psychotic drugs if necessary, and examine his state of mind to see if his thinking was delusional.

The Air Loom, if Matthews revealed its existence under questioning, would now be recognized immediately as a classic paranoid delusion. But in 1797 it was something which had never been encountered before, and it would emerge as the main *leitmotif* of a case which was unprecedented in almost every imaginable way. Subsequently, it would become one of the most celebrated delusions in medical history, and the first recorded example of an 'influencing machine': a fantastic device which sends messages and controls minds. For everyone who has since had messages beamed at them through their fillings, or their TV sets, or via high-tech surveillance, MI5, Masonic lodges or UFOs, James Tilly Matthews is Patient Zero.

The next task for today's psychiatrist would be to establish whether these delusions could be shaken or dismantled. But, as we shall see, Matthews was nothing if not tenacious. He had many reasons for persisting with his story, some very good ones among them. He was convinced that his mission could not possibly be of greater importance, that he was the only person capable of stopping Europe from destroying itself through war, and that he had no choice but to continue to attempt this by any means necessary. Apart from anything else, quite a lot of his story was true. Now, as then, most doctors would assume that his mental derangement was an adequate explanation for his wild claims. Few would consider the possibility that he might have become mad in the course of an adventure which was every bit as extraordinary as he said it was.

There's little doubt that, at the end of his twenty-four-hour assessment, Matthews would still be adjudged to be in the grip of a delusional crisis – in other words, psychotic. In this case he would now be detained under a Section 2, which would confine him to a mental institution for three months on a regime of anti-psychotic medication. If at the end of this period he still stuck to his story, and was unwilling to remain confined or to accept treatment – as he almost certainly would be – he would be put on a Section 3: compulsory detention with a review every six months. What would happen at this point is very hard to judge. Matthews was a mould-breaking patient who would push the eighteenth-century system to its limits, and how he would play his hand today is impossible to predict.

His eventual diagnosis is easier to guess. Today, once enough of his story had fallen into place, he would almost certainly be labelled a paranoid schizophrenic whose delusions had been precipitated by his obscure but clearly stressful adventures in Revolutionary France. In fact, many psychiatrists and historians have already diagnosed him as such. But retrospective diagnosis is a tricky business at the best of times, and schizophrenia is notoriously difficult to recover from history. There are remarkably few clear accounts prior to the nineteenth century of what we would now call schizophrenia – so few, in fact, that many have argued that the condition didn't even exist in former times. In 1987, an analysis of over two thousand cases of madness in sixteenth- and seventeenth-century England found only a handful whom we would today diagnose with schizophrenia. The disjunction between a past where it's so elusive and a present where it's so tragically common is so striking that many have concluded that schizophrenia must be a disorder spawned by the modern industrial age. Those with a Marxist bent have argued that it's an extreme manifestation of the alienation produced by division of labour in advanced capitalist societies; others have proposed that it's an organic disorder, possibly viral in origin, which spreads in proportion to population density.

There are, however, alternative explanations, which show how this disjunction between past and present could be an artefact of historical methods rather than a dramatic change in the human condition. The vast majority of cases of schizophrenia would never have been recorded. When they were, the language around them would be full of terms we no longer use

and have great difficulty translating into modern diagnostics –
frenzy, mania, folly, melancholia, idiocy, madness, fancy,
dotage, unreason. To look back before 1800 is to peer into
another world where the number of institutions for the mad
was a tiny fraction of today's, and what we would now call
mental disorders were often understood as religious ecstasies
or diabolical possessions. And historically, of course, no-one
was looking for the category of schizophrenia. It was only
around 1900, when the German psychiatrists Emil Kraepelin
and Eugen Bleuler witnessed the same patterns of behaviour in
patient after patient, that the new word was coined to describe
a disparate group of symptoms which had never been systematically associated before.

Even in the century since the term was coined, the exact
meaning of schizophrenia has proved uncomfortably slippery
and difficult to standardize. Broadly speaking, it's a form of
psychosis, thus a disorder characterized by delusions such as
hallucinations, hearing voices or believing that your mind is
controlled by a machine. But within this range there are many
diagnostic categories – schizophrenia, paranoia, paranoid
psychosis, schizo-affective disorder, paranoid schizophrenia –
which are still shifting in sense, being applied differently in
different cultures and being superseded by new formulations.
A survey of academic papers on schizophrenia in 1975 concluded that the term is too vague to comply with the usual
criteria of modern scientific usage. French psychiatrists, for
example, find the British definition too 'Cartesian', too rigid
and narrowly medical. The American and Russian definitions
of schizophrenia are almost unrecognizable as the same condition. In recent years, patients have tended to distance
themselves from the label, preferring to refer to their schizophrenia as a 'diagnosis' rather than an actual condition – and
many doctors are now following them.

Whether or not James Tilly Matthews suffered from schizophrenia, and whether or not it was a new illness, it seems that

something dramatic did happen to madness around 1800 – if not to the condition itself, then at least to the way in which it was understood. Sanity, and even reality, are defined by how we view madness, and reality was changing fast. Just as politics had developed a new orientation and a new language, and yesterday's moderate reform had become tomorrow's treason, so the context of madness, and thus madness itself, was altering. We may dub James Tilly Matthews the first case of modern schizophrenia, but perhaps this tells us less about the man himself than it does about the world around him. By the time Matthews had finished with Bedlam, the institution would have changed a great deal more than the patient.

Of course, outside the world of madness and psychiatry, an entirely different interpretation of Matthews' case is possible: that the Air Loom was real. As we shall see, there are those who still argue this today, though it's only fair to point out that they inhabit what are generally considered to be the crackpot fringes of conspiracy subculture. Yet the idea is undeniably tempting, and there are points in the story where it almost seems like the simplest explanation. Matthews is worryingly plausible as a man who, having discovered an incredible secret, attempts to make it known as clearly as possible and to deal with his adversities as rationally as he can. Of course, we can never technically prove the negative statement that the Air Loom didn't exist, nor can science yet offer a full explanation of exactly how imaginary machines can be created by neurological impairments and imbalances of brain chemistry. But to take the Air Loom literally is to close off the most interesting avenues of enquiry, avenues that suggest it was both less and more than a real machine, and that the truth is even stranger than the conspiracy theory.

Perhaps we can say that the Air Loom was real – but, at this point, only to James Tilly Matthews.

*

Bedlam, where the next act of Matthews' adventures unfolded, is the most famous madhouse – or lunatic asylum, or mental institution – there has ever been, and it always will be. Its image, still familiar, is as close to hell on earth as any in the Western imagination. This image, epitomized by the final painting in William Hogarth's series *The Rake's Progress*, was much the same in 1797 as it is today. Then, as now, the facts were rather different.

Bedlam, properly the Church of St Mary of Bethlehem, was founded in 1236 by Simon Fitzmary, an alderman who was twice Sheriff of London. The story goes that, while he was fighting in the Crusades, he became detached from his party and found himself wandering alone in the desert at night, lost behind Saracen lines. Casting around helplessly in the darkness of the Holy Land, he found a fixed point, a bright star over Bethlehem, which he followed to safety. On his return to London he gave thanks for salvation from his dark night of the soul by donating his land at St Botolph Without Bishopsgate – more or less the spot now occupied by Liverpool Street station – to the Church of St Mary to establish a priory.

A century later, the money from Fitzmary's bequest was beginning to dry up, and the priory petitioned the City of London for financial help. In exchange for funding, Bethlem was given over to twenty-four aldermen from the City, and the resident monks began to take in travellers and the infirm. By 1403 several resident guests of unsound mind had been recorded. In the following years bequests began to be made for the care of the sick and insane, and the 'succour of demented lunatics' is recorded on the 1437 Patent Roll, the medieval equivalent of a charitable mission statement.

This first incarnation of Bethlem came to an end in 1536 with the dissolution of the monasteries, but even if the monks were now surplus to requirements, the care of the mad was still a pressing concern. In 1546 Henry VIII gave the building and institution over entirely to the City of London, who continued

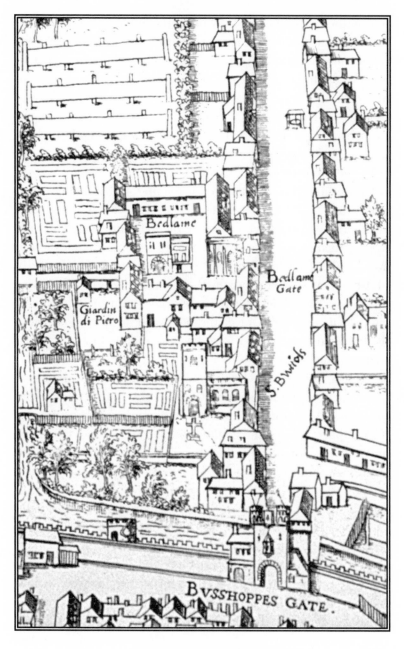

Bethlem at Bishopsgate

to use it to house the mentally disturbed poor. Conditions were extremely spartan and there was no attempt at treatment, but it was nevertheless (with the possible exception of a house in Toledo, Spain) the first public institution in Europe specifically dedicated to housing the mad. Nobody was turned away unless they had friends or relatives who were prepared to pay for private care, and patients could stay for a year, after which they were deemed either 'curable' or 'incurable', and were in either case released.

Up to this point, it was rare for the mad to be distinguished from the poor, the homeless, beggars, vagabonds, petty criminals and others who were unable to fit into society or take care of themselves. It was rare, too, for them to be locked up. We might (perhaps romantically) imagine James Tilly Matthews in this era having the protected status of a 'wise fool', possibly under the wing of some minister who might cherish his ability to speak the politically unspeakable. More likely, though, he would have been abandoned or mistreated with no means of redress. Typically the mad were mocked, scapegoated, locked up by their families and, above all, feared. Then, as now, madness posed terrible, often intractable social problems. On a practical level it was disruptive and destructive: it tore apart families and communities, it was costly to manage, and it brought with it the threat of shame, violence and suicide. And on a deeper level its very existence was at best uncomfortable, at worst terrifying to contemplate. It seemed to open a window on to the dark side of nature, to ask troubling questions about the human condition, and to compel the sane to band together against it to assert their own identity.

By the seventeenth century, the most visible mad people were 'Tom o'Bedlams', the Bedlam incurables, many of whom took to the road after their release, begging and being whipped on from village to village. The fear – or, in some cases, pity – they struck into those who saw them was noted by other beggars, many of whom copied them; gradually, the 'Tom o'Bedlam' became a specific type of beggar, dressed in rags and spouting gibberish. They rapidly came to outnumber the genuine Bedlamites, and Bethlem itself issued disclaimers pointing out that begging was not authorized by the hospital. Shakespeare's Tom o'Bedlam in *King Lear* – the subject of much retrospective diagnosis of schizophrenia – is Edgar in disguise, teasing us with the difficulty of distinguishing the genuine madman from the impostor.

The real Bedlam and its popular image were also, by this stage, beginning to diverge into quite separate entities. There was the hospital itself, but now there was also the proverbial world of the mad that shared its name. *King Lear* (1604–5) was followed by a fashion for setting scenes of plays in 'Bedlam'. Jacobean tragedies such as John Webster's *The Duchess of Malfi* (1612–13) and Middleton and Rowley's *The Changeling* (*c.*1622) use its name to set the scene for plays-within-plays and worlds-within-worlds where reality and fantasy are allowed to blur. Many of London's theatres were round the corner from Bishopsgate, and the real Bedlam was a familiar sight, but these representations were not seeking documentary realism so much as a kind of looking-glass world where the audience could suspend their disbelief, the characters could immerse themselves in a dark dream and the impossible could briefly seem to be true.

The next incarnation of Bedlam was forced on it by the Great Fire of London. The building wasn't destroyed, but many of its governors' residences were, and their owners were forced to move into it as temporary accommodation. A few days' hardship convinced them of a fact they had been able to ignore for centuries: with stone floors, no heating and no windows, it was completely inadequate for habitation. But this discovery offered an opportunity. The late seventeenth century had seen the beginning of a profitable 'trade in lunacy', where secluded accommodation was offered to the mad whose friends and relatives were prepared to pay. Boarding-houses and resident care homes were beginning to spring up, offering rooms and service – maids, attendants, doctors' visits. For the proprietors, this was a financially attractive option: most of the clients were on a long-stay basis, and they could refuse the troublesome minority. It was decided that Bethlem should be remodelled along these lines, and, befitting its status as the original and best-known madhouse in the land, the new building should be conceived with grandeur on a previously unimagined scale.

A site was chosen at Moorfields, just north of London Wall, and Robert Hooke, colleague of Christopher Wren and pioneering craftsman of microscopes and other scientific instruments, was hired to realize a building that would be both a monument to the institution's antiquity and a sales pitch to place it at the pinnacle of the new trend. What emerged, and what James Tilly Matthews would enter over a century later, was a madhouse in more senses than one. To indulge in a little retrospective diagnosis, it was schizophrenia in stone.

Its façade and grounds were almost impossibly grand: in the words of its first official history, 'an illustrious monument to British charity'. For all but the most wealthy, the first sight of the new Bedlam must have suggested that the new patients would be living in a splendour far greater than their sane relatives. The building was approached through an entrance gate whose stone piers were surmounted by a pair of famous and highly regarded statues depicting the twin images of 'Raving Madness' and 'Melancholy Madness'. These opened on to a palatial layout of tree-lined lawns and gardens networked with free-stone promenades. Behind them rose the astonishing façade, over five hundred feet long, modelled on the Tuileries Palace in Paris. Its portals were supported by Corinthian columns, above which its royal arms were carved in stone and embellished with wreaths of flowers. At its centre, a stone balustrade led the eye up to an octagonal turret crowned with a shining cupola. 'England's Bastille', as it

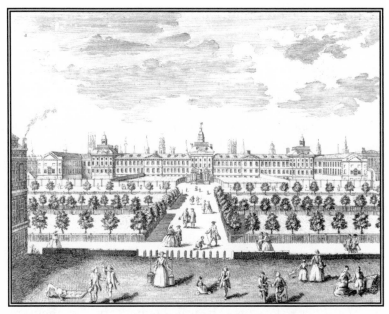

Bethlem at Moorfields

would later be known, looked more like England's Versailles.

But the face Bedlam presented to the world concealed a raw, gaping void that was little more than a ruin. For all the 'grace and ornament' of its exterior, it had literally no foundations. It had been erected on waste ground which had previously been the city ditch; six inches below the ground, the red brick gave way to rubble and loose landfill. Behind its palatial façade, the building had been thrown together with little more care than a theatre set. There were no ties between the different sections of the building; each of them tottered on its base of rubble in independent directions, rent by gaping cracks and rotting plaster. By the time of Matthews' arrival the roof, far too heavy on account of its decoration, had crushed the inadequate structure, bowing the walls, and the interior flooded whenever it rained. By the 1770s, the disaster had become a permanent crisis. The governors had allocated a few hundred pounds for repairs, but every patch and bodge revealed flaws which would cost thousands to fix. Plans were vague: a new site might be found, a grant from Parliament might solve the problem. Meanwhile, like the House of Usher, the edifice of madness sank deeper into the mire, and the symbolism of a façade of care concealing a black hole of neglect became ever harder to ignore.

The interior of Bedlam was as minimal as the exterior was extravagant. It was simply two galleries, one above the other, with individual cells running down each side. Iron gates in the centre divided the men from the women. The day-to-day running of the asylum was handled almost entirely by menial workers: basketmen, maidservants, cooks, washerwomen, gardeners, nightwatchmen. The care of the inmates was undertaken by keepers and attendants who had no special training but were uniformed in the blue 'charity worker' coats and dark round hats that can be seen in *The Rake's Progress*. It was compulsory for them to be resident in the hospitals, and to sleep on the wards.

The daily routine began with a breakfast of watery gruel, bread, butter and salt. The basketmen would cut the bread and butter, clean the men, assist them shaving and bathing,

Raving and Melancholy Madness

34

and 'attend' them, often with physical restraints, when they were being bled or given medicine. A matron supervised the nurses who performed the same tasks for the women. Further meals included meat three times a week – beef, pork, mutton or veal in prescribed servings of eight ounces. Non-meat days, known by the archaic nautical term 'banyan' days, supplemented bread and butter with rice-milk and cheese.

It was during the early life of this building that Bedlam first attracted the image that clings to it to this day. Around 1700 the superintendent, Richard Hale, decided that it would be good for the patients, and certainly for the treasurer, if visiting days were instituted during which the public could interact with the inmates for an admission fee of 2d. This proved popular but problematic. Crowds flocked to the new attraction, followed by fruit and nut sellers, pickpockets and, particularly, prostitutes: the Grub Street journalist Ned Ward's scurrilous guide book, *The London Spy*, claimed that 'a sportsman, at any hour of the day, may meet with game for his purpose'. Staff and patients pitched in, the Bedlam keepers providing beer in exchange for bribes and the patients selling poems and drawings (by 'genuine lunatics') to the visitors. Some patients would ask a penny for a song, usually being canny enough to demand the penny up front. This is probably the origin of the figure of speech, picking up a bargain 'for a song'.

Bedlam, the only public collection of mad people in the country, became proverbial for madness itself. But it also became something more, and something that still endures: a metaphor for the world outside its walls. This enduring image found its first memorable expression in Jonathan Swift's scabrous satire *A Tale of a Tub*, which features a digression on 'the use and improvement of madness in a commonwealth'. Bedlamites, Swift suggests, represent a tragically wasted opportunity in our mad times. Are we, to take only one example, short of generals for our new armies? We have only to send our ministers to Bedlam to find all manner of suitable candidates. If we find a patient who is 'tearing his straw in piecemeal, swearing and blaspheming, foaming at the mouth, and emptying his piss-pot in the spectators' faces', then, Swift proposes, we should 'give him a regiment of dragoons and send him into Flanders among the rest'. Surely we will also find plenty of ideal lawyers, businessmen, poets and politicians among Bedlam's sorry and neglected ranks.

The theme was too good to pass up, and many subsequent satires milked this pungent image of the topsy-turvy modern world. Ned Ward returned to his old subject with a metaphor inflated to bursting point: *All Men Mad, or England a Great Bedlam*; the moralizing minister Thomas Tryon pronounced that 'the world is but a great Bedlam, where those that are more mad, lock up those that are less'; the author and politician Horace Walpole announced a plan 'of shutting up in Bedlam the few persons in this country that remain in their senses . . . it would be much easier and cheaper than to confine all the delirious'. This is no longer the dream-world of Jacobean theatre; it is a bolder vision of madness, where Bedlam is the lens through which we can perceive the nonsense all around us. It's in this tradition that we should read the final panel in Hogarth's *Rake's Progress*, set in one of Bedlam's galleries and featuring its instantly recognizable blue-coated keepers, but in fact illustrating a grander theme. The clue is not in the famous painting itself, but in a subsequent etching of it produced by Hogarth in 1763 where the emblem on the back wall becomes a coin bearing the image of Britannia: this is not Bedlam we are gawping at, but Britain itself. Does the mad bishop, Hogarth is asking us, have any less a grasp of reality than the bishops outside? Does the real monarch have any more concrete a claim to power than the fake orb and sceptre gripped by his Bedlam counterpart? Do real-life scientists have anything more to tell us than the idiot peering through his telescope?

Even during its public heyday, this was a mythical Bedlam.

A Rake's Progress *(William Hogarth)*

Not everybody came to jeer and mock the afflicted. Bedlam was a new addition to a still-familiar London leisure circuit – the Tower, Westminster Abbey, the zoo, London Bridge, the Exchange, the gardens and parks – which was increasingly patronized by respectable families. The diarists Samuel Pepys and James Boswell both visited it, finding an 'extraordinary' and 'remarkable' spectacle. Beyond the freak-show it maintained an edifying dimension as a spur to counting one's own blessings and making charitable donations to the unfortunate, and as a source of moral lessons. Though we associate such sentiments with the Victorians, they began to be expressed much earlier: in the 1740s the novelist Samuel Richardson was moved to contemplate 'such misery as, being wholly involuntary, may overtake the most secure', and another visitor ten years later took home the salutary lesson that 'we may learn to moderate our pride, and to keep those passions within bounds, which if too much indulged would drive Reason from her seat'.

At the same time as the image of madness was becoming firmly fixed on Bedlam, the first laws appeared to deal specifically with the condition. The Act of 1714, under which James Tilly Matthews would be confined, was the first to make a legal separation between lunatics and other undesirables. A dangerous lunatic could now be apprehended and, with the acquiescence of two or more Justices of the Peace, locked up. The costs of pauper lunatics were to be paid by their parish of origin. This rudimentary benefits system was a further driver for the private trade in lunacy, as parishes would often board out their lunatics in private guest-houses or, increasingly, specialist madhouses.

By mid-century, the strains of this *ad hoc* system were beginning to show. Private madhouses abounded, to the point where it's now impossible even to estimate how many there were. They clustered together to share attendants, doctors and facilities; in London, Hoxton and Chelsea became the twin centres to east and west. Reports of abuses abounded, of patients being beaten and chained and sane subjects confined by conspiracies of families and magistrates. A House of Commons Select Committee was convened to discuss the matter in 1763 and its recommendations were finally co-opted into a 1774 Madhouses Act which attempted to regulate the chaos. All madhouses were now subject to licensing and inspection by designated professionals: in the provinces by doctors and Justices of the Peace, and in London by five Commissioners in Lunacy, to be appointed by the Royal College of Physicians – a star chamber with whom James Tilly Matthews would later memorably lock horns.

This arrangement was only a very modest improvement. The Commissioners in Lunacy were a toothless body whose powers to enforce their recommendations were either unclear or non-existent. But the same period saw the beginnings of more effective reform by the 'mad-doctors' themselves. In 1751 the Bedlam physician William Battie broke away from the old institution and set up a new hospital called St Luke's where the mad would be better cared for and, for the first time, medical students would receive specialist training in treating them. In 1758 Battie published his *Treatise on Madness*, laying out the basics of his system and launching a broadside against his former employers. He blamed Bedlam, as the country's leading madhouse, for the shortcomings of the profession as a whole. It was backward and insular, unwilling and unable to shake off its obscure traditions and engage with new ideas. The reply from chief physician John Monro was the first time a Bedlam doctor had ever ventured into print, and it was a less than encouraging start. 'Madness', he pronounced, 'is a distemper of such a nature, that very little of real use can be said concerning it.' The condition would be 'for ever dark, intricate and uncertain', and new theories, ideas and initiatives might be well-meaning but were, sadly, doomed. The mad could not be cured, they could only be, at best, 'managed'.

Thus it was that the Bedlam which greeted James Tilly Matthews was not so much a carnival of filth and depravity as an exhausted and run-down public institution, its fabric falling apart and its professional image tarnished. The free-for-all public visits had been scrapped in the 1770s, as a result of the same broad civic unease that was leading to the questioning of public executions. Selected guests now had to buy advance tickets and be escorted in small groups by a keeper. Preachers, including John Wesley, were banned on the grounds that their passionate sermons tended to make the patients madder. The conditions – plain food and straw bedding – were no better and no worse than those in hundreds of workhouses, almshouses and prisons up and down the country. With its

Thomas Monro

institutionalized staff and patients and its numbing routines, it was perhaps a comparable experience to many public mental hospitals today.

The regime which was to preside over Matthews mirrored the motley patchwork of the architecture. The financial crisis brought on by the collapsing building had been made worse when Bethlem's treasurer, William Kinleside, was declared bankrupt and the ensuing shuffle had exposed a mysterious black hole in the books of six thousand pounds – several hundred thousand in today's money. In 1792 a Select Committee of Inquiry had found the record-keeping lax and the accounting 'extremely obscure and defective'. From this point on, any attempt at reform or renewal would be further hamstrung by chronic underfunding.

The 250 or so patients, including around a hundred long-term 'incurables', were overseen by three medical staff. The physician in charge was Thomas Monro, son of John Monro and scion of a family who had been associated with Bethlem for most of the century. But Thomas's heart wasn't in the family profession. He was supposed to oversee prescription to patients on Mondays and Wednesdays, but in practice he showed up about once a week, in a more or less ceremonial capacity. The only statutory condition of his generous hundred-pounds-a-year salary was that he should attend the weekly Saturday morning meeting of the Governors Subcommittee, but as often as not he would present his apology by letter and claim other pressing business. The rest of the time he pursued his hobby of painting, commissioning and exhibiting watercolours, a field in which he was far more expert. Turner was among his protégés.

The largely absent Monro had two medical staff under him. One was a surgeon, Bryan Crowther, a heavy drinker and frustrated medical man who would eventually publish a book whose title gives a vivid sense of his interests:

PRACTICAL REMARKS
ON
INSANITY
TO WHICH IS ADDED
A COMMENTARY ON THE DISSECTION
OF THE
BRAINS OF MANIACS
WITH SOME ACCOUNT OF
DISEASES INCIDENT TO THE INSANE

Dissecting the brains of lunatics was Crowther's passion, but not his job. Lunatics were separated into 'curable' and 'incurable', and he was responsible for carrying out physical treatments to remedy the curable. Chief among these was bleeding, which was held to calm the nerves and prevent the violent passions from overheating. This was a seasonal practice, concentrated at the beginning and end of summer. The inmates' bodily functions were also in Crowther's domain, and his favoured treatment was the administration of purgatives to constipated subjects: he notes in his book that 'insane persons are subject to costiveness' and 'mad persons will occasionally retain their urine for a long time'. By the same logic, emetics were commonly given to make patients vomit; like bleeding, this was rationalized in terms of keeping fluids moving through the system. Crowther insisted that 'I never saw or heard of the bad effects of vomits'. The syphilitic were, like all syphilitics, prescribed mercury. Most other afflictions, especially the violent paroxysms with which the mad were often afflicted, were treated with opium. This was the most effective medicine in the eighteenth-century pharmacopoeia, not to mention the only treatment the inmates would probably have undergone voluntarily, and was used more or less as a general panacea. Since one of its most obvious side-effects is constipation, this explains the need for the endless regime of purgatives. It's likely that opium was administered in large doses, as Crowther quotes the physician Dr Mead's remark that 'maniacal people, as is frequently observed, require a quadruple dose of opium, which will scarce produce any effect'. Cold baths were another ubiquitous standby.

This was a tired old therapeutic regime, barely changed from the seventeenth century, and one which from a modern perspective seems to have little rhyme or reason. But it had long since evolved for reasons related not so much to the needs of the patients as to those of their keepers. Crowther was

LUNACY BY TYPE

mischievous *743*
not mischievous *886*
attempted suicide *323*
murderous *20*

LUNACY BY CAUSE

misfortunes, troubles, disappointments, grief . . . *206*
family/heredity *115*
fevers *110*
religion and methodism *90*
childbed *79*
love *74*
drink *58*
fright *51*
study *90*

LUNACY BY OUTCOME

cured *924*
incurable *1694*
relapses *535*
deaths *250*

Table of lunacy by John Gozna, apothecary at Bethlem, 1772–95

responsible for up to three hundred 'lunatics', a disparate group with a variety of disorders – or, in some cases, probably none at all. They were contained in the most spartan of surroundings for twenty-four hours a day, adequately fed, but most of them with their mental and physical conditions deteriorating as the inevitable result of their confinement. Apart from opium, there was barely a single effective remedy in the doctor's bag, and certainly nothing that had the slightest chance of ameliorating their mental afflictions. Thus it's hardly surprising that the time-honoured treatments were simply the ones that made the patients easier to manage. Bleeding weakened them and made them more tractable; purging and vomiting did the same. Cold baths distracted them, immersing them in overwhelming physical stimuli, and opium sedated them. Most of these measures were unpleasant – 'treatment' in the sense of punishment as well as cure – and could be withheld from well-behaved patients and intensified for troublesome ones.

The other member of the medical staff, alongside Crowther, was a man of substantially higher calibre; a man with a clear and steely theory of madness and its treatment that would eventually mark him out as a major player in the profession. It would also make him the major player in the next stage of James Tilly Matthews' ongoing drama, forcing him into a conflict which would define the future for both of them. This was Bedlam's resident apothecary, John Haslam.

Haslam was a recent addition to the staff, and a sign that the winds of change blowing through the trade in lunacy might finally be about to disturb the dust of Bedlam. In theory, all three doctors – physician, surgeon and apothecary – had to be elected each year by the Bethlem governors, but in practice these elections went through on the nod, and it was only the death of the previous apothecary John Gozna, who had been in residence since 1772, that brought in Haslam in 1795.

In stark contrast to his superior Thomas Monro, a wealthy underachiever *par excellence*, Haslam was poor and extremely ambitious. He had begun with a medical apprenticeship which had afforded him the chance to become a student at St Bartholomew's Hospital, where he had worked his way up to become a house surgeon. This had paved the way for two years at Edinburgh University, the best medical college in the land.

John Haslam

Completing the course would have brought him an MD and the title of doctor, but for some unknown reason he failed to do so; we can guess it was more likely to have been lack of resources than ability or ambition. He moved on to study at Uppsala in Sweden, and then Pembroke Hall at Cambridge, where once again he was forced to leave before qualifying for a degree.

We don't know exactly why, at this point, Haslam decided to specialize in mad-doctoring, but it was a decision compatible with his combination of humble origins and professional ambition. The trade in lunacy had never been the most distinguished branch of medicine, and the stigma attached to it had rarely made it the first choice of the wealthiest or best-qualified members of the profession. But the private madhouse trade was expanding fast, and the treatment of madness had recently captured the public imagination through the most high-profile case of the eighteenth (and perhaps any other) century: the madness of George III.

When the King's mind began to unravel in the second half of 1788, mad-doctoring was caught for the first time in the full beam of the spotlight, centre stage in an unprecedented national crisis. Huge constitutional questions hung on the nature of the King's illness and his likelihood of recovery, and the leading politicians in the land developed a sudden interest in the medical experts' every word. The royal doctors treated their subject almost like a Chinese emperor, unable to command the monarch and barely daring any physical examination. Arcane diagnoses were bruited about by a mystified but impressed public, but the star of the show turned out to be a man who had emerged from nowhere, the Rev. Dr Francis Willis, a humble superintendent of a provincial private madhouse whose claim to have 'cured nine out of ten' flew in the face of the fatalistic assumption that 'once a lunatic, always a lunatic'. Ignoring the learned taxonomies and diagnoses of the court, Willis embarked on a short, sharp and brutal regime of management and restraint, and the King gradually recovered his senses.

Of course, thanks to the most celebrated retrospective diagnosis in medical history, it now seems plausible that George III's illness was not true madness at all but porphyria, a physical ailment that produces symptoms of dementia. This is, as it happens, not so far from the prevailing view at the time – almost all parties thought the condition physical rather than mental in origin – but in any case the irony of the episode is that neither the court mandarins nor the progressive country mad-doctor are likely to have had much effect on the progress or duration of the royal condition. Still, the message received by both professionals and public at the time was that the treatment of madness, whatever its cause, might be awakening from a long slumber and awaiting the touch of medical genius to transform it. Although Haslam was later dismissive of Willis in print, the message received by this young doctor with few financial and social advantages was that here was a specialism where talent and persistence might find a level playing-field on which to compete.

Thus, when Haslam applied for the post of apothecary at Bethlem, it's likely that he and the governors thought each was doing the other a favour. From the governors' perspective Bethlem was a household name, the mad-doctoring trade was beginning to boom, and apothecary in a metropolitan charitable institution was a worthy post for a man without means or doctor's certificate. But Haslam would have been well aware that he was to be subordinate to a man far less qualified than him, and obliged to live on the premises and not to absent himself for a night without the governors' leave, and all for the same salary Monro received for doing virtually nothing. Nevertheless he took no chances, bribing the Bethlem clerk with a guinea for a list of the governors' names so that he could make his case to them in advance. Either the ploy worked or it was unnecessary, as he won the appointment by a very comfortable ninety-two votes to six over his only rival.

The administrative structure was slightly adjusted on his arrival, as part of the continual but vague attempt to demonstrate that Bethlem was cleaning up its act, but the main effect was that the burden of work shifted rather more heavily on to Haslam than had been the case with his predecessor. He was to be responsible for 'the general health of patients', obliged to make a round every morning, dispense advice and medicines, and 'direct the keepers in the management of the patients'. Both Monro and Crowther had contrived to offload part of their jobs on to him, leaving him with quite a serious remit as the only doctor among hundreds of patients and a couple of dozen unskilled staff. Nor was he allowed to hire, fire or discipline the keepers and other staff with whom he worked every day, despite his frequent complaints that they were drunk. Surrounded by the poor, mad and unskilled in an institution few cared about, and in a menial role barely considered part of the medical world at all, any ambitions Haslam had to turn his job to his professional advantage must surely have cohabited with the grim realization that beggars can't be choosers.

The extent of his daily grind also hampered his progress in the crucial business of supplementing his salary with other sources of income. Despite his poor grasp of medical detail, Monro's position and lineage enabled him to charge handsome fees for consulting with wealthy private patients; Haslam, by contrast, had to make do with small kickbacks from private madhouses for placing his discharged patients with them. Eventually a few more opportunities opened up: as the number of state lunatics increased with the influx of armed forces casualties from the Napoleonic Wars, he made contacts that allowed him to earn modest fees from visiting other madhouses to inspect them.

But he had a string to his bow that was not shared by Monro: well trained, energetic and hungry for recognition, he would write his way out. By the time James Tilly Matthews arrived, Haslam was already preparing his first book for publication, a monograph entitled *Observations on Insanity* that would paint a revealing picture of the character into whose care Matthews was about to be entrusted, and the type of methods he favoured.

Observations on Insanity opens with a flourish that would become more and more pronounced through Haslam's writing career: the vigorous rubbishing of all the competition and any opposing views. With the sole exception of John Monro's reply to William Battie's *Treatise on Madness*, which it would have been most impolitic to criticize, all previous English writings on the subject had been mere verbiage: 'there is no work on the subject of mental alienation which has been delivered on the authority of extensive observation and practice'. Any competing contributions to the subject had been either long taxonomies of different types of madness bolstered with classical allusions, or scrappy, anecdotal collections of a handful of case histories. What Haslam had to offer was, by contrast, based squarely on 'the treatment of several hundred patients' and 'an astonishing number of cures'.

The core of Haslam's theory was this. Madness is no soul-sickness or spiritual malaise but a physical disease, an organic disorder of the brain. Its manifestation can be defined as 'an incorrect association of familiar ideas', which is 'always accompanied with implicit belief'. The reason that mad people see objects and hear sounds that aren't there is not because their eyes and ears are deficient, but because their brains are not functioning correctly. Nor is their intelligence necessarily at fault: Haslam, quoting the philosopher John Locke, explains that they 'will frequently reason correctly from false premises'. This may lead them to all manner of strange behaviours, but doctors have been wasting their time in trying to categorize the mad on this basis, because all the varied manifestations of madness proceed from the same cause.

Mania and melancholy, for example, could not be more different in their effects, but Haslam 'would strongly oppose them being categorised as opposite diseases'. We should not be looking at what the mad think is happening to them, but at the condition that underlies their thought processes. We do not treat fevers by listening to the patient's babbling.

From this follows, for Haslam, the first principle of effective treatment: we have to ignore the contents of the insane mind entirely. To listen to what the patient says, to attempt to reason with him, is to head promptly down the darkest of blind alleys. Haslam's experience with lunatics has taught him 'to disentangle myself as quickly as possible from the perplexity of metaphysical mazes'. There is no such thing as a disease of ideas, which can be cured by reason: 'to endeavour to convince madmen of their errors by reasoning is folly in those who attempt it'. The mad are, by definition, deficient in reason; one might as well attempt to cure the blind by showing them beautiful pictures. 'There is always in madness the firmest conviction of the truth of what is false, and which the clearest and most circumstantial evidence cannot remove.'

Against admittedly weak competition, this was by far the most robust expression of medical opinion that had ever emerged from Bedlam. Much of it has since been vindicated: for an eighteenth-century doctor, Haslam had a remarkably good hit-rate against subsequent scientific discoveries. He certainly managed one spectacular bull's-eye. Drawing perhaps on Crowther's ghoulish area of expertise, he inspected the brains of twenty-nine Bethlem inmates *post mortem* and claimed to observe pathological, 'morbid' damage in all of them. Inspecting the nature of this damage, he noted that the lateral ventricles in the brain, holes in which the cerebrospinal fluid wells and drains, were 'larger in maniacs', and confirmed this by spooning water into them to measure their capacity. Not until the twentieth century and the modern technologies of pneumo-encephalography, CT scanning and magnetic resonance imaging would this observation be confirmed. Today it's well known that schizophrenics have a larger ventricle-to-brain ratio than average; two hundred years ago, the discovery excited little attention.

But if Haslam had hit upon a remarkable number of modern psychiatry's truths, he also had to contend with its nagging problem: assembling data about brains is one thing, but converting these data into practical therapeutic benefits is another. His first problem was endemic in the state of medical knowledge at the time: if madness is an organic condition, how can it be physically recognized? The limitations of physiological data such as these still loom large today. While, for example, the average size of lateral ventricles is clearly significant of something, it's a far cry from a diagnosis, and further still from treatment. Not all people with large lateral ventricles develop schizophrenia, and other people develop the condition without them; overall statistical correlation is one thing, its diagnostic value in any individual case quite another. Similarly, Haslam's claim to find madness 'uniformly accompanied with disease of the brain', however prescient, was an assertion with no obvious application. How could he even prove it was the brain damage that was causing the madness, and not vice versa?

The second problem Haslam faced when turning his observations into practical recommendations was that he wasn't in charge of treatment at Bedlam. The regime of bleeding, purging and vomiting was a hangover not just from Thomas Monro's father but from his father before him. It seems likely that Haslam was privately sceptical about its usefulness but unable to criticize it in print. Instead, he was forced to paint effective mad-doctoring as a form of genius composed of infinite pains, as a mastery of countless techniques of management that could be acquired only by lengthy experience. The goal of these techniques was for the doctor to 'obtain an ascendancy' over the patient, a process comparable to training a dog or breaking in a horse. So long as the patient was allowed to set the agenda in any way, no progress could be made; only when the doctor had control over all the patient's moods and circumstances might 'the most violent state of the disease' begin to lift.

This was not necessarily a cruel process, however, and it was certainly not to be confused with punishment. Haslam was explicit that 'corporal punishment upon maniacs' was 'disgraceful and inhuman', not to mention counterproductive. 'Wounding the pride' of lunatics was essential, but 'severity of discipline' was a last resort. 'Improper behaviour' by a patient should, in the first instance, be dealt with by 'confining him to his room' and by 'withholding certain indulgences he has been accustomed to enjoy'. Only when patients were determinedly violent were they to be placed in physical restraints such as straitjackets or chains. But the more skills and techniques the doctor masters, the less the trappings of authority are needed. Haslam ends on a note of rosy optimism, with the insistence that 'I can truly declare, that by gentleness of manner, and kindness of treatment, I have never failed to obtain the confidence, and conciliate the esteem of insane persons, and have succeeded by these means in procuring from them respect and obedience'.

Haslam's idea of treatment, therefore, was a one-way street. The doctor must dominate the patient; any possibility that the two might seek a solution together, or that the doctor might empower the patient to work towards his own cure, was strictly ruled out. The effectiveness of this method, not to mention the truth of Haslam's claims, would be sorely tested by the arrival of James Tilly Matthews. The irresistible force of the new patient's extraordinary convictions would be set directly against the immovable object of a determined doctor bent on single-handedly dragging Bedlam into the nineteenth century. Something was going to have to give.

3

HABEAS CORPUS

*'If they are not mad when they go into these
cursed houses, they are soon made so.'*
Daniel Defoe, *Augusta Triumphans*, 1728

MATTHEWS DID NOT SETTLE INTO BEDLAM VERY WELL. HE REFUSED
to associate with any of the other patients, on the grounds that
they weren't lunatics at all but agents placed there by one of
Pitt's secretaries. Whenever he left the interior of the building
for the capacious grounds, he was spied on by agents in the
street. He refused to drink the water, which he believed to be
poisoned, and complained about drugs being secretly hidden
in his food. He complained further about the chemical and
magnetic influences in the hospital, which were affecting him
adversely. As far as he was concerned, 'his being under confinement was only part of a grand conspiracy to deprive him
of his liberty, which has for many years been attempted in
the different Courts of Europe'. He was entirely unimpressed
by Haslam's efforts to 'wound his pride' and 'obtain an
ascendancy' over him: in his view the apothecary was
merely a functionary of the Duke of Portland under orders
to restrain him in the hospital, and on whom he would

shortly be revenged for his unjust confinement.

Haslam was equally unimpressed with Matthews, who was not the only patient who claimed to be involved in momentous affairs of state. Among Matthews' companions were Urbane Metcalfe, who believed he was heir to the throne of Denmark, and Margaret 'Peg' Nicholson, who had briefly achieved notoriety in 1786 when she had presented a petition to George III and then struck at him with a concealed (very small and blunt) knife. When apprehended she claimed it was a slip of the hand, but later revealed the truth: the crown was hers by rights, and if she was deprived of it England would drown in blood for a hundred generations. After a year in Bedlam she was assessed and transferred in perpetuity to the incurable wing, on the grounds that she might still present a danger to His Majesty. She had spent most of her working life in service to minor aristocratic families, but some time before the royal incident she had been caught having an affair with a valet; this had cost her her job, and she had been reduced to scraping a living from needlework. In the incurable wing she took up needlework again, along with other menial jobs, worked extremely hard and was very eager to please, delighted to be rewarded with small gifts, of which her favourite was snuff. At the age of eighty-two, after thirty-six years in Bedlam, she developed an aversion to bread and never ate any again. Apart from this she showed very few signs of madness, and remained without complaint in the incurable wing until her death at the age of ninety-four.

The perpetrator of a more serious assassination attempt on George III also found himself in Bedlam, arriving a few years after Matthews in 1800. James Hadfield had been a British soldier in the Revolutionary Wars against France and had, oddly enough, been a bodyguard to the Duke of York at the precise time when Matthews believed the Duke's forces were detailed to obstruct his activities. Hadfield had been badly injured at the Battle of Lincennes in 1793, receiving massive

Peg Nicholson's attack on George III

head wounds and brain damage. He was discharged on grounds of insanity and returned to London to work as a silversmith, during which time he fell under the sway of a Pentecostal preacher and became convinced that the end of the world was nigh. Gradually he developed the idea that he was God's instrument, and that if George III was killed the Messiah would return. After a mercifully abortive attempt to murder his own son on God's orders, he decided that he would kill the King and thereby also sacrifice himself by forcing the royal bodyguards to shoot him. On 15 May 1800 he entered the Drury Lane theatre with a pistol and, as George III leant from the balcony to blow a kiss to his subjects, fired into the roof of the royal box, missing the King by inches.

Hadfield's case precipitated an important change in the law, which offers a marker of the ways in which the notion of madness was being reconceived. He was arrested and charged with high treason, but the trial was waylaid by his lawyer's argument that Hadfield was a religious maniac, not in his right mind and therefore not legally responsible for his actions. This plea led to a verdict that had never been heard before: 'not guilty: he being under the influence of insanity at the time when the act was committed'. As this was essentially a not guilty verdict, Hadfield had to be set free. This prompted a public outcry, and a new law was rushed through Parliament, the Act for Custody of Insane Persons Charged with Offences, which created a new category of prisoner, the criminal lunatic. Such cases would now be detained in state madhouses, or future institutions specially designed for them. Hadfield was sent to Bedlam.

Hadfield was not one of Matthews' favourite companions: he found him 'insolent and daring', and thought it inappropriate that such violent patients should be foisted upon the harmless ones. He was also convinced that Hadfield had been under the control of the Air Loom. But Hadfield didn't trouble him too long: he escaped in 1802 and got as far as Dover

James Hadfield shoots at George III at Drury Lane

before being recaptured. This time he was sent to Newgate Prison where he remained for fourteen years before, as Matthews had long ago recommended, a separate criminal lunatic wing was built at Bedlam and Hadfield was returned there. He kept pet cats and birds, and wrote poems which he sold, spending the money on tobacco. The governors bought him a wig to cover his unsightly scarred head, and when he died in 1841 his post-mortem revealed extensive brain damage.

On 18 March, a few weeks after James Tilly Matthews' admission, the Saturday morning meeting of the Bethlem Subcommittee was interrupted by a woman who addressed the members with the following words: 'I am wife to Mr. Matthews and demand to know by what authority my husband is detained.' The governors dug out the petition of 28 January that authorized Matthews' admission, and read it to her. She wasn't satisfied, and continued to insist that her husband was in his right mind, and should be released and allowed to go home with her. The governors asked her to step outside while they conferred. One of them proposed a motion 'that the Committee do not comply with the request made by Mrs. Matthews'. Another seconded it. Mrs Matthews was called back in and 'made acquainted with the above resolution'. She left.

A psychoanalyst once proposed that 'madness is when you can't find anyone who can stand you'. This is not such a flippant definition as it might at first appear. In practice, the mad are created when those around them can no longer cope with them, and turn them over to specialists and professionals. They are people who have broken the ties that bind the rest of us in our social contract, who have reached a point where they can no longer connect. But by this definition James Tilly Matthews, paranoid schizophrenic or not, was not mad. It is striking that throughout his story, even at the prodigious heights of his delusions, there are always those around him who trust him, and he consistently inspires sympathy, affection and love. In the end, this is the trump card he holds over John Haslam. Haslam may be right, he may be the doctor, his authority and statutory powers over Matthews may be almost unlimited, and all this gives him an advantage that will enable him to assert his will over his patient for many years. But when the chips come down, those around Matthews will stick with him and those around Haslam will coldly settle old scores.

The minutes of the Bethlem Governors Subcommittee are a threadbare and rather desultory record. Year in and year out, they record little more than the names of those present, frequently noting apologies from the absent Thomas Monro and brief notes of any arrivals or departures among the patients. But the spring of 1797 sees them stung into life by a flurry of activity around James Tilly Matthews. The week following Mrs Matthews' visit, the churchwarden and overseer of the parish of Camberwell, Matthews' sponsors, are present.

So is Dr Monro, who informs them that Matthews continues to be insane. The governors tell the visitors from Camberwell that they have considered Mrs Matthews' request very carefully, but have decided that 'they could not, consistent with their duty, discharge her husband unless they were so directed by higher authority'. Mrs Matthews, waiting outside once more, is brought in to hear the unanimous pronouncement.

Like most ordinary people of the time, Mrs Matthews is a ghost in the historical record. We know her only from references in official documents connected with the case of her husband, but her belief in him is unshakeable: she remains convinced of his sanity throughout, and despite her near invisibility is a crucial player in the drama that follows. Always outnumbered, always outgunned, she and her friends nevertheless persist with their demands to free her husband, and it's likely that without their persistence Matthews would have been forever forgotten. This brusque official rebuff from the Bethlem governors was, in her view, far from the end of the story. But several weeks later, the committee was called upon to ratify an unusual order: that Mrs Matthews was no longer allowed to visit her husband, 'his disorder being increased in consequence of her visits'.

Banning visitors from Bedlam was extremely unusual. Although the free-for-all of public visits was a thing of the past, anyone could visit by appointment unless, like preachers, they disrupted the hospital's therapeutic regime. Normally, this was not a judgement passed on next-of-kin; certainly John Gozna, Haslam's predecessor, had not been in the habit of barring relatives. But Haslam was determined to drive his theories through into the practice of patient management. It's clearly impossible to assert an ascendancy over a patient whose thoughts are taken up with plotting and engineering his release. Haslam felt that Matthews was in the grip of an acute mania that would only subside once the doctor, not the patient, was setting the agenda: the doctor must have mastery over the patient's moods if the 'most violent state of the disease' is ever to pass. Part of his delusion is that he is sane, and his wife is reinforcing it; cruel as it may seem, she must be banished. In this exchange we see, perhaps, an early example of a theme that has run through psychiatry to this day: medicalizing the mad and placing them under the care of specialists is a two-edged sword. Even when humane in its intentions, its effect can be not to liberate the patients but to imprison them further.

Separating Matthews and his wife seems to have temporarily calmed things down. No more ructions were reported, and the dismal routine of Bedlam ground on. But Matthews was still failing to recover anything Haslam would recognize as sanity. The patient was not forgotten: given his large workload, Haslam seems to have taken notes on Matthews' state of mind with some diligence. Conspiracies among the crowned heads of Europe continued to dominate his view of the world, along with even stranger convictions. On 10 January 1798 Haslam records Matthews' delusion that there was a figure of a man on top of Bloomsbury Church. The man had a book under his arm, the Doomsday Book – a record of everything, which no-one but Matthews could read.

Shortly after the Doomsday Book incident, Matthews' year in Bedlam, the usual duration of stay, expired. He was assessed and categorized as incurable. But, unlike most incurables, he wasn't released. He was apparently adjudged to be still a threat to the safety of the King and his ministers, and thus became one of the rump of a hundred or so long-term incurable patients.

This had, according to Haslam's notes, a marked and detrimental effect on Matthews' state of mind. His delusions became more intense and systematic, the conspiracies around him more grandiose, until 'he conceived himself to be Emperor of the whole world'. Ascendancy over his will was plainly distant, and if anything still receding. Rather than cruelty,

Haslam seems at this point, in accordance with his theories, to have chosen kindness. Matthews was allocated his own cell, a room about twelve feet by eight with a bed, a door and a sluice pipe for waste. He was allowed to tend a small garden plot among the ruined exterior walls, which he eventually 'brought to a high state of cultivation'. He was also given access to pen and paper, and began to write voluminous notes on his own condition and the affairs of state that were playing out behind the scenes. All these favours, though, remained at Haslam's discretion: again, they are kindnesses when looked at from one angle, but from another they add to the doctor's range of punishments the threat of their withdrawal.

This new dispensation might have made life easier for Haslam, but Matthews' family was still unwilling to accept his diagnosis of lunacy. They continued to press for his release: shortly after he was pronounced incurable, they petitioned the governors for a second opinion. Matthews was taken from Bedlam for the first time since his arrival and driven by carriage to Lincoln's Inn Fields and the home of Lord Kenyon, the Lord Chief Justice.

The only record of this hearing is Haslam's notes; we can imagine that Matthews' would have been somewhat divergent. The interview was short, though long enough for Matthews to explain the true facts behind the Affair of the Necklace, a French court scandal held by many to be the beginning of the French Revolution. In 1785, one of Marie Antoinette's courtiers had apparently been persuaded by a young lady calling herself the Comtesse de la Motte Valois to buy a valuable diamond necklace on the Queen's behalf. Money, necklace and countess then all disappeared. A furious Marie Antoinette put the courtier, and the obscurely involved Count Cagliostro, on trial, tracked down the countess and had her stripped, flogged and branded in public. The countess escaped, protested her innocence, denounced the Queen, and Marie Antoinette was never able to appear in public again without being mocked and jeered. In Matthews' version, the countess had been set up 'by the Queen of England for treasonable purposes'. Lord Kenyon apparently had little hesitation in confirming Haslam's diagnosis.

So Matthews was back in Bedlam and, from Haslam's perspective, continuing to get worse. Matthews felt the conspiracy was closing in on him: his abduction from Bedlam for the opinion of Lord Kenyon had, in his view, been a pretext to implant a magnet into his brain. This meant that others could more easily control his thoughts, but also made him more aware of the 'event workers and political chemists' who were monitoring him (of which more – a great deal more – later). For a pauper lunatic, a class that normally passed so far beneath the radar of Georgian society as to be invisible, he had already succeeded in bringing his case to the attention of a remarkable number of gentlemen, experts and dignitaries. But he was only just getting started.

Matthews' friends and family might have been convinced that he was sane – they were certainly convinced that he would be better off at home than in Bedlam – but their lobbying had hit a brick wall, and the way around it was by no means clear. The Lunacy Act of 1714 had formalized the conditions under which the mad could be detained, but it said little about those under which they should be released. The 1774 Madhouses Act added little more than a layer of bureaucracy, with no means of redress. What if the doctors were wrong? What if the confinement was based on concealed personal motives – revenge, jealousy or financial gain? What if the patient was being held in the interests of a political cover-up? What if the experts were themselves mad?

The eighteenth century had seen a few high-profile and colourful cases of lunatics protesting their unjust confinement, of whom the best known is probably Alexander Cruden. Cruden is also still remembered as the compiler of the

Complete Concordance to the Bible, a massive tome which he published in 1737 from his small bookshop near the London Corn Exchange and which was received as one of the scholarly masterpieces of the great age of dictionaries and encyclopaedias. He came from a strict Presbyterian background in Aberdeen and was highly devout, but also prone to uncontrollable sexual arousal and intense romantic infatuations. His parents had already had him locked up to forestall his obsessive pursuit of his female love-objects before he came to London, and shortly after the *Concordance* was published the same thing happened again. This time the woman in the frame was a wealthy widow called Mrs Payne, and there was another man involved, an elderly Scot recently arrived from Edinburgh called Mr Wightman, who had Cruden carted off to a private madhouse in Bethnal Green.

Cruden lays out the whole story in his subsequent pamphlet, *The London Citizen Exceedingly Injured*, subtitled *A British Inquisition Display'd* and demanding to know how 'a Citizen of London, Bookseller to the Late Queen' could be 'in a most unjust and arbitrary manner' sent to a madhouse by 'a mere stranger'. The diary format records 'the Prisoner', as Cruden calls himself throughout, being 'chain'd night and day' and only able to comfort himself with 'his Bible and his devotions'. He was bled and vomited and attended by the physician of Bethlem, Dr James Monro, Thomas's grandfather, who seemed to Cruden to be 'Wightman's devoted creature' and with whom he heard that Wightman was plotting to transfer him to Bedlam itself. For Cruden, this was the ultimate threat, 'the sorest evil that could befall him, and which he dreaded more than Death'. The threat spurs him to action, and he begins to cut through the bedstead, to which his chain is attached, with a knife. He perseveres with this task (though not on the Lord's Day) and finishes the job on the morning of his birthday, at which point he performs his devotions, takes up his chain and bed-leg, escapes via the window into the garden, mounts the wall with much difficulty and runs all the way to Mile End.

Cruden, having won his freedom, went on the offensive. His case was picked up by the newspapers, and he took his 'Inquisitors' to court for wrongful imprisonment. His pamphlet widened its complaint to the entire system: the Prisoner 'has acted more reasonably than his adversaries', and 'if all lovers were to be sent thither, there would a necessity to erect Bethlemical cities instead of hospitals'. Until his case is addressed, 'what man in England can be safe?' But the court didn't see it Cruden's way. He was arguing that he hadn't been certified as mad by two Justices of the Peace as stipulated in the Act of 1714, but the defence pointed out that this applied only to paupers being admitted to public madhouses. Private madhouses could run whatever system they wanted.

For the rest of his life, Cruden continued to whirl irregularly and chaotically around the twin attractors of religious and romantic passion. He found work as a proof corrector, and began to publish pamphlets under the name of 'Alexander the Corrector', in which he became a semi-biblical corrector of the nation, savagely condemning the immorality he found in public life and, in equal measure, the cruelty with which the objects of his affection treated him. He was committed to several more madhouses, by his sister among others, and even had an extended infatuation with a woman he had never met but whom God had ordained as his 'predestined lady'. He died on his knees in prayer at his lodgings in Islington.

Cruden's complaint of wrongful confinement in private madhouses recurred through the century, but Bedlam was another matter. The private madhouse trade was of interest to the reading public, to the extent that it would be their own recourse if madness visited them or their loved ones, and articles and pamphlets on its injustices were saleable popular fodder. But Bedlam was a state institution for the abandoned poor and mad who were, then as now, both silent and always with us.

The year before Matthews' admission another public complaint had come closer to home, not against Bedlam itself but against Thomas Monro, who had attended a patient called William Belcher at a private madhouse in Hackney, much as Monro's grandfather had attended Alexander Cruden. Belcher argued that he had been entirely sane when he was confined (by a committee who never saw him), but after the experience of trying to get out he was no longer sure he was in his right mind. As a 'victim to the trade of lunacy', having had to fight his way through a tangle of 'managers, commissioners, attorneys, counsels, doctors, lawyers, committees, rent-gatherers, madhouse-keepers, and other respectable brutes', he now thought it would be better to remain a lunatic. His *Address to Humanity: Containing a Letter to Dr. Thomas Monro; a receipt* [recipe] *to make a Lunatic, and Seize his Estate* also contains 'A Sketch of a True Smiling Hyaena [Thomas Monro] by which the author was severely bitten'. This pen-portrait reduces Monro to a cruel but recognizable caricature: a hungry scavenging beast, his 'visage smiling, especially at the sight of shining metal, of which its paws are extremely retentive . . . he doth ravish the rich when he getteth them into his den'.

The notion of unjust confinement was familiar; so was the notion that those diagnosed mad might be sane, and that those treating them might be on to a profitable scam. But no-one had yet reasoned their way out of Bedlam.

Ten years passed.

We know little of this period, except that various charges were primed that would detonate later. Matthews was swallowed up by the tragic invisibility that obscures the vast majority of the mad. He stayed in his private cell; he wrote prodigiously; he and Haslam conversed at length. Haslam made no progress whatsoever in breaking Matthews' will, nor Matthews when it came to convincing Haslam of his sanity, but later events will make it clear that they nevertheless spent a good deal of time together. Haslam rarely saw his colleagues Monro and Crowther, both of whom he disliked in any case, and Matthews must have offered more stimulating company than the average lunatic. Matthews, remaining deprived of family visits throughout, had few other options for conversation. Haslam began to keep a dossier of Matthews' writings, and even asked him to write and draw particular parts of his story. He might have had the first stirrings of the idea that Matthews represented a goldmine of psychopathology such as might come along only once in a lifetime, and that the combination of a talented doctor and an extraordinary patient might somehow add up to more than the sum of their parts.

In the outside world, too, things were gradually stirring. Another group of people largely invisible to history, Matthews' friends and family, had not forgotten him. If they had, we would never have heard from him again. But in the autumn of 1809, a solicitor's letter was presented to the Bethlem Sub-committee. It was an order to the governors of Bethlem Hospital 'to shew cause why a writ of Habeas Corpus should not issue to them commanding them to have James Tilly Matthews before the Lord Chief Justice of this Court at his Chambers in Serjeants Inn Chancery Lane'. In other words, if they wanted to keep Matthews in Bedlam, they were going to have to explain why to a court of law.

Habeas corpus – the right of an individual to be free from arbitrary imprisonment – was one of the most prized settlements of the Glorious Revolution of 1688, a marker of the end of the despotic powers of the King. It had recently and controversially been curtailed by Pitt's government as part of the raft of emergency powers that followed the French Revolution, but had been restored when Pitt lost power in 1801. The case for the prosecution was that Matthews was sane, and it came in the form of a series of affidavits sworn before the King's Bench that November.

This was not a trial: the opposing sides didn't meet, the witnesses weren't cross-examined, and the contested subject, Matthews himself, played no part. Documents were presented and compared, and supplementary documents added. Although Matthews is the focus, at this stage we are forced to try to make sense of him at second hand and in the third person, testifying in echo and interrogated by proxy. Later, when we hear his own authentic voice at length, we may begin to understand how so many witnesses could hold such entirely contradictory views.

The family's opening testimony was dramatic: two affidavits signed by independent doctors named George Birkbeck and Henry Clutterbuck. Both were fully qualified MDs and, as it transpired, each had paid no fewer than six extended visits, together and separately, to Matthews in Bedlam over the preceding months. Both, too, were in complete agreement. According to Birkbeck's testimony, he had 'attempted by every mode of examination he could devise to discover James Tilly Matthews' real state of mind', and 'the result of such careful & repeated & unprejudiced examinations has been that the said James Tilly Matthews is not insane'. Haslam – not, of course, a qualified MD – had taken no part in their examinations, but Birkbeck and Clutterbuck had discussed the case with their colleague Thomas Monro. They had asked Monro whether there were 'any particular subject or subjects which on being mentioned within Matthews' hearing did produce maniacal hallucinations'; Monro replied that he 'was not acquainted with any such subject but that he believed him to be insane'. The examinations continued, and Birkbeck and Clutterbuck reported their opinion to Monro. Monro's response was limp: 'although he might not succeed in convincing them that Mr. Matthews was deranged he had a feeling on which he could rely that Mr. Matthews was insane or words of the same import'.

Not for the first time, a Bethlem doctor looked lost for

words, and Birkbeck hammered home his diagnosis. The most marked symptoms of Matthews' condition were 'his inflexible resistance to the admission of his alleged insanity' and 'his unabated hostility against the Physician and Apothecary to whose care he had been entrusted during his long confinement'. Surely these 'symptoms' were liable to an obvious interpretation, that they were no more nor less than we should expect from a sane man unjustly confined? 'The mind of James Tilly Matthews', Birkbeck concluded, 'is sound.' Clutterbuck's second opinion echoed Birkbeck's precisely: 'he could not discover any thing that indicated insanity in James Tilly Matthews and he verily believes him to be perfectly sane'.

Monro's opinion more or less ridiculed, Haslam's simply ignored. But the prosecution had more. The next affidavit was from a merchant named Robert Dunbar, friend of the Matthews family and voice of the coalition that had been organizing itself behind the scenes. His contention was straightforward: that Matthews 'should be removed from Bethlem Hospital, conceiving him to be recovered from his malady and capable of providing for himself and family'.

As well as acquainting the court with the resolution the family would favour, Dunbar also had a couple of unexpected grenades to lob. A few months before, he stated, he had been dining in a tavern in the City of London when, quite by chance, he noticed John Haslam in the same establishment. Haslam was showing his dining companion a manuscript written by one of his patients, which Dunbar 'observed to be the handwriting of James Tilly Matthews'. He introduced himself, told Haslam that he knew Matthews and asked after him. Haslam replied that he saw Matthews twice a week, and that he was 'very well'. Dunbar pressed him on his state of mind, especially the subjects 'upon which he used to be incoherent'. Haslam told him that Matthews 'never now touched upon these subjects but that he was perfectly quiet', and furthermore that 'it was a thousand pities he could not be restored to his family as he considered him a very clever man'.

After this incident, Dunbar had made further enquiries and turned up another very odd detail. He had approached the parish of Camberwell and urged them to look into the Matthews business. They had arranged a meeting with the Bethlem governors, to which Dunbar and his friends were refused admission, but Dunbar had later spoken with one of the governors who had claimed that Matthews was being confined 'in consequence of a letter from Lord Liverpool, directing his being there detained'.

This, if true, was more than curious. It suggested a possibility which had hitherto never been raised: that Matthews' madness or sanity wasn't, after all, the issue. Was he actually in Bedlam not because he was mad, but because he was an enemy of the state, and specifically of Lord Liverpool? In short, were his persecution fantasies real?

Dunbar's claim was restated by the next witness, Joseph Sadler, a carpenter who was also one of the overseers of the poor in the parish of Camberwell. Sadler confirmed that Matthews' family and friends had told him in August that their relative was now perfectly sane, and that 'they would take charge of him if he were released from the Bethlem Hospital and exonerate the Parish from any further charge for his maintenance'. One of the Camberwell churchwardens had followed this up with the Bethlem governors, who told him that Matthews 'could not be discharged from the Hospital as he was one of the worst of lunatics'. But the churchwarden had persisted: Matthews was their pauper, and they were unwilling to keep paying for his upkeep if there wasn't anything wrong with him. At this point the parish of Camberwell were informed that Matthews 'was a State Prisoner and the Parish would no longer be required to contribute to his maintenance'.

Matthews had entered Bedlam as a ward of the parish of Camberwell, who had paid his bond, not as a state prisoner. Now, if all this was true, his status had changed without anyone being informed, and once this had been brought to Camberwell's attention, Matthews' bill had been quietly picked up by the Home Office. This was becoming more than a plea for compassion from an unfortunate lunatic's family; it was starting to look like a serious institutional irregularity, perhaps even a major political scandal.

But the family were not out for blood: their final affidavit made it clear that they hoped not to create problems but to solve them. They concluded their case with a possible resolution in the form of a guarantee offered by three of their number: Robert Dunbar, Richard Staveley (Matthews' nephew by marriage) and another family friend named George Hodgson. What they proposed to Bethlem was 'restoring Matthews to his friends and thereby relieving your highly valuable institution from any further charge and rendering his family happy after a separation of thirteen years'. They would take over responsibility for Matthews from the parish of Camberwell and personally guarantee his behaviour with 'any security they may require'.

It looked like a tight case, with all the angles covered. Independent experts had pronounced Matthews sane. The parish of Camberwell had no interest in continuing to pay for a patient who had recovered. Matthews' family and friends would take full responsibility for his release. Bethlem seemingly had two choices: either to explain how a lunatic could appear so thoroughly sane, or to admit that Matthews was being confined for some other more shadowy, and perhaps less constitutional, reason.

The affidavits on behalf of Bethlem opened on the first front, and with far bigger guns than Matthews' family could muster. Their first medical testimony was from the Commissioners in Lunacy themselves, the highest statutory body in the land, along with several of their colleagues from the Royal College of Physicians. They were headed by Sir Lucas Pepys, Physician to his Majesty, and Robert Darling

Willis, son of the Rev. Dr Francis Willis, both of whom had attended George III during his illnesses. All four commissioners and four other members of the Royal College of Physicians had been to visit Matthews in his cell, and their report took up a good deal less space than their credentials and honorifics. All they had to say was that 'they took considerable pains in ascertaining the state of his mind and that it is their positive and decided opinion as a result of such examination that the Patient is in a most deranged state of intellect and wholly unfit to be at large'.

Thomas Monro's testimony was similarly brief and, like that of the commissioners, more an assertion of personal authority than a presentation of evidence. 'From his intimate acquaintance with the patient', he recorded, he had 'never felt the smallest doubt with respect to his insanity and does now believe him to be a most insane and dangerous lunatic and wholly unfit to be at large, having scarcely in the whole period of his professional practice and experience known any patient more completely and unequivocally mad'. Emphatic repetition, Monro seems to have hoped, will compensate for the lack of detail. He made no reference to any discussions with Birkbeck and Clutterbuck, or to their opinion that his grip on the facts of the case was alarmingly vague. Monro was nominally responsible for hundreds of lunatics, routinely labelled curable or incurable without complaint. He adduced no evidence, no details of his personal observations, nothing that demonstrated he even knew which patient was under discussion.

So Bethlem's big guns roared, but their ammunition was rather underpowered. These were men from the world of private doctoring turning out the kind of statements private doctors turned out every day: certificates, prescriptions and sick-notes where the letters after the doctor's name counted for more than the stock phrases scribbled below them. The Commissioners in Lunacy were a statutory body whose existence was a response to, and a safeguard against, scandals in private madhouses; given a pauper lunatic to pronounce upon, they seem to have done little more than append their signatures to the governors' request. If they were aware of Birkbeck and Clutterbuck's testimony, they made no attempt to refute it. Madness was a diagnosis that was somewhat academic, especially for those abandoned in Bedlam. In private madhouses the sane might be conspired against for their wealth or property, but who could possibly gain from calling a pauper mad?

The affidavit of Mr John Haslam, Apothecary to Bethlem Hospital, was a very different document. Conspicuously lacking the professional or social credentials of his superiors, he made it equally conspicuous that his knowledge of the case was far superior. His testimony is extremely detailed, longer than all the other affidavits for prosecution and defence put together. He refers to extensive case notes and documents written by Matthews, and offers to produce more if required. He lays out in detail the conspiracies and treasons occupying Matthews' mind on his admission to Bedlam, and his delusions of poisoning and covert observation. He also attempts to bring much-needed clarification to the diagnosis Matthews received after the first year of his stay: he was kept confined as an incurable because of 'his madness having assumed the most marked features of hostility & vengeance to their Majesties and many branches of the Royal Family'.

Haslam goes on to develop this theme at some length. Matthews' delusions, he claims, developed extravagantly along these lines. After his visit to Lord Kenyon, Matthews 'more particularly directed his threats towards his present Majesty and the Royal Family, deriving his own rights to the Crown from King Edward III'. Haslam has in his possession, and offers to display, various documents in Matthews' hand 'denouncing vengeance and death against his Majesty, the Members of the Privy Council, Secretaries of State, Judges,

Governors of the Hospital and all authorities, offering different rewards for their lives'.

There can be little doubt that, among Matthews' voluminous writings, there were accusations that George III was an 'impostor and usurper'; Haslam, after all, would hardly have made such a show of offering them to the court if they didn't exist. As we shall see, some of Matthews' surviving *oeuvre* tends quite spectacularly along these lines, but although he denounced the King his threats of actual violence against him were, to say the least, fantastical and obscure. The act that brought him to Bedlam – crying treason in the House – was far from one of homicidal mania: on the contrary, it was one which scrupulously followed due constitutional process. There is a hint of entrapment here, and opportunism on Haslam's part. With the well-publicized cases of Peg Nicholson and James Hadfield before them, everyone knew there were lunatics who wanted to kill the King, and that Bedlam was where they were kept. It was uncontroversial that such cases should be confined indefinitely; in fact, the new designation of criminal lunatic had been specially created for them. Haslam's best chance of making Matthews seem to the court to be dangerously mad would be, either by evidence or by association, to bracket him with the notorious regicides.

As the affidavit proceeds, Robert Dunbar's story of his chance meeting with Haslam receives some circumstantial corroboration. Haslam goes on to admit that, in the last couple of years, Matthews has improved. Recently 'he appears to have been aware that his particular hallucination or weak part was politics, & that when he has been interrogated on the subject of his former opinions he has generally replied that he should give no answer to such questions'. In other words, he understands that part of his mental world is regarded by others as delusional, and has learnt to avoid talking about it.

The question is whether this means that Matthews is now recovered. This is, of course, a question about madness itself, and this is the area where Haslam takes strong issue with Birkbeck and Clutterbuck. The two independent doctors have interviewed Matthews at great length, and established that he's perfectly capable of holding sane, even remarkably cogent conversation. He can clearly pass for sane in society, and can no longer be provoked into madness by any topic of conversation. How many of the rest of us can claim as much?

But for Haslam this is not enough. In order to be sane, the patient must recant his previous madness. To be sane is not, in Haslam's view, about the ability to behave normally in company, it is about the true state of the inner man. Matthews, when pushed on the subject of his madness, will still maintain 'that he never was insane at any period of his life but always in his perfect senses'. His new-found grasp of how to behave in society is analogous to Galileo blithely swearing before the Inquisition that the Earth doesn't move, quietly convinced that his confession makes no difference to the universe at large. But Haslam is a sterner inquisitor: he's not interested in what Matthews has decided to say, but whether or not he believes it. It is not enough for the mad to learn to play society's game; a doctor must be able to rub salt into their former wounds, and see no evidence of pain. For Haslam to be satisfied, Matthews must submit entirely to the mastery of the doctor's paradigm. He must, as it were, truly love Big Brother. Haslam's conclusion is that 'as a medical question he is well warranted in putting the question of Matthews' sanity or insanity upon such issue', and that ultimately 'the patient is not now of sound mind or he could have no objection to converse or be questioned upon those subjects where he is well aware that his derangement would be manifest'.

As a final proof of this derangement Haslam offers up, for the first time on public record, the Air Loom. Within the last week this allegedly sane patient has testified, before Haslam and other physicians, 'that there had long been & was then an immense machine underground near the Hospital under the management of powerful and evil agents with whom Matthews had frequently had intercourse, by means of which machine the said Matthews was acted upon and impregnated to his great and serious injury'. The actions of the Air Loom were, moreover, not confined to Matthews: 'many other persons were likewise under such malignant influence & the infallible proof of such agency being exerted upon any particular persons was that at the time of such persons swallowing, a noise was heard by them like the creaking of a wicker basket when pressed together'.

Here was big game from the far shores of madness, the kind of palpable insanity impossible to invent and, by the same token, a demonstration of Haslam's prowess. Birkbeck and Clutterbuck might have the letters MD after their name, but they could have conversed with Matthews till the end of time and found nothing but sanity. Haslam, by contrast a specialist mad-doctor, could materialize the awful machine of madness at will.

To Haslam's testimony is appended a brief response to Dunbar: he had never met the man in any coffee-house (the location has changed from Dunbar's tavern), and first clapped eyes on him in Bethlem a few months earlier. The only explanation could be 'some inaccuracy or misconception on the part of Mr. Dunbar'. It was one man's word against the other.

After Haslam's statement, one final and unexpected piece of medical evidence was cited: the affidavit of a man named Peter Mortimer, who submitted that he had known Matthews before his admission to Bethlem. He had met him on a ship returning from France, and had proposed at Dover that they should split the costs of a carriage to London. Matthews told him that he would be glad to, and that he had already ordered a coach and four horses. Mortimer balked at that, saying 'he never travelled in so expensive a style'; he was thinking of two horses. Matthews replied that, in that case, he'd happily accept a smaller contribution. They set off, and no sooner had they left Dover than Matthews ordered an outrider, for whom he had also paid, to gallop ahead and line up fresh horses at Canterbury. If they were waiting when the coach and four arrived, he would pay the outrider half a guinea, and the same to the postillions who provided the horses. At Canterbury they found fresh horses waiting. Matthews paid everyone, and they pressed on. The same happened at Sittingbourne, and again at Rochester, and then again at Dartford. Here, Matthews told Mortimer that he had to leave him because 'he must turn off into another road'. Mortimer protested, pointing out that he had paid for a passage to London. Matthews swore that Mortimer 'should not be a loser by him', and paid for another carriage to take him to London.

The next time Mortimer saw Matthews he was 'in Bethlem Hospital, where he was brought as an insane patient'. He had seen him several times since, and 'firmly believes him to have continued insane and to be so at this present'. He added that 'the particular turn of Matthews' lunacy has been politics', and that he 'considers from his peculiar opinions that it would be highly dangerous and unsafe to the state if Matthews were permitted to be at large'.

Here is an independent witness testifying to Matthews' insanity, but Mortimer's story surely raises more questions than it answers. We find ourselves here in a completely different world, as far from Bedlam's incurable wing as it's possible to imagine. Matthews' vital mission is abruptly not merely in his head, but palpably on the road. Our pauper lunatic is suddenly galloping through the night on urgent business, spending money like water, and giving every impression of being a capable, purposeful and remarkably generous man of means. This is a glimpse of a far bigger and previously unsuspected story, presented without comment or explanation and not dwelt upon for a moment longer than was necessary.

The next affidavit, that of the Bethlem governors, may have been expected to tie up some of these loose ends, but it rather did the opposite. Richard Baldwin, the treasurer at St Bartholomew's Hospital and one of Bethlem's governors, submitted the most baffling statement thus far. It opens sedately on message, with the statement that Baldwin 'firmly believes Matthews to have been insane throughout the period of his confinement & still to continue so', and repeats the refrain that 'from the bias of the patient's mind towards political subjects, his being at large would be likely to be highly dangerous to the safety of His Majesty's Person'. Thereafter, it veers off alarmingly into territory that confirms Dunbar's evidence of strange dealings behind the scenes. Baldwin, along with other members of the subcommittee, had examined Matthews in September 1809 'in consequence of a letter having been sent by Order of the Lord Chancellor which stated that the Patient's friends had represented to His Lordship that he was not in a state of derangement'. As a result of this examination the subcommittee decided that Matthews was still insane, but also that 'they could have no objection to deliver him to his Friends upon the application of the Parish of Camberwell provided the Lord Chancellor should consider it proper for them to do so'.

At this point the case for the defence appears to be unravelling fast. Thus far they have insisted that Matthews is mad; now, suddenly, whether Matthews is mad or not is no longer the issue. The question has somehow, mysteriously, become political. But the Lord Chancellor's reply, it turns out, bounced the decision back to Bedlam. His secretary sent a letter 'in which he stated that he did not consider the case of said patient to be one in which his Lordship's authority could be exercised'. He recommended that the only way to resolve the issue would be a writ of habeas corpus, and that he had communicated this to Matthews' family and to Robert Dunbar.

Like Matthews' midnight ride, the Lord Chancellor has been

briefly whisked on stage only for the curtain to be abruptly dropped, the opposition once more reduced to Matthews' friends and family. At this, the Bethlem governors seem to have recovered their fighting spirit. Their case is now that 'it was very unlikely Mr. Dunbar and his other friends had any intention of preventing said patient from being at large', and that 'it was no more than a public duty in them to prevent said patient from being let loose upon society unless some further opinions should first be taken upon his case by such medical persons as are duly commissioned by the College of Physicians to visit insane patients'. In other words, the governors' strategy would now be to take a back seat and allow the David-and-Goliath struggle between Matthews' friends and the Commissioners in Lunacy to play itself out.

But Dunbar's evidence has exposed the back-story. We begin to understand why the case has taken so long to reach the courts: it has already been kicked around the highest reaches of government, and habeas corpus has emerged as the only legal recourse at the suggestion of the Lord Chancellor him-self. Presumably, up until this point, the Bethlem governors had taken the line that Matthews' confinement was not a question of his madness but of state security. But the pressure exerted by his friends had blown their cover, and the Lord Chancellor had washed his hands of the case. It was now, once again, a question of his state of mind – and the awkward question of why, in an overcrowded and cash-strapped Bedlam, the governors were confining a man who seemed to be entirely capable of handling himself in the outside world and who had sponsors queueing up to take responsibility for him. Could it be that this awkward question concealed an even more awkward answer: that Matthews was indeed, as he had always maintained, the victim of a high-level political conspiracy?

Mad, a state prisoner, mad once more; and another twist was yet to come. This took the form of a final piece of testimony from the governors, hurriedly scribbled, presumably a last-minute response to the facts that had unexpectedly emerged. In addition to the previous affidavits, it added, 'it may be necessary to state that at the time when the Parish of Camberwell and the friends of the patient appeared so desirous of his discharge, it was considered by the Governors as merely their duty to state the facts of such application to the Government of the Country'. Their previous evidence had implied that they were approached by the Lord Chancellor after the family petitioned him; the fact that they had approached him first had, it seemed, slipped their minds. And the reason they gave for doing so turned the entire case on its head again: they had, they now asserted, 'always considered the Patient as virtually a Government patient although not in the Hospital under a letter from the Secretary of State'.

Curiouser and curiouser. Now Matthews' madness seems never to have been the issue; but neither is he a state prisoner, except 'virtually', whatever that may mean. And whatever it means, it has apparently been the case ever since he was admitted. Thus the recent discussions with the Lord Chancellor, the Commissioners in Lunacy's evidence, Matthews' visit to Lord Kenyon, even his assessment as incurable over a decade ago, have all been charades. Matthews' condition, and his indefinite confinement, had by this account been set in stone before he even stepped through the gates of Bedlam.

But the governors' scribbled and garbled testimony concealed a killer blow. It was a cover-note to the briefest, perhaps the clearest and certainly the most influential statement of the entire hearing. The governors now revealed that they had, upon being summoned to the King's Bench, solicited clarification of Matthews' position from on high. Two months previously, they had written to Lord Liverpool, now Home Secretary, and had received the following brief note:

Whitehall 7th Sept 1809

Gentlemen,
I recommend that you do continue to detain in your hosp. as
a fit and proper subject James Tilly Matthews a lunatic who is
at present under your charge, & care shall be taken that the
customary Expences of Cloathing &c together with the
Expences of his funeral in case he dies there shall be
defrayed.

I have the honour to be
Gentlmn
Your most obedient humble servt
Liverpool

This was clearly the biggest gun of all, and one which the
governors admitted they were hoping they wouldn't need to
fire. It had, they wrote, 'hitherto been judged advisable on the
part of the Hospital to give it no prominence on the present
occasion'. But the family's evidence had forced their hand, and
once fired, the heavy artillery rendered all their previous
defences unnecessary. The remainder of their cover-note
effected a swift retreat from their former position, and
effectively retracted the evidence presented by Haslam, Monro
and the Commissioners in Lunacy. The governors now recast
the narrative with the question of madness relegated to the
technical footnotes. They confessed that 'the patient first came
in it is true, from the Parish of Camberwell', but insisted that
he was 'always considered as in the Hospital by the order and
with the knowledge of Government'. The reason for this
anomaly was that Matthews' admission predated the Criminal
Lunatic Bill precipitated by James Hadfield's attempt on the
King's life, and there had been no proper procedure at the time
to legitimize his confinement. This regrettable loophole was
now closed, and Matthews' case was unique.

Having taken this line, the governors were now prepared to extend a generosity towards Matthews which contradicted all their expert medical testimony. As far as they were concerned, Matthews' discharge was now 'truly desirable', not merely because he was a burden on their charitable resources but also because of 'the very great and most improper trouble occasioned for many years past by the detention of this particular patient'. But the judge must decide the proper weight to give to Liverpool's request. The governors, for their part, would only add that they were 'not unmindful that they have a serious duty to perform by the Sovereign and public as well as by the patients and their friends'.

All that remained was for the magistrate to weigh the interests of the Home Secretary, the King and the general public against those of a pauper (and possibly criminal) lunatic and his accomplices. The writ of habeas corpus was rejected.

The verdict was, in one way or another, a disaster for all concerned. Bedlam might have won, but its case was a shambles of contradictions and evasions. The profession's statutory body, the Commissioners in Lunacy, had presented the thinnest of evidence, which had turned out to be irrelevant in any case. The governors had used their own physicians to support their case and then instructed the judge to ignore their professional opinions. It was a victory that would turn out within a few years to contain the seeds of their destruction, a calamity in which Matthews' case would play a conspicuous part.

It was no less of a disaster for Haslam. He had presented the only medical evidence of any quality, and in return had been humiliated with another casual reminder of how little authority he held, even within an institution so sorely in need of professional competence. His opinion had been contradicted by Birkbeck and Clutterbuck, and no conclusion had been reached except that his attempts to set the question of Matthews' state of mind on a proper medical footing were of little interest to his employers.

Once again, Haslam's medical theory was ahead of its time. Psychiatrists today are well aware of how psychoses can be, in the modern term, 'encapsulated'; hours of casual questioning on general subjects can fail to expose well-defended delusional thinking. They are agreed, too, that in such cases it's crucial to probe for deeply buried signs of mental disturbance: even encapsulated delusions can, on occasion, erupt into violence or self-destructive behaviour, and a doctor who failed to identify this possibility would be negligent. Haslam's insistence that such patients are only apparently sane is, in the modern view, not a hair-splitting technicality but a *sine qua non* of secure diagnosis.

Haslam was back to square one: still in Bedlam, with Matthews still in residence, and still a painfully long way from making his mark in the world. If he had hoped that mad-doctoring was soon to propel him to prominence within the profession, his prospects must at this point have looked bleak indeed. But, just as Bedlam's victory contained the seeds of its defeat, so Haslam's ignored testimony contained the seeds of the work for which he would be remembered to this day. James Tilly Matthews' continued confinement would bestow blessings, and curses, Haslam could not have foreseen.

It was Matthews, of course, for whom the verdict was the greatest disaster. Not only had he failed to escape from Bedlam, but the anomalous and inconclusive nature of the judgement made it highly unlikely he would be granted the chance to appeal again. His family and friends had assembled an impeccable case, most of which had been ignored. The testimony of the expert witnesses, whom he had convinced of his sanity over a long series of interviews, had gone for nothing. The governors had admitted that, as far as they were concerned, there was no good reason why he should still be there. According to the letter of the law, he was neither insane nor a political prisoner. No wonder the most prominent symptom of his supposed madness was persecution mania.

To make matters worse, the architect of his persecution had been exposed, and nobody had paid the slightest attention. Whatever had happened in France, it had ended with Matthews accusing Lord Liverpool of treason. Now, twelve long years later, Lord Liverpool had personally intervened to make sure that he stayed in Bedlam until his death. It was surely obvious to everyone that there was more behind this than an isolated incident in the House of Commons one afternoon in the previous century. If this was the whole story, then the Home Secretary's persecution mania was surely more extreme than that of the alleged lunatic. Matthews had by nobody's account even threatened violence against Liverpool – at least, until he entered the looking-glass world of Bedlam. Witnesses were now queueing up to take responsibility for him, stressing that he was no longer a public nuisance. It was barely credible that Liverpool should have even remembered Matthews' interruption unless it concealed a bigger story, one in which the Home Secretary had something quite serious to hide.

The habeas corpus hearing leaves us begging for the real James Tilly Matthews to stand up. It presents us with a veritable platoon of Matthewses, many of them mutually exclusive. We hear of the Matthews who was 'perfectly sane', not presenting 'any thing that indicated insanity'. We hear of the 'most insane and deranged lunatic', the 'most completely and unequivocally mad' inmate of Bedlam. We hear of the violent Matthews, with his 'most marked features of hostility & vengeance to their Majesties', and also of Matthews the victim, whose release would do no more than 'render his family happy by his return'. We hear of Matthews the international man of mystery, and Matthews the parish pauper; a man understood by the doctors to be a political prisoner, and by the politicians to be a lunatic. Which Matthews would we find if we were to reconstruct the verifiable details of his life, and hear from him in his own words? Would we winnow out the true version, or would we find all of the above, and more besides?

The clues were in plain sight, but there was no-one to ask the obvious question: what had actually happened in France all those years ago?

4

REVOLUTION

'Bliss was it in that great dawn to be alive
But to be young was very Heaven!'
William Wordsworth, *The Prelude*, 1805

JAMES TILLY MATTHEWS GHOSTS INTO HISTORY UNDER THE WING OF
a more famous man: David Williams.

Williams, like Matthews, was a Welshman who found himself in London in the 1780s. At the age of fourteen he had
promised his father on his death-bed that he would become a
dissenting minister at Carmarthen, but as his teenage years
rolled on the company of women, as he puts it in his autobiography, 'seduced me into the paths of pleasure', making his
father's career choice inappropriate. Instead, he began to
write, lecture and network prodigiously in radical political
circles. The progress of reason and happiness in life, it seemed
to him, was terminally hamstrung by religious differences.
Opposing religious sects were, in essence, the tinpot local
deities of different tribes and interest groups, and thus a
disastrous basis for national politics. He began working with a
like-minded group on a constitutional document that would
transcend sectarian divides, requiring only belief in a Supreme

David Williams

Being, 'the regulating principle or Good of the solar system'. This was published in 1776 as a *Liturgy on the Universal Principles of Religion and Morality*, to international acclaim: the great French *philosophes* Voltaire and Rousseau both welcomed it warmly. In Britain, though, it proved more divisive. One of Williams' colleagues on the working group was Benjamin Franklin, who had become *persona non grata* in government circles because of his support for the independence of the American colonies. Franklin fled the country, stashing his personal papers at Williams' house in Chelsea, and the project for an enlightened constitution was forced underground.

Williams' zeal for reform soon found other channels. Lecturing became his main source of income, and education one of his specialist subjects. Opposed to learning by rote, he insisted that children should learn by asking questions until they had evolved their own point of view. Increasingly, he began to teach not just children but adults, mature students and foreigners, about the political world and the theories that underpinned it. He gave courses in Pall Mall, in Great Russell Street, and at Carlisle House, where his School of Eloquence held weekly debates.

Williams presented himself as an expert on teaching, rhetoric and theory, but the hidden agenda of political reform was never far below the surface. The Glorious Revolution of 1688, which the mainstream of British public opinion held to have ushered in the most advanced and enlightened political system in the world, was to Williams seriously flawed. In his view, it had concentrated far too much power at the centre of government, out of fear of political instability, and as a result had subjugated the happiness of the people to a cabal of parliamentary cronies, who naturally fell into corrupt horse-trading behind closed doors. How, Williams asked, might it be possible to 'get the will of the people freely and properly expressed'? What was the most effective way of 'organising society into a body'? His *Letters on Political Liberty* proposed new democratic systems: 'tythings', 'hundreds', 'counties', with the will of the people expressing itself from the bottom up, rather than a handful of politicians imposing policy from the top down.

It is in this milieu of lectures and public debates on free-thinking and secular reform, edging already into a political radicalism that was shortly to be labelled treason, that we hear first of James Tilly Matthews, as one of Williams' pupils. In Williams' account, and many subsequent official documents, we also receive a second snippet of context: Matthews is a businessman, a wholesale tea-dealer. This locates him in a second milieu that dovetails neatly enough with the first.

The late eighteenth century was boom-time in the tea trade. Tea had been one of the great success stories of the century, but for most of that time the traffic had been sewn up by the East India Company, which had a monopoly on imports from China. Increasingly, though, the company's restrictive practices began to haemorrhage money to a parallel trade: smuggling. By 1780, smuggled tea, and legal tea adulterated with local leaves such as sloe, was on the point of overtaking the volume of official imports. William Pitt was forced to introduce a Commutation Bill in 1784 which reduced the tax on imported tea from its extortionate level of 119 per cent down to a modest 12 per cent. Prices dropped, smuggling waned, consumption rose; the number of shops with a licence to sell tea tripled to 150,000. Pitt filled the hole in the Treasury accounts with the infamous 'window tax'.

The boom also had a dramatic effect on the trade's social profile. The gentlemen-adventurers of the East India Company still sent the contracts out to China and received the bulk shipments at the East India Docks, but now a crowded tier of subsidiary dealers emerged under them, buying up large consignments, blending them, packing them, and selling on to the new retail customers. Tea auctions were held four times a year at East India House in Leadenhall Street, now the site of the Lloyd's building. Auctions were held 'by the candle', the hammer coming down on each lot once an inch of candle had burned. Behind the grand classical frontage of East India House a labyrinth of small offices hummed with constant activity. Matthews' office, in Leadenhall Street, was right in the heart of the action.

Many of the new dealers, like Matthews, had come from the

Tea auction at East India House

provinces. Even during the company monopoly, a small number of wholesale traders had made spectacular fortunes. Twining's Tea had been founded by a weaver from the Cotswolds driven to London by the eclipse of the local textile trade; within a couple of generations the family had built up a substantial trading empire with over a thousand customers. Mary Tuke, of the York Quaker family, had begun selling tea in 1725; despite a fine and a rap on the knuckles for not being a member of the Company of Merchant Adventurers, she had persisted and thrived, and her company still trades as a subsidiary of Twining's.

Tuke Mennell & Co., as they became, were also at the forefront of another tendency in the growing numbers of provincial tea-traders: philanthropy and progressive reform. Many of the families entering the business were Unitarians, Quakers or other dissenters, and by the 1780s the trade had developed solidarity, and a degree of political clout, around their favoured causes. They campaigned vociferously for the suppression of smuggling and for a reduction in taxes, not just out of self-interest but from the moral high ground: many refused to deal in the cheaper and more lucrative smuggled tea. They supported the American colonists in their struggle for no taxation without representation, and refused to claim compensation after the Boston Tea Party. They agitated for the fair treatment of Chinese growers, and against slavery. They spoke out for peace in times of war; many were early partisans of the French Revolution. And the Tuke family in particular, as we shall see later, were important pioneers in the humane treatment of lunatics.

So the two second-hand traces of Matthews in the 1780s – pupil of David Williams and wholesale tea-merchant – combine to cast a circumstantial shadow: a Welshman come to London, in the thick of a bullish world of trade, with an office on the edge of the City and a young family, spending evenings educating himself in politics and philosophy, surrounded in work and leisure by the intoxicating spirit of progress and humanitarian reform. Of course, this context offers no certainty as to what is really going on inside a man's head, but Matthews' later writings confirm abundantly that the image conjured here is close to the image he held of himself. Of Williams, he was to say simply: 'he is my tutor and as all mankind knows his staunch republican principles, it cannot be wondered at that I should possess the same principles'.

A third faint trace locates Matthews with some precision in Camberwell Grove, in the centre of the south London suburb, in a smart town house just down the hill from the estate of Dr John Lettsom, founder of the Medical Society of London, philanthropist and owner of Lettsom Park, an estate with extensive gardens, views over the City, a menagerie and a famous collection of curios. Much later in Matthews' story they will meet in Lettsom's official capacity as doctor, and both will recall a previous meeting, around 1785, when Lettsom showed Matthews around his private collection.

But none of these circumstantial snippets accounts for Matthews' journey from a wholesale tea-dealership in Leadenhall Street to the dizzy heights of the world political stage. These heights were not attained by years of struggle so much as by a happenstance that would, years later, be transformed by a far greater force: the French Revolution.

Along with Matthews, another pupil of Williams' in the early 1780s had been a young French journalist and *littérateur* named Jacques-Pierre Brissot de Warville. Brissot was the scion of a well-to-do family from Chartres, and had been sent off to Paris to train as a lawyer, where he had added the aristocratic suffix 'de Warville' to his name; he would shortly lop it off again. He was in London trying to set up a forum where artists and scientists, French and English, could meet, debate and correspond, and to publish a journal of its transactions. Such ventures were becoming dangerous within old-regime France, and Brissot was keen to cross-pollinate the French intelligentsia with their radical counterparts in England and America by locating his *lycée* in London, and importing the journal back into Paris as the organ of an international movement. To begin with, the adventure flourished. The *Journal du Licée de Londres* emerged, self-published by Brissot, and French financiers began to take an interest. Brissot even approached the distinguished political philosopher Jeremy Bentham, who approved of Brissot's initiative. But investment failed to materialize. Brissot ploughed in all the cash he could, and called in favours to keep his fledgling enterprise from collapse, but collapse it did, leaving backers exposed and Brissot in debt, under a cloud of fraud allegations. He was briefly jailed, then released and returned to France. Ten years later, once he had become Foreign Minister in the Revolutionary government, this incident would be raked over by both sides: the British would expose his

bankruptcy and misspent youth, and his Jacobin rivals would
find in his prompt release from jail evidence that he had been
a British spy.

During his ill-fated British adventure, Brissot had been
deeply impressed by Williams and his civilizing mission. Here,
for Brissot, was a man who fitted the international ideal, someone who transcended national sects and prejudices and
embraced the common cause of humanity. Williams, in turn,
found Brissot a man of integrity whose international scheme

Jacques-Pierre Brissot

was 'benevolently designed' but 'extravagant and impracticable'. When the *lycée* project foundered, Williams was one of the first to whom Brissot had turned for help; Williams had offered him a post teaching at his Pall Mall lectureship, but Brissot was by that stage too far in debt. Back in Paris, Brissot continued to correspond, drawing heavily on Williams' ideas for his own formulation of republicanism, referring to him in print as his 'mentor', 'oracle' and 'English master', and effecting a far higher reputation for Williams in France than he had at home. He promulgated Williams' educational theories, claiming that the French would have to master them before they could nurture a nation of true republicans, and he translated *Letters on Political Liberty* into French, furnishing them with footnotes rather more radical than the original. The book was seized by the French government and Brissot found himself once again in jail, this time in the Bastille.

He was released quickly for a second time, and the incident did little harm to his future revolutionary credentials, which were in many ways impeccable. Throughout the 1780s he was a tireless proselytizer of the great *philosophes* Voltaire, Rousseau and Diderot's message: the more science and enlightenment, the less God and aristocracy, until the inevitable moment when humanity awakens and casts off its shackles. He was ambitious both for his causes and for himself, and a tireless formulator of grand schemes. His enthusiasm for undertaking the impossible and his persistence in carrying on regardless were both his strength and his eventual weakness.

Come 1789, he found himself in the thick of the first phase of events. He was a member of the National Assembly, a founder member of the radical Jacobin Club where he earned a reputation for fluent and passionate demagoguery, and a participant in the Tennis Court Oath by which delegates swore to 'live free or die' and not to rest until France had its own constitution. After the fall of the Bastille he began to publish his own newspaper, the influential *Le Patriote Français*, and he worked with the Constitutional Committee to produce the Declaration of the Rights of Man and the Citizen. By 1791 he was one of the best-known members of the Legislative Assembly, the new governing body formed after Louis XVI finally agreed to accept the new constitution and turn over the reins of power to the representatives of the people.

Throughout the momentous events he kept in close touch with Williams, who felt starved of impartial news from across the Channel: he claimed that Pitt's government was spending a fortune on corrupting the British press and fostering anti-republican propaganda, and he wanted to start a sister paper to *Le Patriote Français* in London. In August 1792 the new Republic included Williams in a select group of a dozen or so honorary French citizens, along with Joseph Priestley and Thomas Paine. And in November Brissot, now Foreign Minister, in conjunction with Roland, Minister of the Interior, wrote to Williams formally inviting him to Paris to work with the committee on drafting a new constitution for the Republic.

David Williams accepted, and James Tilly Matthews went with him.

We think of 1789 as the date of the French Revolution, and the storming of the Bastille as its defining event. Yet as late as halfway through 1792 most of the familiar images of the Revolution had yet to imprint themselves on the public consciousness. Louis XVI was still King, and the Assembly was negotiating a new constitutional arrangement alongside the monarchy, not so different from Britain's Glorious Revolution of 1688. The power and property of the Church were being gradually dismantled by political and legal means. France was at peace with its neighbours; in February, Pitt had told the House that fifteen years of peace had never seemed more likely. A visit to Paris in the spring of 1792 would have been more or less a routine matter. But the next few months changed everything, and by the time Matthews and Williams arrived in December they were treading a precarious line between being French spies or British traitors. They had received their invitation via a secret French agent in London, were travelling undercover and virtually on enemy soil, in a country militarized under a brutal police state, and were about to witness the most convulsive political events in living memory.

First, there was war. At the moment when Williams was being declared an honorary French citizen, the Prussian army was beginning incursions into French territory, threatening to destroy Paris if the King, at that point under house arrest, was harmed. In 1789, war had been pronounced an act incompatible with the pursuit of liberty, a last resort to be undertaken only in self-defence. But now the calls for peace, particularly from the old-guard generals of the *ancien régime*, looked like treason, a stitch-up between Europe's monarchs to sabotage the Revolution, subject France to partition by its neighbours and reverse the gains of democracy. The Assembly called for volunteers, a National Guard to defend *la patrie*; a huge detachment arrived in Paris from Marseilles, singing for the first time the bloodthirsty battle-hymn thenceforth known as 'La Marseillaise'.

With war came martial law, and the beginnings of the Terror. The most graphic symbol of the Revolution, the guillotine, had made its debut earlier in 1792 after a series of trials on live sheep; by August, it was installed outside Bedlam's architectural model, the Tuileries Palace. A national emergency was declared, and panic followed. Those who were not with the Revolution were against it. Thousands were rounded up, with no trials and mostly no evidence; nobles, priests, beggars, profiteers and 'enemies of the people' filled the Paris jails. As the National Guard trooped east to fight the Prussians, fear gripped the deserted city. The prisoners, many still rich in gold, were bribing their jailers to enter and leave at will; others were forging the new paper currency, the *assignat*, so liberally that its street value was plummeting. Rumours abounded that, with the help of undercover fifth columnists, the counter-revolutionaries were about to escape *en masse* and take over the capital. On 2 September 1792, hundreds of Parisian partisans, the raggedly dressed *sansculottes*, broke into the jails, dragged out the prisoners and butchered around 1,400 of them over four days.

The September Massacres were the first mass slaughter of the Revolution, indeed of the modern era of politics. As news of them leaked out to the outside world, it awoke to the realization that what was going on in France was something unprecedented, even unimaginable. This was chaos. The Assembly was powerless to stop the massacres, and they were prosecuted by makeshift and unpredictable kangaroo courts. Some were lenient: prisoners who pronounced themselves royalists but uninterested in politics were sometimes spared, and many found themselves embraced by those who a moment before had been bent on killing them. Others were brutal: prisoners were executed on the basis of spiteful gossip, or simply for having the same name as a known troublemaker. Rumours of thousands dead and the streets of Paris running with blood were accompanied by the sentiment that this was no revolution along British or American lines, but a ghastly collision of reason and nightmare, civilization and barbarism, whose end could no longer even be guessed at.

Yet even the Massacres were rapidly overtaken by other events. On 20 November the rag-tag National Guard volunteers, fighting with suicidal bravery in defence of the Republic, defeated a far better-equipped Prussian army at Valmy. Euphoria at the news was uncontained, and volunteers rushed in their thousands to extend French territory to the Rhine and the Netherlands. This was a new type of war, a war of liberation where the army offered its fraternity to the oppressed beyond their borders. 'War on the castles, peace to

The September Massacres

the cottages' was the battle-cry; they were not fighting their enemies, but defending them. 'Tyrannicides' were proposed, international hit squads to eliminate monarchs and despots across the globe.

Brissot threw his weight behind the new militarized Revolution. The 'mob' which massed daily on the Paris streets was a frightening beast to lead: unlike their medieval forebears, they were well informed, neither easily fooled nor easily scared, and constantly suspicious of those who had taken power in their name and were, as their mouthpiece Jean-Paul Marat put it, 'trafficking in our rights, our fortunes, our liberties, our lives'. War channelled their destructive energies into vital territorial gains. 'We cannot be calm', Brissot declaimed to the Assembly, 'until Europe, all Europe, is in flames.'

Such incendiary rhetoric, combined with the slow-burning horror of the emerging tales of massacre, had their effect on Britain. Public opinion swung fiercely behind King and country; Edmund Burke's dire warnings about the fate of revolutions became the new orthodoxy, with dissent aggressively marginalized. Loyalist militias began to arm themselves across the country, under the banner of Preservation of Liberty and Property against Republicans and Levellers. But Pitt and his Foreign Secretary, his cousin Lord Grenville, retained a studied neutrality. Public opinion was secure, and France not yet a military threat. Let the Revolution burn itself out, or others destroy it.

Despite war, massacre and international terror, the question emerging as the polarizing issue, both within France and outside it, was the fate of one man: Louis XVI. The original accommodation between King and Assembly had staggered from one crisis to another. Louis had dragged his heels at almost every stage of reform, attempted to flee the country and been constantly suspected of subterfuge and plots against the Revolution with the other crowned heads of Europe. On 22 September 1792, the Assembly had finally declared France a Republic and the new date Year One of Liberty, and within a few weeks had put the King on trial for treason.

This was a momentous decision. It led the Revolution deeper than ever into uncharted waters, and was the catalyst for a growing split within the Assembly itself. The trial was triggered by Brissot, who insisted that the *émigrés* – the French citizens, mostly aristocrats, who had fled the country after the Revolution – should have their assets seized by the state. This Louis refused to ratify, confirming suspicions that his true loyalties lay with preserving a future power-base for the nobility to reclaim. But, once the trial was in motion, Brissot and his colleagues began to back-pedal. Now they had a Republic, it was surely not necessary to try the King, still less to invoke the death penalty, a provocative move that would risk martyrdom, foreign invasion and civil war. Nor would a legal trial, with the King publicly arguing his case, do any favours for republican morale. Best to leave the King's guilt or innocence in abeyance, and the man himself a hostage against future eventualities.

But there was a more radical strand within the Assembly, increasingly identified with its after-hours haunt, the Jacobin Club, where the volatile entente between the Assembly and the mob was brokered. This 'Jacobin' power-base had come to focus not around the eloquent Brissot but the fastidious and squeaky-voiced provincial lawyer Maximilien Robespierre, whose presence in the Assembly was querulous and weak but whose clear-minded pragmatism carried much more weight in the huddles of the club. For Robespierre and the majority of committed Jacobins, Brissot's plan was unthinkable.

Maximilien Robespierre

Those who were not with the Revolution were against it, and prevaricating on the fate of the King was a betrayal of the patriotic fervour on the streets. The Paris mob was demanding his summary execution; why a legal trial at all, when he had been clearly guilty time and again of attempting to impede the progress of the Revolution? To hesitate on eliminating the monarchy was to show failure of nerve, and to allow the forces of counter-revolution to reorganize behind their most obvious and potent symbol.

This was only one issue on which the Jacobins were increasingly aligning themselves against Brissot and his allies, whom Robespierre began to call 'the faction of the Gironde', as several of their leaders were from the provinces around Bordeaux. The Girondins, as they became known, held that the declaration of the Republic had fulfilled the original aims of the Revolution, and that the task at hand was now to consolidate the new system, regularize the new political institutions and allow the people to resume their normal lives. Across the country as a whole the Revolution had been a patchy, often local affair, and support for it was waning in many of the regions. With liberty and equality in place, it was time to get on with the creation of national wealth and stability.

The Jacobins around Robespierre tended to have a very different constituency, and very different goals. Their power-base was the *sansculottes*, the working class who had been the heroes of the early Revolution and who could still be summoned onto the streets of the capital in their thousands by the ringing of the *tocsin*, the bell that had become both a familiar call to arms and a stirring motif of mob rule. To the Jacobins, the Girondins were foot-draggers, even back-sliders: comfortable professionals, lawyers and journalists who wished to hold on to their wealthy provincial bases and keep the Paris workers in their downtrodden place. For them, the Revolution had only just begun; to stop now would be to allow all the old oppressors – the Church, the aristocrats, the bourgeoisie – to pick up the pieces as before. Although neither Girondins nor Jacobins were political parties as such, the balance of power between them became ever more crucial. By the autumn of 1792 it was clear that the Girondins had overall control of the Assembly, but the Jacobins, if they played their cards right, were better placed to bring the people with them. The elected representatives might decide one thing, but the mobs on the street the next day could demand another.

This was the state of affairs in November, when Williams was invited to Paris. But between his acceptance and his arrival with Matthews in early December, relations with Britain had taken a further step into the abyss. The French army had crowned a campaign of extraordinary successes by defeating the Austrians at Jemappes and pressing on to occupy a large swathe of Belgium, and was now threatening the Netherlands. For Britain, this changed everything. The balance of power in Europe had been kept in check for 150 years by the Treaty of Westphalia, which France had now broken; a French Republic spread across the North Sea coast would mean that the entire coastline facing Britain would be in Republican hands. On 1 December, Pitt passed an Act of Parliament declaring a state of emergency and mobilizing militia armies across Britain, ratcheting up both his 'reign of terror' at home and the sabre-rattling across the Channel.

The next aggressive move, on either side, would have to mean all-out war.

A few days after Pitt's declarations, Williams and Matthews arrived in a Paris that was ominously quiet, the streets deserted in the raw winter, the uneasy feeling of a calm before a storm. The Revolution had changed the physical landscape of the city very little; the Gordon Riots a decade previously had done ten times more physical damage to London than three years of mob insurgency here. To the Welsh travellers, neither of whom spoke French or had visited Paris before, many of the recent changes would have been much less obvious than they were to the locals. There were fewer horses and carriages in the streets on account of the mass exodus of wealthy *émigrés*; fewer powdered wigs, with rich and poor alike reverting to the street mufti of artisan smocks. Street names had been changed to revolutionary themes; royal statues had been melted down. The streets themselves were plastered with posters and littered with pamphlets, as the Assembly promulgated their decisions daily and even hourly to the people. Life had a strange but often subtle sense of dislocation, with so many people doing jobs they had never done before, and new figures of authority unsure of their powers replacing old ones unsure of their lives.

Williams and Matthews checked into a hotel together. It's far from clear exactly why Williams invited Matthews to accompany him on this first visit. It's much easier to imagine why Matthews accepted: for an enthusiastic radical to have a ringside seat at the most momentous events of this or any other era was the chance of a lifetime. Matthews might also have known Brissot from his London adventures, although he himself is untypically silent on the subject. We have only Williams' account, written several years later – which, as we shall see, is rather disingenuous. Because of the way events turned out, Williams is at pains to play down his connections with Matthews to an implausible minimum. His version is that Matthews, with whom he had 'some acquaintance', 'followed me to Paris, as he protested, for the assistance I might afford him to see and understand the occurrences of the time'. Matthews, then, a former pupil with an interest in republican politics, is tagging along simply as a well-wisher and observer of the great drama. Once in Paris, Matthews pretends to be ill – a subterfuge, according to Williams, to avoid going out on his own, and to cling instead to his reluctant companion and observe his comings and goings. All this is a far from adequate account of events – apart from anything else, the political situation was

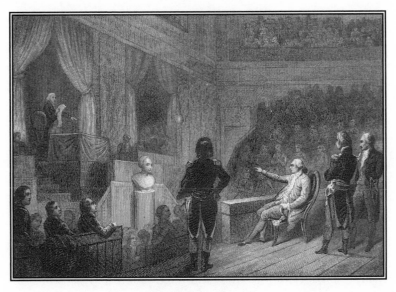

The trial of Louis XVI

hardly congenial to casual tourists visiting on a whim – but the pieces will fall into place soon enough.

Williams' activities, though, are a matter of public record. Things got off to a bad start: factional struggles between Girondins and Jacobins made it impolitic for him to attend the actual meetings of the constitutional committee, and he didn't speak French anyway; he was engaged instead to write out his criticisms of the 1791 Constitution in private at his hotel. The committee's work, in any case, more or less came to a stand-still when the King's trial began on 26 December. Williams attended proceedings throughout, and was appalled. Central to his theories was his belief that public affairs should be conducted with fastidious decorum, and he was shocked at the chaos and public denunciations flying from all sides, the 'criminal confusion' about what sort of legal or judicial system was in operation. The Assembly, it seemed to him, was fissuring into factional chaos before his eyes, while the Commune of the Paris *sansculottes* waited in the wings for the chance to seize power and bring the 'whole country crumbling into anarchy'. Williams, though a devout republican, was no revolutionary. According to his theories, politics should evolve according to 'the general order of nature, which arrives at its end by degrees'. Revolution, by contrast, opened the door to unnatural acts: 'violence, which may produce anarchy, by the very act of laying despotism in ruins'. But now events had overrun theories, and no amount of tinkering with the constitution was going to right the ship. Williams' vigil through the trial was a grim one, a front-row seat at the spectacle of his life's work being dismembered by violence and human frailty.

But he was also involved in a flurry of chaotic activity outside the trial. On 1 January 1793 a Committee of General Defence was formed in response to the looming hostility with Britain in order to formulate a foreign policy and present it to the Convention. Foreign Minister Brissot sat on it; so did Foreign Secretary Charles Le Brun, a former nobleman and partisan of Brissot from Bordeaux. Williams, both a French citizen and an expert on British affairs, was invited to attend, but the back-room committee sessions inspired him no more than the court procedures. The fact that Brissot was the Foreign Minister at all was, in his view, a sad indictment of the calibre of the revolutionary leaders. Brissot had been appointed on the strength of his foreign travels as a journalist, which was the closest to relevant experience the Assembly could muster; despite Williams' respect for his integrity, he felt he had 'neither genius nor knowledge for the part destined for him'.

Brissot's view of Britain was an all too relevant case in point. His time ten years earlier in the radical milieu of London had left him with the unshakeable impression that the British people were ready and willing to rise up in support of the Republic. Williams was unable to persuade him that the majority of Britain was unaware of his coterie's progressive views, or that the glory days of the 1780s, such as they had been, were now crushed under an iron fist of loyalism, counter-revolution and state repression. Brissot was equally bullish in his assessment of Britain's military will. The country was bankrupt, its colonies were vulnerable, its king was mad, Ireland would support the French; Pitt's government might rattle its sabres, but they knew that war with the patriotic armies of France was a disaster to be avoided at all costs. The two nations could bark at each other across the Channel all they liked, but in the end Britain would stay neutral.

Meanwhile, Matthews had recovered from his 'pretences of indisposition' and, according to Williams, pleaded pressing business engagements and slipped back to England. But his actions on his return were hardly those of a tourist recovering from illness. He made a bee-line for François Chauvelin, the French ambassador in London, introduced himself as a friend of David Williams and had at least one discussion with him. Then, on 8 January he wrote to Pitt, who replied presenting his compliments and responding that he would be 'very glad to have the pleasure' of meeting Matthews. They had a private meeting the following day, between eleven and twelve.

Williams – writing with hindsight, while Matthews languished in Bedlam – would have us believe that Matthews was already a lunatic, a plausible maniac who had chanced to overhear some of Williams' discussions and had parlayed them into a bizarre intrigue on the strength of which, in extraordinary times, he had succeeded in contriving a meeting with the Prime Minister. But there was more complicity afoot than this. Williams carried on writing to Matthews after he returned to London, and Pitt was already aware that Williams was in Paris, and that he was privy to confidential discussions about foreign policy. As war loomed, a secret, parallel channel of communication was being kept open. The question is whether, at this stage, Brissot was aware of such a channel – in other words, were Williams and Matthews British spies or French agents? But in another sense the question is academic; within a fortnight such niceties would be meaning-less. At this point both sides were talking war, but feared it. It might split the British Cabinet; it might destroy the Republic. Thus, as the preparations for war were noisily bruited about, a covert scenario for peace was being discussed in whispers.

It was no time to talk publicly of peace, and it was certainly no time for Brissot to test his strength against the Jacobins. The final days of the King's trial were opening up the fissures in the Assembly for all to see, and exposing the core Girondin weakness: they might have the best lawyers and talkers, but their opponents had control of the streets. After the evidence against the King had been presented, the Girondins argued that any verdict would need to be ratified by the people in a referendum. The Jacobins protested that this was a trans-parent appeal to the conservatives in the provinces, a *carte blanche* to thwart the Revolution and spark civil war. Meanwhile, outside the court, the *sansculottes* were pronouncing their own sentence: any verdict except death and they would murder the King themselves, storm the prisons again, massacre all the suspected counter-revolutionaries, and then maybe start on the Assembly itself. The first vote on the King's guilt was passed unanimously. Succeeding votes were tighter: a small majority against a referendum and, on 15 January, an even smaller one – a handful of votes – for execution without delay.

After this, everything happened fast; the only delaying factor was the two or three days it took for news to cross the Channel. Louis XVI was guillotined on the morning of 21 January, in ominous heavy rain and fog and in front of a crowd of twenty thousand in the Place de la Concorde; locks of hair from his freshly decapitated head were sold to the bedraggled spectators. The next day, Le Brun sent a communiqué to recall his ambassador Chauvelin from London, signalling an end to diplomacy and thus a prelude to war. The day after, news of the King's execution reached London. Pitt pronounced it 'the foulest and most atrocious act the world has ever seen', and dismissed Chauvelin before the instructions to recall him had arrived from Paris. This, too, was the last move before a declaration of war. Both sides were simultaneously taking the final step towards the brink.

But James Tilly Matthews was still playing out his mysterious role in London. On 28 January he wrote to Pitt, requesting a second meeting. Now he was presenting himself unambiguously as a British spy, a loyalist who had been taken into the confidence of the French embassy and 'wormed my way into their secrets'. He has done this, he claims, 'without Williams' knowledge'; this intrigue, in other words, isn't more of the same, but a new initiative. His message is that 'chance has given me the opportunity to serve my country by perhaps making these Gasconnades [Girondins] humble themselves to yr. utmost wishes. I shall cheerfully', he offers, 'repair to Paris even tonight.'

This is the first time we hear from Matthews in his own words, and if it were the only time, we would probably have little hesitation in assuming that he was a British agent who had travelled to France as an undercover spy. On the face of it, he seems to be straightforwardly betraying his fellow republicans, going behind Williams' back and scheming to force the Girondins to cave into the British. But, more likely, this is exactly what he wants Pitt to think. Between the lines, we can read this letter as a last throw of the dice, an offer of the only bait he can think of to cajole Pitt and Grenville into engaging once more with the secret peace negotiations. 'Without Williams' knowledge' might be a ploy to whet their appetites, implying that this is a new avenue of opportunity, and one much more to the government's advantage. Perhaps he even plays the role of loyalist spy with too much relish: do such people really describe themselves as 'worming their way into secrets'? In either event, the bait wasn't taken. The letter was ignored, and no meeting arranged.

Back in Paris, the endgame was proceeding dramatically. On 31 January Brissot prepared his report on General Defence and showed it to Williams. It amounted to a virtual declaration of war: a refusal to withdraw from the Netherlands, a savage attack on the British government, and an appeal for the British people to rise up in support of the Republic. Williams was horrified; Brissot was deeply depressed. Williams was unable to believe that Brissot wanted to go to war. Brissot insisted that he didn't, but the Jacobins had left him no room for manoeuvre: anything less than this and he and the Girondins were dead men walking. He was counting on the British to back down – or perhaps, if we credit his involvement in the intrigue, on Matthews and Williams to decode his message in peaceful terms to Pitt and Grenville. That night, Williams had to content himself with correcting the errors in the report and toning down the most bellicose passages. It was to be the last useless contribution he would make to the republican cause. The next day Brissot read out the uncorrected text to the Convention, to tumultuous applause. The delegates voted unanimously for war with Britain and the Netherlands.

That evening, Williams was invited to dinner with Brissot at Le Brun's house. He was still shell-shocked by the day's events, aghast at the declaration of war by men who, like himself, were ideological pacifists. 'You mean to make war like savages!' he remonstrated. Brissot replied like a mournful Pontius Pilate: 'It is done, the Committee would have it; if we had hesitated, the business would have been taken out of our hands.' It was checkmate to the Jacobins.

But, like Matthews, Brissot and Le Brun still believed, or hoped against hope, that there was another throw of the dice to be had. They had a proposal for Williams: they wanted to know if he would be prepared to undertake a private mission to England, to take a secret peace proposal to Pitt and Lord Grenville.

For Williams, this seems to have been the last straw, a final confirmation that Brissot and Le Brun were hopelessly out of their depth. Everything he had attempted so far on their behalf had come to nothing, and now they were asking him to negotiate informally for peace with a country on whom they had only that afternoon declared war. He 'checked the disposition to laugh which the extravagance of the proposal occasioned', and explained once more that his stock was a good deal lower in England than it was in France: in London, he was just another obscure and undesirable radical whose only claim to fame was his association with a French regime to whom the British were implacably opposed. He would be lucky if they let him get past Dover, let alone to Whitehall.

In the end, they reached a compromise. Williams was intending to leave within a few days in any case; if Brissot and Le Brun wished to give him a letter, he would do his best to get it to Grenville. A few days later, they presented him with the brief: an appeal to Grenville that they should keep the ports of Dover and Calais open, to allow for communication between the two governments. Attached to this was a covering note from Le Brun explaining that the proposal was being sent via Williams because 'the conversations I have had with him have for some time allowed me the hope of maintaining harmonious relations between our two countries'.

It was a letter with few parallels in the history of diplomacy, effectively an apology for having just declared war and a simultaneous plea for peace. But there was another message that was stranger still, one which Brissot and Le Brun gave to Williams only verbally, since they knew that its discovery would mean the guillotine for them all.

Although Matthews had claimed to have acted behind Williams' back, and Williams claimed that Matthews was only a vague acquaintance, when Williams returned to London on 12 February Matthews was waiting for him with a carriage. They drove together to the Foreign Office to deliver the letter to Grenville. Williams stated his business, and was kept waiting. Eventually a civil servant emerged, a Mr Aust, Grenville's Under-Secretary of State. Williams explained that he had a communiqué from France: a written request to open the ports and another request that could only be made verbally and in private. Mr Aust was unimpressed. 'The French government has declared war,' he observed. 'I know it,' Williams replied, 'but I also know it would make great sacrifices to preserve peace.' Here again, in exact concert with Matthews' hints to Pitt, is the idea that despite the declaration of war there was another option on the table, one in which the French would be more than generous. Williams eventually left his name and address on a piece of paper. Aust assured him that Grenville would be given the message, that he would send for Williams if he desired. As it turned out, he did not. Williams never heard from Grenville again.

For Williams, it seems, this was the end of the road. Back in England after two tumultuous months, he realized sharply how much the world had changed. The old neutrality towards France, the fear of upsetting the European status quo, had evaporated. There was no longer any status quo to upset: everything was now in chaos and, for better or worse, the future of Europe would be determined by war. And in this war, no quarter would be given to the republican government; the time for gentlemen's agreements and diplomatic soundings was past. If he went back to Grenville, the outcome would be the same; if he put the secret proposal in writing, he would be signing Brissot and Le Brun's death warrants.

He must have said something of this sort to Matthews back in the carriage, but he received an unexpected reply: 'If you would exert yourself, you could prevent the war.' Williams was taken aback and 'laughed at the extravagance of the observation', but Matthews was serious. The next day, he went round to Williams' house to discuss plans. Williams repeated that it was over, he would do nothing, but Matthews had other plans. He was going to go back to France, and he asked Williams for letters of introduction to the government. Williams refused, on the grounds that they would compromise all concerned if discovered, but he agreed that Matthews might make contact with Le Brun and explain why Williams was unable to write.

This was the last time the two ever saw each other. Williams' political adventures were finished – not through fear, he later insisted, but through despair that the greatest chance in history had been fumbled by those 'to whom power seemed to have been delegated only by chance'. The French Revolution, he felt, had not produced any new principles or truths, merely a mass of examples of how things could go wrong. His only hope was that future politicians would study the sad events and use them to forge more scientific and rational governments if and when the opportunity arose again. He devoted most of the rest of his life to establishing a literary fund for struggling writers.

But James Tilly Matthews' political adventures were only just beginning. He was the last one left with the secret that could stop the war.

The stakes were getting higher by the day. On 15 February, Pitt introduced the first reading of the Traitorous Correspondence Bill. This was aimed not just at written correspondence, but at 'all commerce and intercourse with His Majesty's enemies'. Specifically, the borders with France were closed to all those without special passports; the penalty for the guilty was, in the letter of the law at least, to be half-hung and then to have their entrails removed and burned in front of their eyes while still alive. The opposition fought it tooth and nail: Fox called it 'a fundamental attack upon the liberties of Englishmen' and Erskine 'directly repugnant to the policy of the best and wisest of our ancestors, and contrary to the highest authorities in the law'. Not to be outdone, Burke supported it to the hilt: no Englishman worth defending would wish to 'carry on an adulterous intercourse with the prostitute outcasts of mankind'.

As the Traitorous Correspondence Bill headed for its highly charged second reading on 19 March, Matthews wrote to Pitt for the third time. Once again, no reply. Within a month, with the bill a week or two away from becoming an act of law, he was back in France.

The timing of his trip was just as fraught on the other side of the Channel. On 18 March, the day before his arrival, France's six months of military triumphs against the odds had come to an abrupt end at Neerwinden in the Netherlands. The Austrian army had first driven them back, then chased them out of the country entirely, wiping out the entire winter's military gains. In Paris, conspiracy theories abounded: the general Dumouriez, an old-guard noble, had deliberately betrayed the army to Austria. Dumouriez, facing the guillotine back home, deserted to the Prussians and took a party of fellow officers with him. At the same time, the first rumours were seeping into the capital that the district of the Vendée, a counter-revolutionary hotbed, had begun a violent insurrection against the republican government. From north and south, from outside and inside, *la patrie* was, once again, *en danger*.

The Girondins in particular were feeling the heat. It was clear that Brissot wanted to bring an end to the Revolutionary government, dismantle the police state apparatus of the Committee of Public Safety and normalize political life on the basis of a new republican constitution. In the prevailing climate, however, it was all too easy to paint this as a counter-revolutionary agenda, a Trojan horse that would allow the old guard back into power. Brissot's aristocratic suffix 'de Warville' was frequently recalled; rumours and smears spread that he was secretly wealthy, with property in London and contacts with Pitt and the crowned heads of Europe. On 9 March, Jacobin-sponsored mobs had attacked the Girondins' houses and destroyed the presses of *Le Patriote Français.*

Nevertheless, in the heat of the crisis, Matthews was granted an immediate audience with Le Brun. He passed on Williams' message that he was unable to write to Le Brun himself, in the light of the new Traitorous Correspondence Bill. Williams suspected that Matthews also implied that Williams was out of the picture because he was 'a timid man' whose fear had overcome his principles, but that Matthews himself was made of sterner stuff. Matthews then passed on to Le Brun two documents: the first comprised several pages of British military secrets, and the second a thirteen-page peace proposal, in his own hand but purporting to come from the highest levels of the British government.

The peace proposal is a strange document indeed. It is presented in a question-and-answer format, stating the British demands, occasionally expanding on the reasons for them, and then offering an answer acceptable to both sides. The British will demand the release of the remainder of the royal family; the answer is that they should be exiled to any place except Spain or Sardinia, but preferably Britain, to whom France should offer half a million pounds for their upkeep. The British will demand indemnification for its war expenses; the French should 'cede to England an island or two, including Tobago'. France must disarm; England will disarm too, if independent commissioners are appointed to oversee the process. But the oddest thing about the proposal is that the majority of its demands are about French internal affairs, and its new constitution. The new French constitution must include the clergy; they must have two chambers, one for life and the other elective; the Assembly must sit outside Paris; Avignon must be restored to the Pope. Each of these demands has a considered solution, most of which are broadly in line with Girondin policy, but which clearly have another goal: to bring French public and political life into alignment with Britain's.

Yet oddest of all is that, although Matthews' document bore little resemblance to any peace proposal before or since, Le Brun and his ministers took it very seriously indeed. They set to work on meeting the demands and forging compromises, working day and night to assemble a counter-proposal to present to Lord Grenville.

It's extraordinarily unlikely that Matthews' idiosyncratic proposal was actually drafted by the British government. Pitt and Grenville, since the King's execution and the invasion of the Netherlands, had set Britain firmly on the course of war, and had nailed their colours irrevocably to the mast virtually every subsequent day in Parliament. But Matthews still held the secret Brissot and Williams had conceived in January, which he must have attempted to sell to Pitt at their meeting.

As spelled out later by Williams, long after the crisis was past, the secret was this. Brissot and Williams feared that the power of the Girondins was ebbing away, and with it any chance of a peaceful republican settlement. War had worked for a while, but was now spinning out of control. Britain, whose Glorious Revolution of 1688 was the closest model for the Girondin project, was about to become their mortal enemy. Brissot had no choice but to talk up war in public, but there was another possibility. The Girondins could invite Britain on to their side, to destroy the Jacobin power-base – a civil war, but with Britain on one side. Together, they could overpower the Paris Commune and set up a constitutional republic of the kind that had been envisaged in 1791. Britain and France could then move forward as allies, with broadly similar political systems.

No wonder the protagonists kept this plan close to their chests. It would have confirmed every suspicion of Brissot's hidden agenda, and sent the Girondins, not to mention Williams and Matthews, to a prompt and surgical death. For this reason it could only succeed by progressing down the most secure channels possible – which, given the situation in

France, meant channels outside the usual diplomatic ones. It would have needed agents loyal to the plan, but outside the French government – agents such as Williams and Matthews.

The mind becomes dizzy even contemplating what the effects of this plan might have been had it succeeded. No Revolutionary Wars – or, if it had come to war, Napoleon and Wellington on the same side. Beyond that, the entire story of Europe would most likely be unrecognizable from that which the history books now record. It was, as everyone appreciated at the time, a moment of destiny, the crucible in which the future of the world was being forged – a future which the alliance of Britain and France would have sent in an entirely different direction. It would have been almost unique in history for the extent to which a single ordinary individual, James Tilly Matthews, could have changed the world.

The question, then, is whether it was remotely possible that it could have succeeded. The episode certainly doesn't loom large in most histories of the Revolution. British historians have tended to ignore it in favour of the far grander story of the subsequent war, and the French, on the rare occasions when it has been examined, to cite it as a further example of British dirty tricks and double dealing. The great nineteenth-century French historians of the Revolution, Aulard and Sorel, interpreted the peace proposal not as Matthews' invention but as a British government initiative designed solely to elicit French secrets; Matthews is, for them, a *'négotiateur mystérieux'* who vanishes from history after this transaction. The general consensus on the Girondins is coloured by the truism that they were on the wrong side of history: theirs is seen as a doomed holding position that was bound to be swept away by the dynamics of the Revolution as it progressed. But it's hard to dispute that, had the British weighed in on their side, things might have been entirely different.

On the British side, too, the possibility is not inconceivable. Pitt and Grenville were extremely reluctant to initiate war with

France; despite their ideological opposition to the Revolution, it was only the execution of the King and war with the Netherlands that forced their hands. There were many obstacles, but the option of allying with the French moderates against the Jacobin threat was, if unlikely, not unthinkable.

But given the remote possibility of the plan's success, was Matthews himself – tea-merchant, amateur republican and already possible lunatic – in any position to effect it? Williams' assessment that the moment had passed and the die was cast was certainly the most balanced one. Matthews took up the baton at a stage when the Girondins were losing the power to act, and the British had set their faces against peace. His task was immense: somehow to pull the plan up by its bootstraps and re-sell it to two uninterested parties at the same time.

We may suspect that this was impossible from the start, but the fact is that he made a resounding success of the first part of his mission. Le Brun and his ministry formulated a response, and presented it to the Cabinet. They accepted that it offered a chance for peace, and agreed to explore it further. Some of its demands were rejected – releasing the royal family and moving the Assembly were seen as domestic matters only – but on 2 April Le Brun was able to present Matthews with a reply, together with a covering letter proposing that a French ambassador be reinstated for the new negotiations.

Whatever else he had been, Matthews had certainly been brave, and his initiative had placed him at the centre of the web of power. Against all the odds, the secret peace plan was on the move: Britain now had a concrete offer for extricating itself from war. The question now was how to get it back to London – a decision that was effectively in Matthews' hands. From nowhere, he had suddenly become the prime mover in a scheme on which the political future of Europe balanced.

If the diplomatic manoeuvres had thus far been odd, the steps Matthews now proposed were odder still. The letters were not to be sent to Pitt, or Grenville, or their secretaries or MPs, or indeed to anyone in government or the civil service. They must be sent under separate cover to a man named John Salter, the vestry clerk of the parish of Poplar in east London. Salter would receive instructions to deliver the first sealed letter to Grenville; this would turn out to contain a request for a passport and safe conduct for a negotiator. If Grenville bit, he would receive a second letter which would reveal the identity of the negotiator: Maret, a diplomat who had good relations with Pitt and who had been Brissot's choice to replace Chauvelin until war intervened.

Williams, writing of course with hindsight, claims that 'this transaction gave me the first suspicion that Matthews was affected in his head', a statement that has been seized on by subsequent commentators from the world of psychiatry as the first evidence of the crumbling of Matthews' reason. The case for this draws on the pathology of paranoid schizophrenia. The onset of a delusional psychosis is frequently preceded by a period of excitement during which the subject is gripped by extraordinary energy and feelings of omnipotence. This can manifest itself in an intense engagement with grand schemes, a sense that the subject holds the destiny of the world in his hands and, not infrequently, a conviction that everyone around him knows this and is secretly involved. Subjects are often gripped by hunches of obscure origin which they follow with unshakeable conviction, and which can turn out to be unnervingly correct. Their sense of physical energy is certainly no illusion: it can produce palpable physical effects. Those affected often show little need for sleep, and almost super-human tolerance in the face of cold or hunger.

This is obviously a tempting lens through which to view Matthews' state of mind at this point, but serious caveats need to be introduced. The first is that there's no evidence that any-one involved at the time thought Matthews was mad; indeed there's a great deal of evidence to the contrary, since the French government was staking much on his probity. Of course, this in itself could be read as a testament to the manic force of his delusional insanity; but here the diagnosis of paranoid schizophrenia starts to become more of a hindrance than a help. The onset of other psychoses, such as bipolar disorder, can produce a confidence and energy that are highly charismatic and compelling to others, and might be pressed into explaining how Matthews could have seduced the French government into his grandiose schemes. But the onset of paranoid schizophrenia in particular is, by contrast, almost always characterized by precisely the opposite of such charisma. Subjects tend to make connections too bizarre for others to follow, and miss obvious social cues in their obsession with them; if other people figure in them at all, it is most likely as pawns or persecutors. If we are to read Matthews' behaviour here in the light of his subsequent madness, we must reconsider the now standard retrospective diagnosis. Our alternative is to accept that the reason he believed he was suddenly being thrust into a world-changing drama is because he genuinely was.

The incident has also been read in another quite different way by some French historians: as proof that Matthews was a British agent bent on destabilizing the republican government. According to this view, his eccentric peace proposal was canny and highly effective. He succeeded in wheedling out of the French not only the bottom line of their negotiating position on peace, but the extent to which their own internal affairs were up for compromise. In the course of this he also gathered highly damaging information about their internal divisions which could be used to open up splits in the government, and, in a final act of humiliation, he showed up their lack of diplomatic experience by persuading them to sign up to a crackpot and ridiculous plan.

But it's still quite possible at this point to take Matthews at face value, neither madman nor spy. He was both extremely naive in diplomatic matters and, given the Traitorous

Correspondence Bill, forced to be extremely cautious, even devious. Certainly his plan was bizarre, but there is no rule-book for the conduct of covert negotiations, especially when the two interested parties are at war. Sending the peace plan to a public notary, if it was a crazy hunch, was also a good one: it kept him at one remove from the transaction, and also provided legal attestation that the documents had come from the source he claimed. If we look forward to Matthews' career in Bedlam, we find ample evidence to support his frequent claim that he was, first and foremost, a peacemaker. This, too, can be given a pathological reading – in the absence of any information about his early life, we may speculate as much as we wish about family traumas which might have triggered a life-long obsession with reconciling warring parties – but it also offers a motive for his actions up to this point without recourse to either treachery or madness.

The letter was sent, and Matthews headed back to London a few days later, accompanied by Scipion Mourgue, the secretary to the proposed new French ambassador Maret. But crossing the Channel was no longer a simple matter, and they were arrested at Boulogne. Matthews wrote to Le Brun asking to be released and, mystifyingly – perhaps as a follow-up to a previous conversation – for a thousand acres of land in France as a reward for his services. In the end, Mourgue effected their release, and Matthews crossed back into England. It might have been on this occasion that he shared his breathless midnight carriage-ride with Peter Mortimer – evidence, again, either for his delusional extravagance or for the genuine urgency of his mission.

Back in London, things were moving slowly for a man with only days to save the world. Matthews got back before the proposal was delivered to Salter and spent his days taking carriages up to Westminster, attempting to meet Cabinet ministers, but without success. Williams claims in his memoirs that he made several attempts to meet him, but that Matthews avoided him. Matthews sat in on a number of debates at the House of Commons, and heard Pitt stepping up his rhetoric against the 'regicides' of France – 'a crime so extensive in its consequences, as well as detestable in its nature' that it 'demanded reprobation and abhorrence'. Finally, on 27 April, Salter delivered his letters to Grenville. Matthews waited outside the Foreign Office while Salter was questioned for an hour and a half. Then, day after day, silence.

Suspecting that the government was simply going to ignore the approach, Matthews began to put pressure on them from the periphery. He lobbied MPs and lords, including Lord Liverpool, and began rumours about the secret peace plans Britain was hushing up. He sent copies of Le Brun's letters to Lord Rawdon, leader of the independent MPs, and begged him to press the government for a response. Questions were asked in the House, and Pitt was forced to deny the existence of a peace plan. Finally, on 16 May, Grenville replied to Le Brun. He maintained the formal position that the British government did not recognize the republican administration, and that if he wanted to discuss peace he should offer terms to the generals of the allied armies of Britain, the Netherlands and Austria.

Now, Matthews realized, there was little to be gained from secrecy. If Pitt and Grenville were unwilling to contemplate the plan on their own initiative, they would have to be bounced into it. He did his best. He leaked a copy of the papers to the MP William Pulteney, and on 22 May he published the covering letters of Le Brun's proposals in *The Times*. They appeared in large point at the beginning of the news pages: three notes from Le Brun stating that France was 'desirous to terminate all its differences with Great Britain' and offering Maret as a negotiator for the peace. The piece was signed off by 'James Matthews', who confirmed that 'I do attest the truth of the letters, and do hereby authorise and desire the publication thereof'.

But by now it really was too late. Reaction against the Girondins in Paris had spilled over into full-scale denunciations and accusations of treason. On 1 June, the presidency of the Convention switched from the Girondins to the Jacobins, and eighty thousand *sansculottes* massed outside the meeting to make sure that the Revolution would no longer be sabotaged by its enemies. That night, the Girondins hid, afraid to sleep in their own beds; the next day, the Commune stormed their houses and placed them under house arrest while the Committee of Public Safety investigated the charge that they were involved in 'a conspiracy to establish tyranny and the old constitution'. Distorted rumours from London of secret deals with Pitt and Grenville helped their cause little. The Committee of Public Safety formally took over the portfolio of Foreign Affairs.

Here is a point where we may reasonably expect Matthews to have given up, and not to find him wanting in courage if he had. If, unlike Williams, he had believed in January that there was still a slim chance of peace, he could be excused for changing his position as events unravelled. But – peacemaker, madman or spy – he did no such thing. Around 10 June he returned secretly to France and met with officials of the Committee of Public Safety. Unlike Le Brun, they were by no means convinced of his motives: not only had he brought no further developments from the British government, they had serious doubts about whether the original peace proposal had had anything to do with Pitt or Grenville. They strongly suspected Matthews of being a spy, fishing for information. He returned to Dover, under cover and in a hurry.

This third trip had surely made matters worse. Now neither government was taking him seriously, and the only question if he persevered was which one would subject him to the more draconian punishment for treason. But, mad or sane, Matthews was a man of no ordinary persistence. He was clearly not prepared to renounce the peace plan, any more than he would be prepared to renounce his madness in Bedlam. A month later, he was back in France, this time for an extended stay.

The blissful dawn of Matthews' revolutionary adventures was coming to an end, and his dark night of the soul was about to begin.

5

A MOST DIABOLICAL TRAITOR

'. . . a brain confounded, and a sense
Death-like, of treacherous desertion, felt
In the last place of refuge – my own soul.'
William Wordsworth, *The Prelude*, 1805

ON 20 AUGUST 1793, MATTHEWS FOUND HIMSELF IN THE CUSTODY of the Committee of Public Safety in Paris, sitting around a rough, cloth-draped trestle table covered with papers, tobacco, wine bottles, glasses and firearms, surrounded by armed strangers in makeshift revolutionary uniforms and red bonnets speaking a foreign language, and being asked by the only man in the room who could understand a word of English to give an account of himself. He had arrived in a country at war without any papers of commission, and he was requesting a passport for himself and an interpreter, claiming that he had information of great importance to the national security of the Republic. The committee asked him to explain the nature of his business. He sat down and, off the top of his head, wrote a twenty-two-page account of himself in his usual immaculate copperplate hand. It still survives, and is, depending on your persuasion, either a full first-person report of his activities or an elaborate and intricately concocted attempt at high-level espionage – or the first unmistakable sign of his madness.

The title of the letter seems, at first view, to be ample evidence for the last. No name, no date, no subject; simply the statement, in bold capitals across the top:

DELAYS ARE DANGEROUS BUT WITH PERSEVERANCE
AND DETERMINATION I NEVER DESPAIR

Delay is the central motif of this, his first autobiographical statement. 'The present state of things', he begins, 'which would have been avoided by diligence has been occasioned solely by delay.' He returns to this theme throughout: 'I hate delay,' he repeats several times, often underlining the word, and once adding 'even the word itself'. Later, he puts it more poetically: 'I have preserved everything except time.'

We may still be tempted to read more than a hint of mental imbalance into this, an impatience at being surrounded with a cast of characters who don't share his burning intensity, but Matthews again makes a very rational case in the letter for delay being the root of the problems he has been facing all year. He lists all the lost opportunities for diplomatic entente and all the events detrimental to France's interests which have occurred as a result. The British Cabinet, he maintains, have 'the most virulent inveteracy' towards France and her republican ideals, and time has allowed them to reach out to their allies across Europe and forge a 'grand chain of confederation' against her. Matthews, for his part, has sabotaged this plan wherever possible, but as one man alone he has been unable to hold back the tide. He has all too easily been smeared as 'a democrat, a Jacobin, and had such other titles bestowed on me as were most likely to make every word I uttered to be construed into a lie'.

Nevertheless Matthews has remained, in his own account, a true servant of the republican cause – even, at one point,

'a true *sans culotte*'. He has studiously avoided any factions
within the Assembly, never dealing with anyone until 'I was
sure that they would never unite with any set of men, but who
would really act for the good of the Republic'. Clearly, he is
aware of the nature of the men to whom he is now writing:
friends no longer, but apparatchiks of a zealous secret police.
But he has more to say than simply to plead his innocence. The
Republic must know that it cannot survive an encircling attack
from all the other powers of Europe. It must seek peace, and
must grasp how this can be achieved. It must understand the
rivalries and sticking-points between Britain, the Netherlands
and Russia, and exploit them. It must recognize the bargain-
ing chips it holds, and be prepared to lay them down boldly.
This is the diplomacy with which Matthews has been tirelessly
engaged all year: he has pursued the goal of 'effecting a just
and honourable peace, and obtaining an acknowledgement of
the Republic', but his enemy time and again has been
'accursed delay'.

Here, perhaps not surprisingly given his predicament,
shades of conspiracy and paranoia creep into his language.
'The most determined system of mortification and insult' has
been orchestrated against Matthews by the Cabinet; 'a war of
intrigue commenced' between him and Pitt. His claims of his
own centrality in world politics, too, are grandiose. If he had
not been delayed, he would time and again have 'prevented
the completion of a treaty'; sometimes he has succeeded in
'throwing in some trifling obstacles' to keep Britain and
Austria apart. We will find such paranoia and grandiosity
taken to vertiginous heights in Bedlam a few years later, and
with hindsight it is easy to find their roots here, but once again
we must be wary of hindsight's gifts. The French Republic *was*
being plotted against and diplomatically encircled; Matthews
was attempting to juggle the fate of nations, and being conspired against as a result. If we were to read every covert
diplomatic briefing, from Lord Walsingham's Elizabethan spy

network to the CIA, with the spectre of paranoid personality disorder lurking in the background, we may well conclude that the intelligence business has always been staffed by grandiose lunatics.

The real question is, at this point, whether Matthews' account of himself read sanely to his intended readership. Here, again, delay was the major problem. Brissot and Le Brun were gone from the administration; who was Matthews now writing to? The letter is addressed to Georges Danton, the great demagogue hero of the Paris communes with whom, Matthews claims, Le Brun had told him to liaise if for any reason his old Girondin contacts were unreachable. But Danton was no longer the man in charge. A huge, brawling, passionate, ever daring man and an impassioned orator, to many he quite simply *was* the Revolution. He was, in fact, like both Brissot and Robespierre, a provincial lawyer, his scars and broken nose earned not on the mean streets of Paris but on the farm where he grew up. But the *sansculottes* took him as one of their own, and his support for the Jacobins had been crucial to their triumph. He had been given the Committee of Public Safety as his own fiefdom, but his power-base cut uncomfortably across the Girondin–Jacobin divide. Now, for the Jacobins, increasingly he was less of an asset and more of a problem. His instincts were, on crucial issues, ideologically unsound: he saw, for example, no reason why the Republic should be at war, and even no great benefit from having executed the King. In the nooks and alcoves of the Jacobin Club, he was whispered about as a loose cannon, a man with more raw impulse than good judgement.

As Matthews wrote Danton was, in any case, out of town, recovering from an illness at his country home with his new sixteen-year-old wife. But he would shortly be ousted from the Committee of Public Safety, his own creation, suspected like so many others of attempting to block the progress of the Revolution – and, like the others, soon to meet the same abrupt

Georges Danton

end. Seeking Danton's protection was already a less than ideal Plan B for Matthews, but delay had made it worse: it was now a suspicious conduit, an invitation to theories that this was some factional intrigue against Robespierre. Matthews' letter was diverted to more reliable eyes, and ended up with various functionaries of the foreign affairs division of the committee, who held him under arrest while they considered his case.

Matthews was summoned for an interview with Otto, the *chef de la première division* of the department and one of its few English speakers, to whom he delivered a second communiqué in many ways more extraordinary than the first. This was a brief dossier of British military secrets, including an allied plan to split the Republic into three parts and, more specifically, details of an attack on Dunkirk to take place in a few days' time.

How had Matthews got his hands on British military secrets? He claims, both at this point and later, that he bought them from corrupt Whitehall civil servants, on his own initiative and with his own money. He quotes fabulous sums: eleven thousand pounds, the equivalent of over half a million today. He might well have been tempted to inflate this claim: after all, if he had got them for nothing, he would have looked uncomfortably like a friend of the British government. But, as the evidence of Peter Mortimer's carriage-ride will later confirm, money is certainly flowing freely and easily through Matthews' hands at this stage – and so, as we've seen, are negotiations about large parcels of French land. The fact that he begins his adventures as a well-off businessman and ends them as a pauper may or may not account for any or all of this; certainly he is insistent later that the British government made financial promises to him they didn't keep. But unless the British plans were an extraordinarily lucky or well-informed guess on Matthews' part, events would shortly prove that they were genuine. Otto sent an urgent note to the army to strengthen Dunkirk's fortifications and sat down to interview Matthews about the rest of his story.

For Otto, Matthews' sanity was not in doubt. 'The entire conduct of Matthews', he notes in his preliminary report, 'reveals a man of great experience in public affairs, and above all, profoundly versed in the politics of his country. He writes as well as he talks.' The charisma of the mad, possibly; more likely, perhaps, the inexperience of the official. But time, for once, was on Matthews' side. Four days later, the British fleet attacked Dunkirk and Toulon. Dunkirk survived, for which the French readily acknowledged Matthews' advance warnings. Toulon was taken after a three-day siege but liberated only four months later – by a twenty-six-year-old commander named Napoleon Bonaparte, his first significant action in the war.

Matthews now posed quite a problem for the department. His military intelligence had proved extremely valuable, though its source was unclear. At various points in his letter he had talked of greasing palms and buying secrets; his concluding phrase was that delay would soon make it impossible for him to serve the French cause any more, even 'if I have all the money in the national treasury at command'. All this made him look like a spy, and there was nobody in the French government who could vouch for his loyalty. If they were holding a double agent, it would be extremely dangerous to let him go. Even if he was genuinely a republican, he might well be a Dantonist working to strengthen his master's hand against the Jacobin high command. Yet he had shown that, whatever his allegiances, he had intelligence they needed. On 1 September they made a summary translation of his peace proposal under the heading 'Proposal made by a British Secret Agent', and began to consider his case.

The committee had a great deal on their minds besides Matthews. The Convention, freed of the foot-dragging influence of the Girondins, were driving forward the radical plans for the Republic which Robespierre and his allies had long cherished. At the end of August they announced an unprecedented policy called the *levée en masse*. This effectively turned France into a war machine, the like of which had never been seen before. From now on, all resources, public and private, were at the disposal of the Republic. All citizens were obliged to take up arms; all produce and property were requisitioned by the government. If the rights of man were now enshrined in the new constitution, here were the duties that came with them. Those who were with the Revolution were now at its disposal; those who were not were enemies of the state. It was, as so many had cried for so long, liberty or death. On 4 September the Convention passed a motion that 'terror is to be the order of the day'; those whom reason had failed to sway must expect summary justice. A week later, the principle was enshrined in the Law Against Suspects: only acts of patriotism would now be accepted as proof of true citizenship. To have done nothing was now not to be innocent, but guilty.

The Committee of Public Safety – motto, 'Activity, Purity, Surveillance' – was now the front line of government, charged with enforcing the new laws and investigating the loyalty of all those against whom complaints were made. Nevertheless, as the procession of investigations swelled to a flood, they squeezed in a few minutes' consideration of Matthews' case. He had been in France in March and in June to 'propose conciliation'; in August he had written to Danton 'to ask for a passport to communicate objects of great importance'. This much was clear; what was not was 'the object of his mission' and 'the nature of the proposition'. On 6 September they sent a message to his hotel that he was now under house arrest pending further deliberations.

Over the next two days, Matthews sent a stream of letters back to the committee. The truth is now clearly dawning, if it hadn't before, that his situation is at best unpromising, at worst disastrous. His enthusiasm for the cause and his urgency in driving it forward has now led him to confinement in a Paris boarding-house, with all too much time to cool his heels and speculate on where he was now headed. It was one thing to share a passion for republican principles with like-minded Londoners at David Williams' lectures, quite another to find himself in a country where he spoke barely a word of the language, accused of spying for a foreign power in the middle of a snowballing experiment in state terror. All around him, it has suddenly become extremely dangerous to be less patriotic than one's neighbour. The Committee of Public Safety have informers in every street; personal grudges become political denunciations, and the first the victim knows is the dreaded knock at the door in the small hours. Being English is already enough to be in a very precarious position; being English, alone and without a passport, is a good deal worse. Tom Paine, the most high-profile Englishman in town and until a few months ago an unimpeachable revolutionary hero, has become a suspected traitor on account of his Girondin contacts and is being held prisoner in the Luxembourg Palace; he will only escape the guillotine thanks to a bureaucratic error. But Matthews keeps his cool, playing the few cards he has with great skill. He writes to the committee, asking for clarification on a point of procedure: foreigners are not allowed to be resident in Paris without valid passports, and he has not received one. 'I cannot transgress so positive a law,' he tells them, but it's not clear what he can do to rectify the situation. 'I will be obliged to you to speak to the minister of the Committee immediately as I am not easy.'

Having shown his desire to do everything by the book, and having probably kept a copy of his own letter as a last resort for emergencies, he opens up alternative routes. He writes to Hérault, Robespierre's loyalist on the committee, trying to set up a personal meeting with him. No reply. The next day he writes to Danton, telling him that he has both ready explanations for the committee and urgent business in the interests of the Republic; he has been promised a reply and 'I have waited ever since in hourly expectation, but have had none'. No joy from Danton. A further prod to the committee, now claiming that he has additional military secrets to pass on even more valuable than his intelligence about Dunkirk, this time 'of the infamous plan of the combined powers for the dismemberment of France'. Now, a note of desperation is creeping in, and he can't refrain from voicing his fears about his situation. 'It is now over nine months since I have been a volunteer in your cause', he reminds them, 'and have continually been laying before you the various dispositions of the English government at least as far as by a sacrifice of nearly all my fortune I was able to obtain them and I have had to lament that they have not been attended to or else neglected.' A final hook: he has to ask for the return of some of his documents which are in his handwriting and would incriminate him with the British if they were discovered. But from Hérault, from Danton, from the committee, silence. Neither we nor Matthews have the slightest idea what they now think of this puzzling and inscrutable Englishman – or, indeed, whether they think of him at all.

The replies are unforthcoming, but the letters continue. Matthews is sympathetic ('among the numerous duties which occupy your attention, I fear you have quite forgot me'), gently insistent ('I wrote you some days ago on the particular hardship of my cruel situation; you promised my immediate release but you have not performed it'), pleading ('I will be obliged to you to inform me, by what means I am to live, for in another month I shall not have any sous left'). By November, all these ploys are exhausted and he is staring into the abyss. The landlord of his lodging-house has sublet his rooms, leaving him only a tiny bedroom; he can clearly no longer pay his rent, and the story that he's in town on official government business is wearing thin. Worse, his protestations of being a gentleman of

importance are now being met with open disbelief. His landlord, he tells the committee, claims to have spoken to 'some
member of the Committee or the Commissioner for Foreign
Affairs' who 'had told him that I was an impostor, had no
claims whatever on the government, and was here only to trick
the Republic out of a little money, & that done & out of France
the nation might be damned'. Matthews goes on the offensive:
'I can clearly prove from the facts themselves that every step I
have taken since the Republic was first established, has been
those of a warm friend.' His 'cruel and unjust detention' will
inevitably expose him in the eyes of the British, and make a
valuable asset of the Republic worthless. But all this is
happening in a vacuum. The committee stopped paying
attention to his letters long ago. Since he has no French and
writes in English, none of his correspondence can be read
unless someone takes the trouble to translate it. By contrast,
Lord Grenville's sporadic letters to the committee are in fluent
French. One of the systemic ironies of the Revolution is that its
friends across the Channel – Matthews, Williams, Paine –
speak the language poorly or not at all, while its class enemies
make themselves understood effortlessly.

The cruelty of silence is ruthless. Over the weeks and
months, we see Matthews' pretensions stripped away. He is no
longer an ambassador, not even a useful spy. He is no longer a
friend of the cause, but smeared as a venal opportunist. No
longer even a gentleman; he is a pauper, a beggar, living at the
indulgence of an uncaring landlord. At this point his letters
take a turn into an emotional blankness all too familiar to
those who have witnessed or experienced the effects of torture,
kidnap or systematic abuse. He becomes obsequious,
grovelling, painfully eager to suffer anything in exchange for
the knowledge that his suffering is part of some plan. 'I doubt
not', he insists, 'that you have some good reason in thus
stabbing mortally the little respectability left to me in the
house, & which has been well, though so cowardly done.' If

this is all part of the revolutionary plan, so be it: he will drink the poison chalice, indeed will show them 'how deeply I will drink of the bitter cup . . . I invite you to empoison it to what extent you please, I am prepared for it'. He begs to be sent to prison so as not to incur any more debt. He virtually begs to be tortured: 'If it had been in Spain or in Turkey, I might have been put to the rack . . . but knowing the event I should have borne it, and would have despised the tyrannical order with more firmness.' What he is suffering now seems worse than torture: 'Citizens, in the capital of the land of liberty I have experienced a refined policy which neither Turk nor Spaniard would have been at the trouble to look after.' Torture would, at least, be attention. It would be an affirmation that he mattered, even if only as an obstacle – a release from the awful fear that nothing he can possibly say or do or feel is of the slightest interest to anybody.

Finally, on 6 December, he receives a note from the committee. But it is worse than no reply at all. It is a peremptory accusation that he has been secretly receiving letters from England. He forwards the letters immediately, insisting that 'I have not had any correspondence whatever without your knowledge – having received the enclosed two letters from the master of the house where I lodge, I send them to you.' Both are personal, the only shreds of attention he has received since his arrest. One is from a man he travelled with to Ostend in August; the other is from his wife. Though he has missed her terribly, 'having now for some months past renounced the strong affections I have always borne my family which were my earthly gods', her letter provides little comfort for him: it contains 'the confirmation of every evil I have dreaded from such detention'. The Traitorous Correspondence Act is now in force, and any British citizen in France without the King's permission is subject to a mandatory minimum of six months in prison. A traitor in a foreign land, he is now officially a traitor back home; even release from Paris would only mean prison again. Nevertheless, he dates his covering note in the revolutionary style – 17th Frimaire, Year 2 – and signs away the last vestiges of his private life with 'Citoyen minister, I salute you with fraternity – Vive la Republic.'

There was no relief either for Matthews or for Paris. Through the freakishly bitter winter – *le grand hiver*, the coldest in living memory, the Seine frozen for weeks – the death count rose relentlessly. Brissot and twenty of his Girondins were found guilty of treason and died under the guillotine defiantly singing 'La Marseillaise'. Enemies of the Revolution multiplied: food shortages returned, and hoarders, profiteers and thieves were tried and executed in unprecedented numbers. It became problematic that Paris had only one guillotine. 'La Machine' had been adopted the previous spring, not only to promote clinical and humane death equally for peasant and noble (beheading had traditionally been for aristocrats only), but to symbolize the state monopoly on violence: since the September Massacres, violent lynchings were strictly forbidden, and no-one went before the guillotine without a state trial. In this sense, the Terror was not anarchy; rather its opposite. Every one of the guillotine's victims was legally arrested (usually by the Committee of Public Safety), briskly tried, and their death efficiently recorded. Playing to an audience for whom abstract ideas of liberty were a great deal less persuasive than physical demonstrations of the overthrow of tyranny, the guillotine was intended as a clean, dignified and legal alternative to the lynch mob.

There were executions every day in January 1794, but by late spring the guillotine was working almost ceaselessly. Danton had stood up against its excessive use – 'it is a thousand times better to be guillotined than to guillotine' – but he was to join the queue himself in April, the signal for its use to multiply once more. April saw 258 victims, May 345 and June 688. Its operators claimed that it was no longer possible

The Mob and the Guillotine

to maintain its high clinical standards when there was such a pressing queue of victims. Calls for multiple guillotines became frequent, but there were objections both ideological and practical. The single machine had become a uniquely potent symbol of state justice and to create others would be undignified; in any case, more guillotines would cause chaos as the crowds dashed from one site to another to catch the next event. There were plans for a pneumatic guillotine, the machine harnessed to a steam engine driving a conveyor-belt

Jacobins as cannibals (James Gillray)

of victims into an automatic drop-and-raise blade. The combination of food shortages and mass executions even prompted
the Abbé Morellet, a member of the French Academy, to
suggest eating the guillotine's victims as 'a new means for the
Nation's sustenance'. Terror victims should be sold in a
'national butcher's shop', and to encourage the squeamish
there should be 'a law which would oblige citizens to shop
there at least once a week'. Enemies of the state would be
served at 'every patriotic fête' and the dish would become a
'Jacobin eucharist'.

Throughout the winter and spring, Matthews' letters to the
committee continue, though at a gradually slower rate. He has
already told them his situation is hopeless without their help;
he stresses repeatedly that prison would be better than his
present plight. More and more he comes to dwell on the
accusations he has received via his landlord that he is an
impostor, a man without honour, a traitor to the cause. 'I am

told I am an agent of Pitt,' he writes to the committee; 'I answer that if it was so, my conduct would have been different.' It's almost as if Matthews has inadvertently acquired a doppelganger, an evil twin who is destroying his reputation by pretending to be a servant of the British. He begins to spend pages denouncing this phantom, demonstrating how it couldn't possibly be him. If it had been, 'my object would have been to acquire some knowledge of your situation; your preparations; to have fomented divisions etc.etc.etc.'; point by point, Matthews demonstrates how he did the opposite at every turn. Besides, he is British in name only. 'I am Welch,' he informs them, and the Welsh have always, unlike the British, been lovers of liberty and reason: 'from the time of Caesar to this moment, we have pressed our liberty and laws, and history cannot furnish an hundred instances in this period of us having forsaken the cause for which you are now fighting'. Furthermore, he is barely Welsh: 'my mother's family are French, of the name of Tilly, who were obliged to leave France at the revocation of the edict of Nantes; I bear this name, having been christened James Tilly'. His confinement is gradually becoming less of a political blunder and more a case of mistaken identity: the man they are holding is someone else altogether.

This stream of consciousness continues until May, by which point it seems that Matthews is no longer expecting any response from the committee. His letters of protest have become a game of solitaire: he reworks his own motives, his own identity, apparently more for his own purposes than for those with which the exchange began. In May, the paper trail goes cold. Either the committee stopped filing his letters, or Matthews stopped sending them. Here, in the dark heart of the story, we have radio silence.

Outside his lodging-house, the Terror hurtled towards its great climax of self-destruction. Danton had finally been arrested in April, not so much for anything he had actually done as for fear of what he might do. He had raged at the Convention, calling all of them cowards, challenging any one of them to accuse him to his face. They had stayed silent, and voted quietly for his death. The Convention's complicity in this purge had bound them together, whether in conviction or fear that any other dissenter might be next. On 4 June they elected Robespierre their president by 485 votes to nil. Where all others had shown weakness, vice or favouritism, the Incorruptible One had no interests beyond those of the Revolution. He slept two or three hours a night, lived on little but bread and coffee, and had no hesitation in taking the Republic forward into territory where its previous leaders had feared to tread.

Under Robespierre's presidency the Revolution, already highly and visibly branded, reached its pinnacle of ideology and spectacle. Churches were made over into Temples to Reason, and revolutionary mottos and neo-classical motifs sprang up on every wall and street corner, with exhortations towards *patrie* and *liberté* and denunciations of hoarding and profiteering. Robespierre's grandest gesture was probably also David Williams' most direct, though perverse and belated, contribution to the Revolution. Williams had written extensively on the need for a universal religion to transcend sectarian divides, and had drawn heavily on Rousseau's ideas of Nature and the Supreme Being; Robespierre, at this point, decided that the Revolution needed a transcendent ritual to replace that of the Church, and formulated an event which shows Williams' imprint, though elevated to a level of portentous grandeur that would have appalled him. The Feast of the Supreme Being was held on 8 June 1794, stage-managed spectacularly by the artist Jacques-Louis David and presided over by Robespierre in a sky-blue coat, gold buckles, culottes and powdered hair. It combined titanic stage sets and statues with new secular hymns voiced by a hundred thousand *sansculottes*; a vast monument to Atheism (an 'aristocratic' indulgence) was set alight to reveal a statue of Wisdom, perched on an artificial mountain, towering through the smoke and ushering in the new Reign of Joy. The grand gesture had its moments of unintended bathos – the smoke from the burning Atheism turned Wisdom's face black – and the grandiosity of its pretensions inspired some but alienated many more. Knots of *sansculottes* were heard muttering, 'He's not content with being boss, now he wants to be God too.'

The Feast of the Supreme Being was immediately followed by the Law of Prarial, which effectively made liberty or death the only two possible outcomes of any trial: since any crime was a crime against the nation, all crimes were treason. But Robespierre's undisputed leadership was rapidly beginning to work against him. With a leader so incorruptibly above favouritism, no-one was safe; after the death of Danton as their binding act of faith, no-one could take the moral high ground against summary justice. At the end of July Robespierre's house was broken into in the middle of the night, the president, working at his desk in his Supreme Being garb, shot in the face. The next day he was stretchered into the Convention, bleeding and bandaged and missing half his jaw, and condemned as an enemy of the people. His was planned as the last execution of the day, but he was fading fast from loss of blood, and jumped the queue.

Robespierre's death was not the end of the Terror. The next day, seventy of his allies, or 'accomplices', followed him, and the floodgates opened once more. Everyone whose friends and family had been imprisoned or executed by the Jacobins demanded revenge; across the country, where tinpot Jacobin regimes had wielded power over their terrified neighbours, they were shown little mercy in return. But gradually the Terror subsided into mere martial law; and, eventually, we hear from Matthews again.

After a year of silence, Matthews' next letter was always likely to be unpredictable, but what we get is surely stranger than

Robespierre's arrest

anything we could have imagined. We might have suspected that the conspiracies against him had become more florid and fantastic, or that his identity crisis had generated some un-recognizable new life story, or that the causes of the war had blossomed into cosmic conspiracy. What we could never have guessed is that his next letter would make no mention of his predicament, the plots against him, the Revolution, the war, or even of himself. Instead, what we get is a grand plan for the future of French municipal agriculture.

Even by the standards of Matthews' prodigious later work, this is an epic: thirty close-written pages of methodical detail, description and argument laying out a permanent solution to the food shortages and crises that had plagued the country since long before the Revolution. We begin with a brief political preamble – 'in these extraordinary times of penury and distress, active and extraordinary measures on the part of government are very necessary' – and then plunge headlong and without respite into the world of vegetables.

'There must be', Matthews reasons, 'in places around Paris, numerous hothouses, greenhouses and other buildings having a sufficient inlet of light, always to preserve the air from stagnation or intemperance, and which are perhaps entirely void or unoccupied.' Twenty or thirty of these should be selected, and men with barrows should be detailed to fill them with earth to a depth of fifteen or eighteen inches. 'I would then take a sufficient quantity of the seed of the costliest and largest cabbages common to the country, sow it and leave it to vegetate' – heating would be unnecessary in such enclosures – and the plan should then move on to stage two.

'There is in Paris a continual dirt and filth,' Matthews continues, but behind this terrible problem for the inhabitants lurks a brilliant resolution for the food shortage. All the government needs to do is to commandeer the 'considerable body of those idle, or those more unfortunate men of which there are no doubt too many about the town, put brooms into their hands, and scrapers, [and] make them scrape together all the deal of filth which can possibly be picked up throughout the city'. This vast tide of manure could then be transported, by carts or boats, to the hothouses, where it would fertilize the cabbages in abundance and nourish a vegetable supply for the nation.

This would, Matthews admits, require a change in the national diet; but he generously suggests that 'the French naturally are not gourmands, enough is all they want', and furthermore that 'a more than abundant supply of vegetables can be continued through the entire year, a less destruction of fowls, of young flesh such as small pigs, lambs and calves may be contrived, whilst the offal and vegetables will continue to support them'. The government needs to face the fact that the rich French diet may be unsustainable, and also that the reason so few people eat cabbages is that they have become excessively scarce and expensive, 'a cabbage which formerly cost some sous, bringing in today in Paris 25 livres'.

But, lest perhaps he should be accused of monomania, Matthews makes it clear that 'this cabbage scheme is not the only thing which I aim at, although in addition to what I have stated it may preserve much fruit from being gathered and consumed'. Cabbages would only be the beginning; once one vegetable was up and running, others would follow. 'The government', he suggests, 'may find means to obtain from England either by small or large cargoes, say only 1000 bushels of the sound mealy potatoe.' These could be grown in the English fashion – planted in March, at a depth of nine inches – in between the cabbage rows, where they would 'no doubt vegetate well', having sufficient nourishment and a more temperate climate than they were used to.

The plan continues for many more pages, all proposals buttressed with a similarly exhaustive level of practical detail, and gradually expands the scheme from a local experiment in crisis management into an all-encompassing and permanent system. 'If France could be supported one day entirely by such singular modes', Matthews concludes, 'it would be much. They may be made regular in better times, and premiums and encouragements to assist them.' The intensive labour required would be, like the manure from the Paris streets, not a problem but a solution, as it could be 'drawn from an industry that may be established with houses of detention, or seclusion, where now nothing seems to reign but idleness and criminality'.

Is the cabbage scheme mad? It's certainly unexpected, and with the foreknowledge of Matthews' future madness it's easy to read it as grandiose and obsessive. But all technical documents are detailed: if we were shown a railway timetable and told that the author had later gone mad, we might be tempted to reinterpret the mundane as bizarre. The cabbage plan may equally well be read as a cunning ploy, and one which succeeds. Paris had long been renowned for intensive cultivation methods, and the minister to whom Matthews addresses it is apparently an enthusiast. 'You are a master in agriculture, Citizen,' Matthews flatters him, and 'I doubt not that you will be able to improve anything which I shall here offer.' And there is a crucial indication that he has hit the mark. This is the first of his letters for over a year which merits a French translation, though in a somewhat abridged form. As previously, if he were in the early phase of paranoid schizophrenia this type of effective orchestration of those around him is precisely what we would expect to be missing. But mad or not, he has the ear of the government once more; the cabbage plan has succeeded where all his protestations of innocence, conspiracy and injustice have failed.

The first result of his new-found attention appears, on the surface, not to be spectacular: within a fortnight he is transferred to Pleissis prison, just outside Paris. Conditions in the revolutionary jails were, unsurprisingly, poor: with requisition notices for food, supplies, tools and bedding arriving regularly in every district, prisons were usually the first places to be pillaged. Food consisted mostly of a little salt pork or haricot beans eked out with *pain d'égalité*, black bread coarse and gritty from being inadequately threshed and milled; blankets and fires were more luxury than staple. But Matthews had been begging to be put into prison over a year before in order to discharge his debts; we have no idea where he has been in the meantime, although his sign-off comment about 'houses of detention, or seclusion' suggests that he has some experience of them. Nevertheless, his stay in Pleissis will turn out to be brief – and to be his last staging-post before freedom.

It also turns out to be the place where he encounters a new idea that will prove highly influential to his subsequent story. It appears to have been a chance encounter, but one which was crucial in the formation of his future delusional world. It clearly made a deep impression on him as he was able, under John Haslam's prompting fifteen years later, to recall the conversation word for word. It was with a Mr Chavanay, whose father, Matthews also recalled, had apparently once been Lord Lonsdale's cook.

Chavanay opened the conversation with the following words: 'Mr Matthews, are you acquainted with the art of talking with your brains?' Matthews replied that he was not, and Chavanay expanded somewhat obscurely: 'It is effected by means of the magnet.'

This is the wild card in Matthews' French adventures: the disputed science of mesmerism, which of course will eventually become the motive force behind the Air Loom. Was Matthews mesmerized by Chavanay? He doesn't tell us, but it would explain a great deal. To someone grappling with the confusing, overlaid identities that had become so intertwined with both his jeopardy and his survival, the experience of having thoughts and feelings conjured up in his head by another, with no apparent input from his conscious mind, might well have dramatically altered his understanding both of his situation and of himself. Here was an alternative framework of explanation, cutting across the seemingly random parade of inquisitions and detentions that had become his life. If it was possible for some people to control the minds of others, might that not account for everything? Nobody wanted war, yet war had enveloped the world. The British government had avoided it easily enough until Matthews took the stage, and then had suddenly rushed into it. Brissot had not wanted war either, but had stood up in front of the Convention demanding that Europe be consumed by flames. Someone, behind the scenes, had sabotaged the peace plan from both sides. Most strikingly of all, the entire republican project, so carefully conceived and courageously fought for, had been hijacked by a power everyone seemed to fear but nobody could explain. It was not just that Matthews' own intentions and actions had turned out disastrously, everybody's had. Perhaps things were not as they seemed; perhaps no-one was any longer the master of his own will.

Although mesmerism is a wild card, it is far more than a solipsistic obsession Matthews develops in isolation from the real world of politics around him. Mesmerism was an invisible current deeply woven into the fabric of the Revolution, one about which Matthews had probably heard a great deal before running into his first practitioner, and one which was to overlay his story in profound and complex ways. For it had undergone an extraordinary and chaotic journey through the Revolution, its founder having described a trajectory which exactly paralleled Matthews' own, from loyal ally to sacrificial victim.

Franz Anton Mesmer arrived in Paris in 1778 from his home city of Vienna, already trailing the twin reputations that would follow him for the rest of his life and far beyond: that he was a genius whose discovery would revolutionize medicine as Newton had revolutionized physics, and that he was a money-grabbing quack who had made a fortune exploiting the wealthy and gullible. He immediately proceeded to strengthen both reputations considerably.

Within a few months he had set himself up in grand apartments near the centre of Paris, offering his 'magnetic' therapies for a substantial fee. Patients were ushered into a thickly carpeted hall decorated with astrological symbols, accompanied by ethereal music often played by Mesmer himself on a strange glass harmonica which sent shivers through the nerves. The treatment rooms were dominated by three huge contraptions known as *baquets*: circular tubs, large enough for thirty people at a time to crowd round them, containing bottles of water Mesmer had magnetized and arranged in a concentric star-shape. These were submerged in more water which had been filled with iron filings, and magnetized iron rods protruded through its surface for the patients to grasp with one hand while linking the other with their neighbour's to form a 'mesmeric chain' of healing current.

Mesmer's baquet

These magnetic salons, or *séances*, were spectacular. As the 'fluid' moved around the group, patients began to feel twinges and surges of pressure and release. First one, then another was swept up in the mysterious invisible tide; people began writhing, convulsing, speaking in tongues, often passing out. If their convulsions became too violent, they were whisked off to small heavily curtained and mattress-padded 'crisis rooms' where Mesmer would make dramatic hand-passes down their limbs and across their stomachs, bringing their convulsions to a climax from which they would emerge swooning like damp rag dolls. Such crises always presaged cure: once the treatment had begun to force magnetic fluid through the blockages in their system, the patients' bodies would restore themselves to health and harmony.

And so they did, in their hundreds. Patients were cured of muscle spasms, paralyses, epilepsy, stomach cramps, ulcers, toothache, fainting fits, even lifelong blindness. A genuine miracle-worker had set up shop in the Place Vendôme; whether it was science or superstition, it was without doubt worth watching and investigating. The *baquet* sessions had to be booked weeks in advance. One tub had originally been set aside for the deserving poor, but the vast crowds made it impractical; instead, Mesmer magnetized a tree at the end of the road to which throngs of people attached themselves by cords.

But Mesmer hadn't come to Paris to make money. His first appointments had been with the dignitaries of the Royal Academies of Science and Medicine, to whom he had come to have his new science recognized. He arrived with sheaves of testimonies from cured patients, but the academies refused to consider anecdotal evidence. The remissions might have been spontaneous, the patients might not have been ill in the first place; without knowing the case in question, they were not prepared to judge. But as his practice grew, Mesmer continued to petition the members of the academies in person, inviting them to witness the miracle of the *baquets*. Gradually, he began to win influential converts, and in 1784 they agreed to investigate his scientific claims and to set up a commission headed by the American Minister to France, Benjamin Franklin.

The commission needed no proof that Mesmer was curing patients every day. The disputed territory was whether he had discovered a new force in nature or whether doctor and patient were, consciously or not, colluding in some therapeutic fantasy. For though Mesmer's practical results were plain to see, the theory that underpinned them was a great deal more opaque. The basis of his claim was that there existed an invisible influence throughout nature, 'a universally distributed fluid, so continuous as to admit of no vacuum, incomparably rarefied, and by its nature able to receive, propagate and communicate all motion'. His therapies tapped into this influence, boosting the fluid's circulation and curing disease by restoring harmony to the organism. But the nuts and bolts of how all this worked seemed unclear even to Mesmer himself. To begin with, he believed the fluid was channelled through magnets, and thus christened it 'animal magnetism'. Then he became persuaded that the shape of the magnet was significant. Soon, he realized that many types of things apart from metals could also be 'magnetized': bread, silk, water, trees, dogs, human beings. By now, the Society of Universal Harmony that had been founded in Paris to propagate his teachings was beginning to generate multiple systems as his followers shaped their own experiences and techniques into rogue and heretical magnetic doctrines.

The commission had no problem *per se* with new and invisible forces in nature: gravity, after all, had been the greatest scientific discovery of the century. But Mesmer was by no means the first since Newton to propose a mysterious new force: such submissions had become, like perpetual motion devices to the Patent Office, a constant bane. In this case, though, they had to respond not merely to tracts and diagrams but to extraordinary new powers. How could human beings, rational creatures with souls, be reduced to puppets, or machines, with a few passes of the hand? What, if any, was the role of God in such miracles? If Newton had banished Him from the material world by elucidating the mechanics of gravity, was Mesmer now expelling Him from humankind?

These were weighty and unavoidable questions. The commission decided to proceed by trying some magnetic cures on themselves. Some of them felt mild twinges, but overall they were struck by how different the effect was from that generated in the salons by groups of believers. Subsequent double-blind tests showed that even those patients who were undoubtedly cured could nevertheless not distinguish magnetized objects from non-magnetized ones. They concluded that 'there is no proof of the existence of the Animal Magnetic fluid . . . the imagination without the aid of Magnetism can produce convulsions, but Magnetism without the imagination can produce nothing'. But their final recommendations were even more negative: they warned sternly that the 'stimulation of the imagination' and the contagious 'risk of imitation' involved in mesmerism were potentially harmful, and that 'all public treatment by Magnetism must in the long run have deplorable consequences'. Mesmer's claim to a place in the pantheon of scientific genius was emphatically rejected.

It was at this point, in 1785, that mesmerism and revolutionary politics became fellow travellers. Mesmer, shattered by a verdict from which he would never really recover, launched a counter-attack on the academies: who cared what they thought when thousands of patients had witnessed the supposedly impossible with their own eyes? 'It is to the people that I appeal,' he concluded, with ominous revolutionary overtones. And there were many among the radical and excluded who were prepared to flock to his cause. The revolutionary journalist Jean-Paul Marat, self-proclaimed Friend of the People, had also had his invisible-fluid theory rejected by the Academy and had done much to promote the view of the scientific establishment as a narrow, self-interested oligarchy. The Marquis de Lafayette, an early mesmeric convert, had gone off to fight the American Revolution, spreading animal magnetism evangelically as he went. Mesmerist salons went underground, becoming fronts for dissenting corresponding societies and radical self-healing movements.

During this process, the malleable theory of mesmerism acquired a markedly political dimension. Since the magnetic fluid was distributed throughout the cosmos, its principles could apply as much to societies as to individual organisms: the body politic, too, could be healthy and harmonious, or blocked and disrupted. Mesmer's protégé Nicholas Bergasse, a

Animal magnetism lampooned

political radical, conflated his master's work with Rousseau's notion that primitive societies had been harmonious and self-regulating, but modern customs and institutions had disturbed their natural balance. Specifically, he maintained that despotic systems which ruled from above by the constant pressure of brute force always prevented a society from finding its true fluidic form. Only when such shackles were removed could society once again truly live and breathe as nature intended.

This was an alliance of repressed science and politics which appealed to many, not least to Jacques-Pierre Brissot. In the years before the Revolution, Brissot championed the cause of mesmerism with typical vigour, convinced that it was not merely true – as thoroughly demonstrated as any scientific theory had ever been – but a revolutionary strategy whose time had come. It had exposed the largely aristocratic scientific establishment as 'base parasites' and 'oppressors of the father-land', and had opened up spheres of radical thought to a new audience. Marvels of science, he thought, were a better vehicle for radical ideas than political tracts. Mesmerism had become a subject of fascination to a wide reading public, far more than would ever glance at Rousseau's *Social Contract*. 'The time has now come for the revolution that France needs,' Brissot argued, 'but to attempt to produce one openly is to doom it to failure. To succeed it is necessary to wrap oneself in mystery; it is necessary to unite men under the pretext of experiments in physics but, in reality, for the overthrow of despotism.'

But come the Revolution, mesmerism was reinterpreted once more. While some radicals had espoused it, others had not – and, in any case, the old alliance was broken once the under-ground where it had flourished had transformed itself into the establishment. The new revolutionary orthodoxy swiftly adopted the view that, from its beginnings, mesmerism had been an aristocratic fad. Mesmer, by this stage long gone to Germany and Switzerland, had made a fortune from his noble patients, had charged the huge fee of a hundred livres for admission to his Society of Universal Harmony, and had even been offered a fat pension for life by Marie Antoinette. Mesmerism was denounced by the Assembly as vigorously as it had been by the academies five years earlier.

But this dismissal, like the last, was not the end of the story. There was something about mesmerism which was too powerful and disturbing for edicts and prohibitions to undo. It remained easily demonstrated, mysterious and profoundly strange; thousands had felt its effects, had had experiences they would never forget. Although many leading mesmerists had become *émigrés*, there were skilled practitioners still in circulation and, as Matthews' encounter with Chavanay suggests, they could transmit their ideas under the cloak of occult drama which had so intoxicated the younger Brissot. Mesmerism remained a strange power, trailing behind it a mysterious science, transmitted covertly, its discovery now punishable by death.

There were those in England before the Revolution who had seen in mesmerism a new kind of political danger. As it was almost exclusively a continental phenomenon at this stage – the Victorians would be the generation to embrace it with intense fascination, and rechristen it 'hypnotism' – the news of it which crossed the Channel was interwoven with anxieties about the spread of the virus of revolution. 'This power', warned the journalist John Pearson, 'may prove a dangerous engine in the hands of a corrupt administration.' If a politician mastered its dark arts, he might deal with an opponent in the House 'by the eloquence of his fingers, consigning the troublesome member to sleep'. After the Revolution, similar anxieties began to spread through the Republic, particularly through Brissot himself. The power of which he had been so convinced in the early days of the struggle was now, once more, in the political wilderness, and might be reclaimed by those 'who are unhappy with the new order of things and who hope to find in it a means to destroy them'.

The *'contre-révolution des somnambules'* which Brissot feared had quickly, and perhaps not surprisingly, begun to manifest itself. Strange and garbled news of mesmerist plots spread around the new regime as early as 1790. The first was a conspiracy to free Louis XVI from prison by communicating an escape plan to him by magnetic influence: two counter-revolutionaries had hired an aristocratic mesmerist to imprint their scheme on the King's mind, and were allegedly shocked by their arrest as they believed that they had been made invisible. A few months later, a mesmerist *séance* communicated a conspiracy purportedly hatched by a cell of noble *émigrés* to overthrow the government with the support of the British and Spanish navies.

Against this background, several commentators have proposed that Matthews' mission to France might have been a mesmerist initiative from the beginning. Brissot might have communicated his anxieties about mesmerism to Matthews early in the game; Matthews, losing his grip on reality, might have claimed to the Committee of Public Safety that his peace proposal was magnetically channelled from the British Cabinet. There's much that appeals in this theory: under pressure to admit that he had written the proposal on his own initiative, the idea of mesmerism might have allowed Matthews to finesse a middle ground between truth and fiction, and a committee susceptible to the idea of magnetic plots might have believed him. But the suggestion is, once again, essentially argued backwards from the content of his Air Loom delusions fifteen years later; the events of the time provide no evidence for it and quite a lot to the contrary. None of Matthews' letters or the committee's confidential reports on him mention mesmerism, nor does Matthews himself mention it in his subsequent correspondence with the French government – and, of course, his own later account specifies that his first contact with it was in Pleissis prison.

But there can be no doubt that the idea of 'talking with your brains' – what we may now call telepathy or thought-transference, with the assistance of magnetic powers – impressed him deeply. It arrived at a stage in his life when his sense of identity had been under sustained attack. The previous two years had begun the process of teasing out a series of overlapping but distinct Matthewses: the revolutionary partisan, the British spy, the double agent, the Revolution's saviour and its secret saboteur, and the troubling Matthews of Paris gossip who cut so disastrously across the image he was carefully presenting to the authorities. Magnetic influence, with its implication that people were speaking and acting without their own knowledge, or under the control of an unscrupulous operator, seems to have offered a theoretical framework for making sense of his increasingly complex internal contradictions.

One of the most striking effects of being mesmerized is that the face which stares back at you from the mirror is no longer easily recognizable as your own. If Matthews was already becoming someone who could no longer easily recognize himself in the mirror, the experience might have given powerful external validation to the insight that the world had somehow become a strange shadowplay, its true motive force concealed from all but a few. Within a few years, this insight would have taken root to the point where his first complaints on meeting Haslam would be of magnetic influences inside the walls of Bedlam.

But we hear nothing of this from Matthews yet. What we get, by contrast, is an energetic and focused resumption of his campaign to get himself released. The response to his cabbage plan has clearly reawoken his hopes, and he decides to strike hard while the authorities are once more paying attention to him. He sends two letters, one to the Minister of Foreign Affairs and another to the Directory, and follows them up with a third to the Committee of Public Safety in November 1795. His tone, too, has changed dramatically: gone is the pleading and the wistful chatter, replaced by a brusque attention to business. He has been the victim of an 'infamous calumny', and it's high time that it was redressed. He is sure that the committee 'must be well acquainted with my affair' and 'will not permit to languish long unheard a man so devoted to the nation as I am'. He addresses himself personally to their civic responsibilities: 'I demand justice', he insists, and 'I deny any charge which can be laid against me'.

Again, he hits the target: his letter is translated the same day. But silence descends again. We hear from him next three months later, in February 1796, by which point briskness has shaded into irritation. Once again, he goes straight to the top: Delacroix, the Minister for Foreign Affairs. Matthews has told him everything he needs to know – 'you are in possession of all the pieces which shew the infamy of those who thus keep me here' – and he is losing patience. Now, he speaks the unspeakable. 'I am sorry', he continues, 'after all my efforts to be obliged to think that to have a right to justice in France, I ought to have assisted in its destruction instead of having endeavoured its preservation.' Matthews the diehard republican is, at this moment, dead. He is through with protesting his loyalty to the cause, offering justifications for his actions or evidence that he is on their side. The faith that has bound him through the entire story is now a thing of the past. He no longer cares what they think; for the first time since the early days of his arrest, he is threatening to throw his weight around. 'I demand of you personally,' he concludes, 'in your official capacity, that you lay before the Directory all my papers.'

This is a high-risk strategy: he is threatening to burn his bridges, to lose the ear he has gone to such lengths to obtain. He might have calculated that since nothing else had worked, he had nothing to lose. But writing the letter must also have been profoundly therapeutic. He has lived in fear since his arrest, offered to mould himself to his captors' will, even to sacrifice his life to their designs. Many who had suffered the same might have lived out the rest of their lives in this abject quiescence, perhaps lapsing into terminal depression. But Matthews, somewhere, somehow, has maintained a core of resilience, and a burning coal of righteous anger: he has regenerated the part of himself that refuses to take no for an answer, and the urgency which impels him to demand that the man at the top 'render me instantly my liberty'.

But, once again, he runs into the old adversary which dogs this state of mind: delay. He receives a note from Lacroix's office telling him that his papers have been forwarded to the Minister of Police. He writes back, blazing, 'you delivering my applications to the Minister of Police is neither what your duty commands of you nor yet what I demanded of you'. Again, the cold and professional tone of the man who knows the functionary's job better than him: 'I request you will in your official capacity take the necessary means to enable you to obtain my liberty, by your presenting my papers to the Directory.'

Within two weeks, he is set free.

Matthews' return journey to England is symbolic of how his fortunes have changed over the last three years. No coach-and-horses this time, no lavish distribution of cash tips as he races from post to post. According to his later telling of the tale, he makes his way on foot from Paris to Calais, accompanied by a gendarme, hustled from cell to cell, each night in a different dungeon. He is barefoot for much of the way, his ragged clothes exposing him to the bitter cold. He is sometimes fed scraps, and sometimes beaten. At Calais he has to beg his passage across the Channel, and arrives back in England on 6 March 1796.

He returns to his 'distressed family', who are as impover-ished as he is, in a state of high excitement. In clinical terms, this may be another bout of delusional intensity, a precarious surge of energy after the deep depression of his confinement, but it's not hard to recognize the emotions that would grip anyone, mad or sane, who had suffered the same. He's most clearly 'mad' in the modern sense of angry: the upswing of giddy euphoria that must be accompanying his freedom is swamped by the righteous anger that provoked his release. This anger must feel good, his ability to express it even better; but perhaps, too, he is indulging it too recklessly, and suppressing the troublesome possibility that it might have had little to do with his release. The workings of the revolutionary gulag were impenetrable; hundreds of thousands of prisoners were held, released, executed for reasons they would never discover. Surely Matthews *must* believe that it was his anger which freed him; the alternative, that it was simply a quirk of bureaucracy, a casual decision prompted by general over-crowding or a change of policy, is too painful to contemplate. Here, perhaps, is an entry-point for what psychiatrists would call 'delusions of reference', the conviction that everything that happens centres on you.

If his anger is the motor now driving him, its object is clearly the British government. He undertook his mission on their behalf; he risked his life for them; whatever has happened to him is their responsibility, and they must somehow pay. All we know of his movements on his return is that he spent a great deal of time in Westminster and Whitehall, calling on officials, trying and failing to secure meetings with members of the Cabinet, spending days in the public gallery of the House of Commons. It seems that he received short shrift since, after several months of this, he picks up his pen again and writes at length to Lord Liverpool.

The letter begins coolly enough. Matthews reminds Liverpool that, as 'your Lordship will well remember', they met in May 1793 at Addiscombe Place, at which point Matthews 'made known to your Lordship the certainty I had of being able to effect a total change of principles and measures, then pursuing, or adopted, in France'. Clearly this refers to the peace proposal, and the covert support of Brissot and the Girondins. Matthews remembers, too, 'the pleasure your Lordship seemed to enjoy at the prospect', and 'I confess to your Lordship it acted upon me as a stimulus to push with additional vigour'. Gently, Matthews is implying that this is something of which Liverpool cannot entirely wash his hands.

After this, though, the bad news. The 'triumph of anarchy by the insurrection of the 31st May' – the Jacobin seizure of power – 'seemed as if purposely wrought in contradiction to all the assurance which I had been making', and plunged the plan into disarray. This, Matthews continues, 'necessitated my instant return to Paris', at which point he was on his own and defenceless: 'I became the object of every intrigue, and every other measure which could be practised seemed practised, in order to entrap and destroy me'. There were even, apparently – 'and if true your Lordship must shudder' – those who believed he was a British government agent.

But, despite being beset on all sides, Matthews stood firm; 'it happens that I am not soon frightened by a whole Jacobin army!' He returned to London to rescue Britain from 'the treason of some of its allies', and thence back to France where he had been promised official powers and status (presumably the passport offered by Le Brun). At this point he 'had hopes of saving the unfortunate Princess and her family' – suddenly Matthews is no longer the *sansculotte* but the Scarlet Pimpernel, rescuing trembling aristocrats from the slavering mob. But just as his plan was on the point of success, 'I was put under arrestation, and a law which had been expressly passed two days before, was intended to take away my life'.

By this point, we may feel we are beginning to nudge gently across the boundary, always a porous one, between self-justification and fantasy. Matthews' story is not a fantasy: we can recognize every event. But the frame of reference is some-how shrinking, and grand world events are being rewritten around the actions of a minor player. To begin with, he is scrupulous in explaining that 'it seemed' as if governments were acting specifically to block his plans, but this is the last time we shall hear that 'seemed'. Suppositions are becoming certainties; metaphors are becoming literal truths. Thus far, putting our finger on the point at which Matthews 'went mad' has been a speculative and problematic pursuit, but here we can see clear signs that he is beginning, in crucial ways, to close off dialogue with the world around him.

The warning signs are followed by a sheer drop. 'Letters were fabricated', purportedly from Matthews, 'discovering plots centred in me': other Matthewses are being constructed by invisible hands, troublesome impostors, even ones who are apparently selling British naval secrets to the French. Soon, the French have him tied up in knots, with 'a plausible pretence of putting me to death'. At this point they put his loyalty to the test, offering him ten million livres to 'join in a plan to stir up insurrections in Great Britain'. They have assembled 'an atrocious set' to partner him in this infamy – a gang we may, perhaps, meet later in a different guise. Matthews, of course, refuses, despite the 'tenders of riches and honour, palaces even' they now extend. Huge sums of money are floating around in these international conspiracies to destabilize the British government, and it is being 'pretended by those in power that such sums had passed through my hands'. But Matthews will not budge, 'equally despising their guillotine and their palaces', and he is thrown into prison.

He had 'resolved rather to perish wanting food than suffer the British name to be injured', and this resolve was put to the test over the following years. He was 'continually reduced in wretchedness' until, 'after continual remonstrances and approaches', he was released, and dragged back to Calais filthy and starving. But worse was to come: back in England he discovered that 'other measures to destroy me had been put into practice' – not just the Traitorous Correspondence Act, but 'four or five persons had committed a forgery on the Bank of England, and much pains had been taken to spread abroad that it was me'.

Matthews, then, is in an impossible position. At this stage this is not Lord Liverpool's fault, but Liverpool is among the few who can resolve it. Thus far, Matthews tells him, 'there seems to be much evasion'; if this continues, his only option will be to 'publish to all the world every transaction which has come to my knowledge'. What should he do? He is more than happy to 'do myself the honour of calling on your Lordship's office'.

This letter to Liverpool is perhaps the last point at which the story could have ended, if not happily, at least peacefully. Liverpool could have offered Matthews a meeting, during which he would probably have discovered that it would take very little to satisfy Matthews' pride and honour, to allow him to believe that he had given his country valuable service. But it's unlikely that Liverpool considered this, or even got past the first page of the letter. Even if he couldn't recall Matthews immediately, he would on prompting have remembered his harassment of the Cabinet at the beginning of the war, his publishing of Le Brun's letters in *The Times*, his threats to expose Pitt and Grenville. Now, war with France had become the nation's great patriotic cause, the strange fumblings after peace in 1793 an embarrassment to be forever forgotten. Matthews, by his own admission in the letter, is 'without pecuniary means', and without support on either side of the Channel. He is a peace movement of one.

Matthews, too, could have ended the story at this point by leaving Liverpool alone and letting the whole episode lie. He could, perhaps, have taken a leaf out of his own book and turned his prodigious energies to intensive cabbage culti-vation. But righteous and frustrated anger is hard to turn off, even in the sanest of us. Claims become wilder, demands for redress more grandiose, until we get attention – which is, usually, all we really wanted all along.

There are no prizes for guessing what actually happened. Liverpool ignored the letter; Matthews wrote again. This time, he crossed the Rubicon.

Matthews' second letter to Liverpool, written on 6 December, flips the entire story on its head. 'What I have to say to your Lordship', he announces, 'will be short', though in fact it's the same length as the previous one. But it announces its tone plainly enough in the first paragraph: 'I pronounce your Lordship to be in every sense of the word a most diabolical traitor.'

Now, all the iniquitous dealings Matthews had previously imputed to the French are heaped on Liverpool's head. 'After a long life of political iniquity,' he claims, 'you have made yourself a principal in schemes of treason' which have 'laid your country at the feet of its most bitter enemies'. It was Liverpool who was trying to stop Matthews rescuing the King – in fact, his 'secret cabinet in the court of St. James's' actually arranged 'the murder of that unfortunate monarch' and plotted to replace him on the French throne with the Duke of York. This is a conspiracy theory which was widely believed in France; not all of this is spun directly out of Matthews' head. But all of it, whatever its source, has now been telescoped into a final showdown between him and his adversary. Liverpool was behind the Jacobin seizure of power: 'you and your fellow labourers in iniquity caused the insurrection in Paris'. Liverpool sabotaged the British army; Liverpool handed over the West Indian colonies; Liverpool orchestrated 'the fomenting of insurrections in the different parts of England, Ireland and Corsica'. All this has been done not out of principle but out of greed – 'it has been for bribes . . . to the amount within my knowledge of upwards of three millions' – and all has depended on whipping up war. Throughout, Matthews has 'sought only the honour of rendering France and England as much friends as they had usually been rivals, enemies'; Liverpool has bribed and plotted to scupper any plans for peace. Louis XVI was Matthews' talisman: as long as he lived, there was scope for *rapprochement* between the sides. But Liverpool has played the crowned heads off against each other: 'you have encouraged the desire to destroy each other, and to accomplish the ruin, the death even of all those you have found inimical to your crafty plans'.

Matthews has enough insight not to expect Liverpool to concede any of this: the letter is not a negotiation but a challenge. 'I profess myself to be at open war with you my Lord,' he concludes, 'and with all those your partners or apostles in craft and treason.' He has enough insight, too, to predict the direction in which all this is heading, perhaps even to invite it. 'You may succeed', he signs off, 'in imposing upon the world that I am insane, but I will persevere till I convince you and the world that I am perfectly otherwise.'

This is an extremely unwise letter on many levels. It's treasonous under the Traitorous Correspondence Act for one; it also goads Liverpool into ignoring it at his own peril; it even suggests to him the easiest way to deal with the problem. It's mad, and not just in the sense of angry. Matthews seems to have yielded to a long-frustrated urge to be free of balanced analysis, of equivocation, of factual justification. At least in the heat of writing it, the strain of resisting the grand conspiracy is too great. He no longer cares whether he seems like a reasonable man, whether he's likely to persuade a rational audience. He wants to speak the unreasonable truth, to release the flood of conviction that these are the facts in the case of James Tilly Matthews against the rest of the world.

Needless to say, his letter gets no reply. A few weeks later Matthews is in the gallery of the House of Commons, shouting his accusations at Liverpool in person. A few weeks after that, Matthews is in Bedlam – which, as we know, will prove a great deal harder to get out of than a Paris jail.

6

ILLUSTRATIONS OF MADNESS

'O! Matter and impertinency mix'd;
Reason in madness'
William Shakespeare, *King Lear*, 1604–5

THE HABEAS CORPUS HEARING IN 1809 MIGHT INITIALLY HAVE
seemed like a brick wall for both Matthews and Haslam, but
it turned out to be the catalyst for a flurry of intense activity
on both sides. For twelve years they had been locked in stale-
mate, Matthews ever less likely to renounce his mission and
declare that he had been insane, and Haslam equally unlikely
to renounce his diagnosis and allow his own pride to be
wounded. But in contrast to the silent confinement that
preceded it, the next three years saw both physician and
patient taking up their pens and, in their different ways,
attempting to write their way out of the impasse. The results
would be spectacular. Haslam was to convert his experiences
with Matthews into one of the classic case histories of
psychiatry, the book for which he is still remembered today.
Matthews, in turn, would go one better, producing a remarkable body of work that would rewrite the story of Bedlam
itself.

It was Haslam who struck first, and whose salvo was most clearly motivated by the unfinished business of the habeas corpus hearing. His response came within a few months of the verdict, and its roots are firmly in the detailed evidence he had given at the King's Bench. On one level, it was his personal backlash at the proceedings, and at the divergent notions of madness and medical authority which had been raised; on another, it was a flinty justification of his own actions and statements. But, over and above the details of the hearing, Haslam was working up a much broader agenda. *Illustrations of Madness*, when it came off the press, was a sensational work written not just for the doctors but for a general readership, the first book-length account ever printed of the contents of a prodigiously mad brain, and Haslam's strongest claim yet that he was a master of a profession yet to be properly recognized.

Its title page trumpets this double agenda: beneath the title is the subhead *Exhibiting a Singular Case of Insanity, and a No Less Remarkable Difference in Medical Opinion*. In contrast to his previous books, Haslam introduces himself not as the sober professional talking to his peers, but as the ringmaster in the circus of lunacy, offering a glimpse of uncanny phenomena to the curious. His strategy is to sell the readers on the outlandish and bizarre, but in a way which will leave them eager for details of the professional controversy surrounding it. The remainder of the subhead – *With a Description of the Tortures Experienced by Bomb-Bursting, Lobster-Cracking, and Lengthening the Brain* – spins the head and whets the appetite further, offering tantalizing snatches of exotic nonsense to sweeten any doctrinal pill. And as if that were not enough, the whole is *Embellished with a Curious Plate*.

The title page sells the reader on the sizzle, but Haslam asks us to wait a while before he serves the steak. The first section of the book, after a preamble of classical references, is a detailed run-down of the affidavits served in the King's Bench hearing. Haslam assures the reader that Matthews' 'insanity

ILLUSTRATIONS

OF

MADNESS:

EXHIBITING A SINGULAR CASE OF INSANITY,

AND A NO LESS

REMARKABLE DIFFERENCE

IN

MEDICAL OPINION:

DEVELOPING

THE NATURE OF ASSAILMENT,

AND THE MANNER OF

WORKING EVENTS;

WITH A

DESCRIPTION OF THE TORTURES EXPERIENCED

BY

BOMB-BURSTING, LOBSTER-CRACKING,

AND

LENGTHENING THE BRAIN.

EMBELLISHED WITH A CURIOUS PLATE.

BY JOHN HASLAM.

" Oh! Sir, there are, in this town, Mountebanks for the mind, as well as the body."—*Foote's Devil upon Two Sticks ; Scene the last.*

London:

PRINTED BY G. HAYDEN, BRYDGES-STREET, COVENT-GARDEN :

And Sold by

RIVINGTONS, ST.PAUL'S CHURCH-YARD; ROBINSONS, PATERNOSTER-ROW;
CALLOW, CROWN-COURT, PRINCES-STREET, SOHO;
MURRAY, FLEET-STREET; AND GREENLAND, FINSBURY-SQUARE.

1810.

Illustrations of Madness – *title page*

was most evident' from his first admission in 1797, but that 'his relatives did not possess the faculty of perceiving his disorder' – hence the pointless judicial farrago. But his case is not against the family. In the author's view, they are the innocent dupes of the two real villains of the case: Clutterbuck and Birkbeck. In a writing career marked by savage attacks on his professional colleagues, Haslam never outdid his polemic against the evidence of these 'two learned and conscientious physicians', whom he introduces with heavy sarcasm as 'deeply conversant with this disease, and doubtless instructed by copious experience to detect the finer shades and more delicate hues of intellectual disorder', and who inspire him to his clearest ever statement on the nature of madness and the primacy of the specialist mad-doctor.

He begins by printing their affidavits in full; they are followed by the testimony of the Commissioners in Lunacy. But he intends more than simply to show that the two doctors' opinions on Matthews' state of mind were contradicted by such distinguished company. 'How they could fail to detect his insanity', he claims, 'is inexplicable'; even the other lunatics had not the slightest difficulty in recognizing it. Clutterbuck and Birkbeck had made elementary procedural errors, such as interviewing Matthews together rather than separately; they had virtually no practical experience of diagnosing lunatics. The only reason their opinion was taken seriously at all was because they had the letters MD after their names.

This, for Haslam, is the root of the problem, which has led to such absurdities in this case: 'every person who takes the degree of doctor becomes, in consequence, of taking such degree, a learned man; and it is libellous to pronounce him ignorant'. He may be 'blind, deaf and dumb, stupid or mad', but once he has his diploma we are no longer at liberty to point out that he is talking rubbish, no matter how obvious to all concerned. Here, of course, it is easy to recognize the chip on Haslam's shoulder, the frustration of years of subservience to qualified ignoramuses. But his polemic is no denunciation of the quackery of the medical profession; it's a claim that expertise in the diagnosis of the mad is another skill entirely, for which the standard diploma should no longer suffice.

If being a doctor is not a sufficient qualification for diagnosing madness, then what is? To Haslam, the answer is self-evident: you can recognize the mad by the fact that they are mad. 'Madness being the opposite to reason and good sense,' he patiently explains, 'as light is to darkness, straight to crooked &c., it appears wonderful that two opposite opinions could be entertained on the subject.' Clutterbuck and Birkbeck cannot take refuge behind the idea that madness is in some sense in the eye of the beholder, some abstract or relative concept on which it's possible to agree to differ. 'A person', Haslam insists, 'cannot correctly be said to be *in* his senses and *out* of his senses at the same time.' Thus the only way to proceed in the diagnosis of madness is by careful examination of the facts of the case. As ever for Haslam, high-flown theories and abstract categories are worse than useless; observation is the key, and correct observation of the patient is precisely what Clutterbuck and Birkbeck failed to achieve.

And so to the case in point, 'the peculiar opinions of Mr. Matthews', which Haslam will now proceed to expound. There will be entertainment to be found here – and Haslam will not be slow to point it up, slyly and even occasionally with broad collusion – but it will be served on a bed of edification. Let the reader, while goggling at the baroque edifice of Matthews' madness, simultaneously absorb the cautionary tale that two qualified doctors interviewed him at length half a dozen times and still pronounced him sane. Let the reader, too, learn the elementary lesson of how to observe without theorizing. In this Haslam will lead the way, as he sets out Matthews' views exactly as he found them 'and leave the reader to exercise his own judgement concerning them'. This is, as the title promises, not a theory or a lecture or a taxonomy but an illustration of madness. If the reader wishes to know what madness looks like – well, here it is. Matthews himself will pronounce the diagnosis out of his own mouth, for if what follows is not madness, then what is?

Haslam plays his cards with the pretence of a poker face, but not without a droll rolling of the eye and arching of the eyebrow. The Air Loom is, he warns us, a 'formidable instrument', a 'curious and wonderful machine' unlike anything we will ever have encountered in the world of sanity. Matthews apparently insists that the device is described in Chambers' Dictionary of 1783, though Haslam sardonically adds that 'it is unnecessary to tell the reader that he will fruitlessly search that work for such information'. Instead, the evidence he offers for it is the 'curious plate' of the title page, the literal 'illustration of madness': a technical drawing of the machine by the lunatic himself.

Here is something which surely few readers, then or now, would have anticipated. Where we might have expected to see crazed daubings and frenzied scribbles, we have instead a precise and beautiful image, which at first glance wouldn't be out of place in any scientific or technical journal of the time. Barrels, tubes, levers and cylinders are elegantly rendered and delicately shaded; figures are carefully dressed and artfully posed; components are finished with understated brass fittings and neatly keyed with copperplate lower-case initials. There is a coolness and conviction about the whole image, a sense that the artist has worked carefully to illustrate something highly complex in the simplest and most elegant form. To the reader expecting an illustration of madness, such coolness has a curiously unnerving effect: we wonder if, had we encountered this drawing in a saner context, we might have been convinced of its authenticity. Perhaps we begin to wonder if the artist, even in his Bedlam cell, might have been as plausible to us as he was to Clutterbuck and Birkbeck.

The Air Loom

But the technical accomplishment of Matthews' work merely assists Haslam in his drollery. Taking his cue from the credibility of the image, he explains the machine in Matthews' own words and within the technical rubric of the drawing, a sober naming of parts in accordance with the illustration's key. Thus *a* is 'the top of the apparatus', *b* 'the metals which the workers grasp to deaden the sympathy', *c* 'the place where the pneumaticians sit to work the loom', and so on for a dozen pages of exposition. This mock-precision also frees Haslam from interpreting the workings of the whole: where the drawing fades out into hazy detail, he quotes Matthews' admission that he 'could never ascertain what the bulky upper parts were'. The temptation to try to make sense out of this nonsense is thus avoided, and the claims that the machine works can be mocked obliquely. Haslam is not interested in proving that the machine doesn't or couldn't exist in reality, simply in laying bare the unreasonableness of the very idea.

Nevertheless, there is clearly some mechanical intent to the device, and though Matthews' description of it has been chopped and edited by Haslam for bathetic and comic effect, its essentials are easily reconstructed. It is, basically, what it says on the tin: an Air Loom, whose mechanics are predicated on the idea that invisible airs and magnetic fluids can be 'woven' into different configurations and projected at a subject who is somehow charged to receive them. Within this logic, however, the details are undeniably bizarre. It is powered by a long list of the most putrid substances imaginable – 'seminal fluid, male and female . . . effluvia of dogs – stinking human breath . . . stench of the sesspool – gaz from the anus of the horse' – which are stored and magnetized in barrels. From here, they are fed into the main body of the loom, where their release can be controlled and modulated by an array of levers and keys, functioning perhaps like organ-stops to emit the charged airs in different combinations, forces and frequencies. Thereafter the gaseous magnetic fluid passes into the upper parts of the machine, which were always blurred to Matthews but which seemed to incorporate arrangements of cylinders and canvas sails; from here, the magnetic rays finally emerge, programmed to seek out their subject and render the effect selected by the operators.

Haslam offers no comment on the victim of the rays positioned obliquely in the top left-hand corner of the plate and, like the other figures, rendered not schematically but with a sense of portraiture from life. It's tempting to speculate that this might be a self-portrait, and if so the only surviving likeness of Matthews himself. Who else, after all, might he have been likely to represent in that position? The figure is effectively highlighted, too, in a version of the plate which Matthews coloured by hand. Significantly, he tinted neither the machine nor any of the human figures, but simply washed the rays themselves in a pale yellowish-green. It is the air that is most vivid and alive, not the loom or the gang, and the effect throws a lurid halo around the frozen victim.

Where Haslam has glossed over the details of the machine, he is much more precise about listing the various settings the operators have at their disposal, and which he (or Matthews) describes as the Air Loom's 'effects' or 'workings'. Here, he senses, we are subtly shifting territories into Matthews' descriptions of his own physical sensations: we are moving – still, of course, through a treacle of nonsense – from crackpot theories to the firmer terrain of clinical symptoms. The range of 'event-workings' is a 'formidable catalogue of human miseries', with every operation vividly christened. 'Fluid locking', for example, is the name for 'constricting the fibres at the root of the tongue', which impedes speech; 'kiteing' is a force which 'contrives to lift into the brain some peculiar idea, which floats and undulates in the intellect for hours'; 'lengthening the brain' is an effect analogous to a distorting mirror at a funfair, which twists any serious and important notion until it becomes irresistibly hilarious – significantly, 'it

James Tilly Matthews – a self-portrait?

can cause good sense to appear as insanity'. 'Bomb-bursting' distends the stomach by filling it with gas and remotely detonating it, at which 'a horrid crash is heard in the head'; 'gaz-plucking' is the extraction of precious magnetic fluid, bubble by bubble, from the anus; 'dream-workings' force the subject to endure whatever dreams are transmitted to him in sleep. Many other workings are more or less self-explanatory, such as 'thought-making', 'laugh-making', 'brain-sayings', 'foot-curving', 'vital-tearing' and 'fibre-ripping'. And there are also fatal operations such as 'lobster-cracking', which increases the magnetic pressure around the subject 'so as to stagnate his circulation, impede his vital motions, and produce instant death'.

The third and final part of the Air Loom scenario focuses on the operators themselves, the gang. Here Haslam finds a particularly happy match between Matthews' profusion of curious details and his own jocular intentions, and he lists them with the mock-earnestness of a butterfly collector: 'of their general habits little is known . . .' When engaged in Air Loom business, however, they 'hire themselves out as spies, and discover the secrets of government to the enemy, or confederate to work events of the most atrocious nature'. They are 'profoundly skilled in pneumatic chemistry', and they work out of a cellar near London Wall. Just round the corner, as it happens, from Bedlam itself.

The gang are seven. Their leader is Bill the King, who 'exerts the most unrelenting and murderous villainy; and he has never been observed to smile'. His second-in-command is Jack the Schoolmaster, who takes notes on the machine's operations and sometimes 'makes a merriment of the business', making wisecracks like 'I'm here to see fair play'. Third is Sir Archy, foul-mouthed and low-minded, who wears old-fashioned breeches and is 'always cracking obscene jokes and throwing out gibes and sarcasms'; some of the gang speak of him as a woman in drag, but Matthews is unable to verify this. The fourth and last man is known only as The Middle Man, who is said to be 'a manufacturer of air looms, and possesses the first rate skill in working this instrument'.

The first of the women is Augusta, who seems to be the public face of the gang. She rarely works the machine, and is usually to be found liaising with other spies and 'corresponding with other gangs at the west end of town'. Charming when she gets her way, when thwarted she 'becomes exceedingly spiteful and malignant'. The second, Charlotte, seems to be French and, unlike Augusta, rarely leaves the cellar. She is half-naked, poorly fed and apparently often chained; Matthews believes she may well be 'equally a prisoner with himself'. The final member, known only as the Glove Woman, is virtually part of the machine. She operates it with incredible skill and, despite regular teasing from the others, 'she has never been known to speak'. Matthews suspects that she wears gloves because she has 'the itch' – scabies.

There is more, too. Even for the jaded, thrill-hungry reader, this is impossibly rich stuff, full of crystalline detail that begs for pause and comment. But we are allowed none; richness is served up on top of richness until it becomes indigestible. This is part of Haslam's design: we have asked to be titillated by morsels of madness, but he is stuffing us with it until we beg for mercy. There is almost a sense of revenge being enacted on the reader for the incompetence of Clutterbuck and Birkbeck. How could they have ignored such a torrent of palpable lunacy?

The Air Loom Gang, we are told, is only part of a bigger story. 'Many gangs are stationed in different parts of the metropolis', near every government office and every lunatic asylum. And because the Air Loom 'requires the person assailed to be previously saturated with magnetic fluid', gang members stalk the streets to impregnate their future victims by releasing bottles containing pressurized gas around them, sidling up to them in coffee-houses and theatres. If observed, they grasp magnetized metal rods which make them temporarily invisible. Their most frequent targets are politicians, who are constantly manipulated by the gangs: a secretary at war, perhaps, will be thinking about something else altogether when 'the expert magnetist would suddenly throw into his mind the subject of exchange of prisoners'. Weaving their magnetic webs around the corridors of power, the gangs control everything, yet no-one but Matthews suspects anything.

At this point Haslam turns over the book for the remaining third of its length to Matthews, reproducing a lengthy memoir of plot, counter-plot, conspiracy and magnetic spies which seems to be included for its impenetrable density rather than for any purpose within Haslam's frame. This is rubbing our nose in madness, urging our gratitude to the physician for having taken the trouble to interpret the bulk of the material so diligently. He acknowledges our defeat when he picks up the thread for his conclusion: 'by this time', he interrupts, 'it is probable that the curiosity of the reader is sufficiently satisfied concerning the mischievous and complicated science of event-working'. Unless we are mad ourselves, we are now sufficiently softened up for the moral of the tale: Haslam's diagnosis of madness was surely correct, and his insistence that Matthews should be confined indefinitely is abundantly justified.

Interestingly, Haslam connects these two propositions by breaking his own golden rule that we must pay no attention to the utterances of the mad. On the final page of the book he smuggles in an interpretation of the Air Loom's meaning and psychological significance to Matthews – and a very acute and prescient one. 'The system of assailment and working events', he argues, 'deprives man of that volition which constitutes him a being responsible for his actions, and persons not so respon-sible, in the humble opinion of the writer, ought not to be at large'. In other words, Matthews' delusions have a function: they excuse him from his own actions, and thus from any criminal responsibility. Here is a tacit acknowledgement of some psychodynamic method in his madness, but the possi-bility is left hanging; this is simply the staging-post to Haslam's conclusion that 'there are already too many maniacs allowed to enjoy a dangerous liberty', and that one so patently mad, with such a reckless political agenda and a tailor-made excuse for his own innocence in any situation, ought surely not to be among them.

Haslam leaves us in no doubt what we are supposed to make of Matthews' mental world: this is madness, categorically and without a shadow of a doubt. But the irony of *Illustrations of Madness* is that it's now virtually impossible to read it in the way the author intended. Too much of the zeitgeist of the early 1800s screams out at us from the page; too much of the sub-sequent progress of psychiatry sends beams backwards in time to illuminate this detail or that, and receives answering winks in reply. Most of all, if we have followed James Tilly Matthews' own version of proceedings, we cannot help but notice again and again that we are in a looking-glass version of a story we already know, a version not simply deranged but somehow artful, pointed, inspired, at times even deliberately witty. We would know none of this if Haslam had not recorded it, but we must somehow bypass the author to unlock its true meaning. It is a book that cannot simply be read; it demands to be hijacked.

This is where, for Haslam, the relentless inclusion of detail becomes a two-edged sword. The raw, uninterpreted data – the long lists of different event-workings or Air Loom settings, for example – were included with two purposes in mind: to satisfy the jaded reader's appetite for strangeness and to demonstrate that a specialist mad-doctor could elicit such strangeness from a man whom qualified doctors had pronounced sane. Yet the same febrile inventiveness he heaps rhetorically on the reader to illustrate madness can be re-examined by others, and reclaimed for agendas other than Haslam's.

It is this that has made *Illustrations*, apart from anything else, something of a classic in the world of psychiatry: it is the first case study in history from which the modern diagnosis of paranoid schizophrenia can be convincingly reclaimed. Previous case studies had typically been brief, often a paragraph at most, hung round a ready diagnosis of the time such as melancholy or mania; Haslam, by contrast, presents a wealth of details about lobster-cracking, bomb-bursting, brain-sayings, kiteing, gaz-plucking, the accumulation of which offers the key to a retrospective diagnosis. One of the markers of psychoses such as schizophrenia, as understood today, is that subjects feel a loss of agency: they are watching themselves at one step removed, their own actions seemingly driven by forces over which they have no control. As Haslam himself quietly interpolates in his conclusion, this sense opens the door to a delusional world where outside agencies have taken control of the subject's will, and their thoughts, feelings and memories have been taken over by someone or something else. 'Kiteing', for instance – the sense that messages from out-side are being forced into the brain – is a symptom any psychiatrist today would recognize immediately; 'lengthening the brain', where an important thought is ridiculed, would be equally familiar as the self-sabotaging chatter of internal voices. Such routinely observed symptoms now have their own shorthand classification of 'passivity phenomena', and the Air Loom itself is the prototype for one of the now-standard delusional frameworks for such passivity: the 'influencing machine'.

This retrospective neatness must, as ever, be set against the slippery diagnostic criteria of schizophrenia today. If we consider the syndrome more broadly, it could be argued that Matthews is a less than perfect match. Schizophrenia in males is most commonly a condition with onset in the teens or early twenties. We don't know Matthews' exact age but, as a businessman with a young family, it's likely to be somewhat over the top end of this scale. 'Disordered thinking', another crucial check-box, fits less well, since Matthews plainly pre-sented as sane to casual examination. Again, the highly encapsulated nature of his delusions may save us here. Hearing voices, the first sign most psychiatrists look for in cases of suspected psychosis, would clearly apply, but its validity as a marker of schizophrenia is no longer universally accepted: recent research by Marcus Romme at Maastricht University, who has set up a support group called the Voice Hearing Network for non-schizophrenic sufferers, suggests that this phenomenon is not uncommon among the wider population. 'Emotional flattening' – a loss of affect, and dis-engagement from consensus reality – is hard to assess, partly because we have ample evidence that Matthews was frequently bright and chatty, and partly because emotional flattening is a trait anyone confined in an asylum for twelve years, mad or sane, may be excused. Similarly with 'hostility': if, as Birkbeck and Clutterbuck claimed, Matthews' hostility was limited to those responsible for his confinement, then perhaps it was not without reason.

The *sine qua non* of the diagnosis of schizophrenia, though, is delusion. This, we cannot deny, Matthews has in spades. Yet here too there are extenuating circumstances and parallel readings. There are four types of delusion typically regarded as primary. The first is 'delusions of persecution', the hallmark of paranoia; persecution undeniably oozes from the pages of *Illustrations*, yet the evidence that Matthews was genuinely persecuted could hardly be stronger. The second, 'delusions of reference', describes the subject's belief that everything, including major world events, revolves around him personally. Again, for Matthews, world events for a brief time genuinely did. The third, 'delusions of control', finds its classic expression in the Air Loom, the first device designed specifically to control the mind, body and will of its victim; yet it's hard to think of anyone whose life was genuinely more controlled by malign outside forces than Matthews'. The fourth, 'delusions of grandiosity', refers to the inflation of the subject's life and events into an epic, world-defining drama. Once again, this is hard to separate from the true story of Matthews' life. On the one hand, all the primary delusions of schizophrenia can be extracted with ease from Haslam's account; on the other hand, the uneasy feeling persists that real life was indeed, for Matthews, somehow tailor-made to generate them.

How, then, do such delusions arise in the first place? The theory goes that the intensity of the onset of psychosis becomes, eventually, too exhausting to sustain. Every tiny detail and event signals its hidden significance; thoughts run too fast for tongue or pen to keep up. Meaning is everywhere; sleep becomes impossible; vast worlds of possibility revolve constantly inside the head. At some point in this overheated flux, a fixed point emerges, an all-embracing structure on which this universe of floating possibilities can finally come down to earth. Like a collapsing wave-form, a bursting balloon, the mind is set free. Faster than thought, every wrinkle and detail of the story insinuates itself into the new paradigm, fitting with a neatness that makes it impossible to imagine how it could ever have been conceived in any other way. Indeed, this sense is so overwhelming that the new delusional framework insinuates itself backwards in time, becoming the explanation for events which took place long before it existed, as far back as childhood. Going forwards, too, everything fits: whatever new experiences are received, they are accommodated seamlessly under the carapace of the new framework.

We are still a long way from explaining this process neurologically, still further from being able to demonstrate on any biological model how such overarching delusions find their shape – the content, unique to each, which writes itself into such fully formed and effortlessly detailed patterns. But it's well recognized that such delusions have a tendency to worry and tease at rips in the cultural fabric, interpolating themselves into gaps in the social psyche. Delusional subjects often unsettle those who encounter them not just by the form of their condition but its content: they can reflect back a disturbing, often nightmarish certainty about free-floating anxieties in the broader culture. Disturbing political events, new scientific developments, uneasy cultural shifts and over-the-horizon prophecies and predictions typically worm their way into the frame. Today, for example, those who deal with the paranoid and psychotic hear the same mundane tales of malign neighbours, scheming councils and sinister immigrants with numbing frequency, but most will also have been offered vivid and forcefully elaborated tales involving more intangible, twilight anxieties: designer viruses, computer surveillance, government cover-ups, sleep experiments, terrorist cells.

Sometimes, too, these fixations seem to be doing more than simply reflecting back the current obsessions of the media and broader culture: they seem to be tuning in to faint presentiments of obsessions yet to come. Paranoia is, among other things, a state of hyperawareness. Senses such as hearing and smell are heightened; non-verbal levels of communication are eerily well read. Subjects can seem to have almost supernatural acuity to tiny cues that those around them are starting to doubt their sanity. Is it possible, then, that they may be similarly sensitized to more nebulous cues in the world around them? Can such delusions be not merely pathological but also visionary, even prophetic?

This is the question Haslam's embarrassment of detail tempts us to examine, though to do so takes us straight down his sternly forbidden path. Can we seek out reason in Matthews' madness – not just clues to his own state of mind, but to a broader crisis of reason in the culture around him? If such an excavation of derangement can be attempted at all, Matthews is surely a prime subject. He was intelligent, well informed, and his view of the world had been tempered in the crucible of the greatest event of the modern age. The world of the Air Loom, even when held up to mockery by Haslam, has a power and strangeness that are not easy to shake off. Are its magnetic fluids more than just the solipsistic ravings of a lunatic? Are they, perhaps, invisible currents that were genuinely permeating the wider world outside Bedlam?

The place to begin this investigation is not in Haslam's account of the Air Loom, but in the pages following it which are transcribed directly from Matthews' notes. For this is Matthews' own version of how he drifted into the gang's ken in the first place, and when and where they first began to assail him.

We recognize from the start that this version has diverged from, or evolved alongside, what we know as the facts. Matthews is an unreliable narrator, but this itself is helpful as it makes it clear that we are dealing not with his memories but with a snapshot of his current beliefs. His suspicions about the existence of a magnetic underground – 'how infamous human beings, making a profession of pneumatic chemistry, and pneumatic magnetism, hire themselves as spies' – date back, he now tells us, to the period of his confinement in France, from 1793 to 1796. He became a thorn in the side of the gang due to his peace intrigues which, if they had succeeded, would have destroyed the magnetic masterplan which was, and still is, 'for surrendering to the French every secret of the British government, as for the republicanising Great Britain and Ireland, and particularly for disorganising the British navy'.

Grandiose, paranoid and all the rest; but what leaps out from this telling is that the magnetic masterplan bears a striking resemblance to Matthews' own activities prior to his confinement in Paris. It was he who was surrendering British government secrets to the French; he who was a diehard republican trying to merge the British and French constitutions; he who specifically disorganized the British navy by sabotaging their attack on Dunkirk. The struggle between Matthews and the gang seems to have its origins in a struggle inside his own head, between Matthews the 'true *sansculotte*' and Matthews the loyal British patriot. In his quest for peace, he found himself playing the role of the British spy to Pitt, and of international republican to Le Brun; back in London in 1796, his attempt to find common ground with the Girondins had become, in his absence, flagrant high treason. The question 'Whose side are you on?' becomes ever more crucial: Matthews' true answer, that he is on the side of peace, becomes unacceptable to all sides in a world committed to war. As the British and French national agendas diverged into open hostility, so was the peacemaker torn in half. The most diabolical traitor became Matthews himself. The Revolutionary Wars and Matthews' madness thus become almost one and the same thing – one, at least, a symptom or aspect of the other. As long as France and Britain were still at war, so also would Matthews' mind be.

The phrase that floats, or 'kites', over this struggle is

'double agent'. Matthews was never confused in his basic objective: he was a peacemaker, pure and simple. It was being a double agent which forced him to split in two, to hold mutually exclusive and increasingly hostile views depending on who he was talking to. Eventually, as peace was discarded, his role descended into nonsense: once the two sides could no longer be brought together, the left hand neither knew nor cared what the right hand was doing. Matthews was left holding two opposite positions in his head, with consensus reality rapidly receding from both.

Here, perhaps, we can glimpse how the Air Loom might have made its entrance. It offered an escape hatch for the double agent, a genuine double agency. As Haslam observed, it allowed Matthews to eschew responsibility for half his actions: one agenda could be driven by Matthews himself, and a contradictory one forced into his head by magnetic workers. The two sides could change as fluidly as world events: whoever Matthews was talking to, the other agenda could be ascribed to the gang. His individual agency was, indeed, split into two. The Air Loom, whatever else it might be, was perhaps a *deus ex machina*, a solution to an insoluble problem.

From here on, he tells us, magnetic spies were specially appointed to watch over him. In a magnificent Matthewsism, they began 'confining me within the measure of the Bedlam-attaining-airloom-warp': it was impossible for the gang to divert Matthews from his efforts, far easier to use their event-working powers to make him look mad, and have him locked up. Political events slot effortlessly, one after another, into the all-embracing Air Loom paradigm. In the tangles of conspiracy that follow, some elements are directly illuminated by our knowledge of real events. Erskine's sudden, and genuine, indisposition in the House of Commons, for example, is now preceded by Matthews receiving a brain-saying from the gang that 'We will actuate Erskine'; thereafter, Matthews tells us, 'I feared they intended to make Lord Erskine mad'. His version of the day which saw him committed is now that 'they stagnated Erskine in the House of Commons, by an Air-Loom warp . . . and would have killed him afterwards there as an example in their pretexts but for my exposing their infamous threats'. So Matthews' shout of treason saved Erskine's life, but even Erskine has subsequently betrayed him: 'he now cares no more for me than he does for the dogs in the street'.

All this begins to suggest how a delusional system such as the Air Loom, for all its florid irrationality, might have a function and a rationale, the power to offer a miraculous fix to a breaking mind. But it still barely scrapes the surface of the machine itself. How could such a dizzyingly complex apparatus materialize for Matthews in such intricate detail? Why pneumatic chemistry, why magnetic fluids, why a loom? Crucially, since such a thing had never been conceived before, why a machine at all?

When we think of anxieties about the loom in the early Industrial Revolution, one clear association leaps out: the Luddites, the underground organization of textile workers who smashed industrial looms under cover of darkness and the cryptic banner of 'Lord Ned Ludd'. But Matthews was no Luddite. The early textile industry was originally confined to the north of England, a world away from Wales or London; unless he sought one out deliberately it's highly unlikely that Matthews would ever have seen an industrial loom. Apart from anything else, Luddism was still in the future. Although the 1790s saw isolated incidents of machine-wrecking in response to general trouble at the mill over labour relations, the first mass sabotage ideologically driven by the prospect of forced subservience to the machine didn't take place until 1812. Either Matthews' prescient antennae scored a direct hit out of the blue, or we must look for a less literal and broader reading.

This, as it turns out, is far easier to locate, once we shift our attention from loom to air. The idea of a mesmeric machine would have been presented far more forcefully to Matthews through other channels. The fledgling science of electricity had produced, from the 1770s onwards, a fantastic array of devices, assembled from glass, polished wood and finely tooled and calibrated metals, which had not only released invisible forces and charged ethers around laboratories but had demonstrated previously unsuspected 'animal spirits' in the living. Luigi Galvani's frogs' legs had twitched when wired between plates of different metals; the British scientist Henry Cavendish had even, in 1776, built an artificial electric eel out of metal plates encased in a series of leather pouches which had discharged its mysterious force through salt water into human hands. Mesmerism itself had been technologically driven from the beginning: Mesmer's *baquet* was an outgrowth of this strange technology that transmitted power from machine to man.

And we can locate the spirit of the Air Loom with equal clarity through its central science, pneumatic chemistry, which plunges us straight into the turbulent waters of the culture wars in which Matthews was so deeply immersed. The

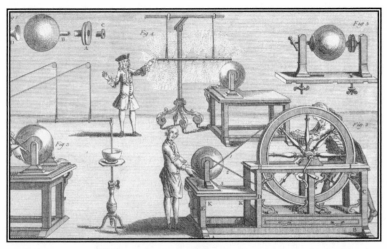

Eighteenth-century electrical machines

Joseph Priestley

discovery of gases was new and, in Britain, associated most prominently with one man: Joseph Priestley. Priestley was originally a dissenting minister, political reformer and vocal partisan of American independence, whose interest in chemistry was a hobby. His ministry in Leeds in the 1760s was next to a brewery, and he became interested in the 'airs' – carbon dioxide – that bubbled out of the barrels during fermentation. He collected them, added them to water and found that they dissolved, leaving the water sparkling and pleasant to taste. 'Soda water', on which he refused to take out a patent, became a popular health craze.

But his greatest discovery came in 1774 when, after heating mercuric oxide, he produced a gas that seemed to be more

vibrant than air itself. Candles burned brighter in it, mice
lived longer simply by inhaling it, and when he breathed it
himself he found his spirits elevated and his health restored.
His 'dephlogisticated air' was oxygen, and though other
chemists were discovering it independently around the same
time, it was recognized by scientists and public alike as
Priestley's crowning glory.

From the beginning, this new science was charged with
political meaning. Nature was changed: man's dominion over
it had spread into the realms of the invisible, and opened up
the possibility of separating its elements and reconfiguring
them in new and powerful ways. For Priestley, religion, politics
and science were all pointing in the same direction. The old
certainties of Church, state and monarchy had evolved in a
world that was now being superseded. Scientific discovery was
opening the door to new, more rational forms of government.
'The English hierarchy', he wrote in tones that might have
resonated with Matthews, 'has reason to tremble even at an air
pump or an electrical machine'.

Priestley's politics were unambiguously radical. He was a
hero in the republican milieu where Matthews first met David
Williams; he was a hero in revolutionary Paris, too, where
many of the new leaders were also scientists, and he was
nominated an honorary French citizen along with Williams
and Tom Paine. As France and Britain headed towards war
and the British press and public opinion lurched to the right,
rhetoric flared into violence, and Priestley was an obvious
target. One clear night in the summer of 1791, Priestley was
forced to flee his laboratory as mobs under banners 'For
Church and King' set about destroying it. They were unable to
burn it as they had no fire – Priestley, from a mile away,
heard people offering two guineas for a lighted candle,
and discovered later that the crowd had spent some time
trying to generate a spark from the large electrical machine
in his library – but by the time he returned the next

Priestley and Paine's 'Pact with the Devil' (Isaac Cruickshank)

morning it had been demolished virtually to the last brick.

So the pneumatic chemistry of the Air Loom brings with it a heavy freight of political significance. For Matthews, it is intimately linked with his own original cause: the pneumatics were his people, socially, ideologically and politically. But his people, effectively, no longer exist: they have either defected to the counter-revolution, like the Romantic poets, or been consumed in the Terror. The Revolution has become a sightless, violent beast that has, in the famous phrase of the time, devoured its own children. Across the Channel the other genius of pneumatic chemistry, Antoine Lavoisier, had been arrested in 1793, a few months after Matthews, and guillotined the same day. Scientist to the last, he announced to his assistant that he would attempt to establish how long a decapitated head survived by blinking as many times as he could after the blade fell. From the basket, his head performed twenty blinks. Pneumatic chemists, it seemed, were an endangered species.

Matthews, then, is no Luddite, protesting the new world of

Antoine Lavoisier

power relations predicated on the machine; he is no William
Blake, for whom the new science is nothing but godless evil.
For him and his ilk, pneumatic chemistry is a clear symbol of

the hope of reason and progress which was offered to mankind and spurned by it, its bearers trampled to death. But the science has not died with them; rather, the world has lurched forward into a new darkness where the gifts of enlightenment have been carelessly scattered, looted by criminals and terrorists. This is the world of the Air Loom, one where the tools of the new dawn have been hijacked by vandals seeking to bend the world to their own destructive ends. Matthews himself, a creature of the false dawn, has been sacrificed as surely as Lavoisier to a world that no longer has any need of him.

We can, therefore, build a picture – like Matthews' own illustration, a little hazy at the edges – of how the Air Loom might have inserted itself so forcefully into the consciousness of a double agent, and why it might have taken the pneumatic form it did. But why was it the first of its kind? Today, such machine delusions are commonplace. Clinical psychiatric case notes hum with secret radio transmitters, omnipresent surveillance systems, devices implanted in TVs or heating systems or the subject's brain, controlling beams from political elites or alien craft. Their function for the subject may be similar to the Air Loom's; they may even resonate with the same sense of loss of a brave new world. But, unlike these, the Air Loom creates a new form, and thus requires a further level of explanation, not just for the machine itself but for the very idea of a machine.

Here we approach once again, from a different angle, the historical problems of schizophrenia. We are dealing, in the *Illustrations*, with two things at once: Matthews' unprecedented delusions and Haslam's unprecedentedly detailed record of them. If we wish to discover why it was that Matthews might have birthed the influencing machine, descriptions of previous cases would be a good place to start. They are few, but perhaps the most promising – certainly the one most frequently excavated for retrospective diagnoses of schizophrenia – is that of a German painter named Christoph Haizman. The remarkable aspect of Haizman's case is that we have a full record of it in his own hand, in the form of a diary and nine paintings.

In 1677, Haizman was in church when he was 'seized by certain unnatural convulsions to the horror of all present'. Questioned by the local prefect, he confessed that he had sold his soul to the Devil nine years before. Since that point, he had been tormented with dreams, visions and shadowy intimations of the Devil, who gloated that he would soon be back to claim his prize. Even while attempting prayer and confession, Haizman would be snatched away, transported in his mind to scenes of temptation. He recovered gradually, though whenever he drank too much wine the Devil would reappear and try to lure him into another pact.

Haizman's diagnosis by the doctors of the time was unhelpful to modern psychiatry – 'cacodemonomania', or demonic possession – but his first-person account suggests a psychotic disorder, and was famously interpreted by Sigmund Freud as paranoia caused (as always, in Freud's view) by repressed homosexual panic. Compared to Matthews', it has undoubted structural similarities, but a marked difference in content. Where Matthews has the Air Loom, Haizman has the Devil; where Matthews has the gang assailing him to act against his will for their political ends, Haizman has a struggle against temptation and a supernatural pact. Somewhere in the century in between we have crossed over an invisible border, where the frame of divine or demonic possession, as old as history, has been usurped. The underlying clinical condition may be the same, but the subject's experience of it has lurched into a new nightmare. God has been replaced by the machine.

This is, of course, the grand story of the Age of Reason. But one of its most telling and precise examples is furnished by mesmerism itself. When Mesmer began his miraculous cures in Austria in the 1770s, he had a rival: a Jesuit priest named

Father Gassner was performing similar miracles under the rubric of exorcism. Like Mesmer's, Gassner's sessions were a public sensation, and cries of fraud competed with those of miracle-worker. The Catholic Church was uncomfortable with Gassner's unorthodox methods and high profile; the local elector asked Mesmer, their scientific prodigy, for his views on the priest's actions. Mesmer explained that Gassner was using magnetic phenomena, probably to genuine and positive effect, but that he had a primitive and superstitious understanding of his own powers. The elector ordered Gassner to cease and desist, while Mesmer, armed with an apparently scientific explanation of his powers, went on to Paris and, among other things, his own subsequent denunciation.

Here, exorcism and mesmerism virtually blur into one; the difference is merely in the sales pitch. But, for those on the receiving end of the experience, the implications of this difference are vast. It is one thing to be the tool of supernatural forces, quite another to be puppeted by a machine with a human operator. When Matthews is brain-lengthened or gaz-plucked or kited, it is not just the Air Loom that is a machine, but Matthews himself. He is reduced to a puppet, an auto-maton, a thing of pumps and levers, pulleys and air-jets; in turn, the levers, pumps and air-jets of the machine built to tor-ment him are constructed in his image. This is the deeper meaning of the machine: that it has mechanized the man.

The intensity of psychosis is often such that those who experi-ence it cannot help but frame it in the most all-encompassing terms available. For most, this is God: they are in direct con-tact with the power behind the universe, playing the central role in a cosmic drama. But for Matthews, a citizen of the future, this was no longer the big story: he had slipped his fingers into a new rent in the cultural fabric, and ripped hard. What if the invisible power behind the real is no longer God, but a machine? What if we are being controlled by this machine, just as the mesmerist controls his patient? And what if those who think that they control our affairs – politicians – are themselves being controlled? What could we do about it? Indeed, would we even notice?

In the centuries of history leading up to Matthews' time, these questions are almost entirely absent; most of them could barely even have been understood. But in the two centuries since they have been asked with increasing frequency – casually, flippantly, seriously, in fiction, satire, science, journalism, even mainstream politics. The phantoms of a futuristic machine age which flicker through Matthews' delusions, while still profoundly strange, are a great deal less strange to the modern mind than they must have been to his contemporaries. He was the first victim of the Air Loom, but by no means the last.

Thus far, perhaps, we can illuminate the machine, but what of the gang behind it? Here, again, Haslam has provided a wealth of detail. Where in previous accounts of madness we hear of nothing more than insubstantial figures, devils or creatures of the night, here we have seven characters drawn with hallucinatory clarity. Bill the King, for example, is either sixty-four or sixty-five; he 'resembles the late Dr. De Valangin, though his features are coarser; perhaps he is a nearer likeness to Sir William Pulteney'. In Matthews' mind, at least, these are no shadowy, nightmarish abstractions but real people. Not only do they have precise visual descriptions but individual sets of skills, verbal tics, idiosyncratic behaviours. They speak to one another, for example, in a shared patois designed to disguise their regional accents: they pronounce 'you' as 'yho', 'catch' as 'ketch', 'preserve' as 'presearve'. They have complex motivations: the character of Charlotte, the quasi-prisoner, is 'that of a steady, persevering sort of person, who is convinced of the impropriety of her conduct, but cannot help herself'. As with all well-drawn characters, we get the sense that Haslam's recorded observations are merely the tip of the iceberg, and that Matthews could have given us dozens of pages of further details – as many or more than he could give of his own family, friends or Haslam himself.

But this doesn't necessarily mean that the gang are real people. Delusions can be fantastically intricate: places, people, events leap fully formed and immaculately rendered into the mind, sometimes more real than reality itself. People with delusions are not deluding themselves. The reason their experiences are persuasively real is that they are so seamlessly woven into the consensus reality they share with others that it's impossible to tell where one starts and the other stops. Matthews has been in the same Bedlam cell for the last twelve years, deprived of any stimulus beyond its damp and rotting walls. The gang are denizens of the far richer world inside his head, hyper-real composites of half-remembered people, half-forgotten fears and ghosts from the machine.

It's significant that the part of Matthews' world where the gang have the most powerful and regular control over Matthews is in his dreams. It's when he sleeps that they assemble their new projections, 'forcing their phantoms and grotesque images on his languid intellect'. They begin to manipulate 'puppets of uncouth shape, and of various descriptions' into obscene travesties of the waking world, simulating scenes and studying Matthews' reactions to them; thus they 'glean his waking opinions on the mysteries which, during the night, have danced in his imagination'. When he wakes, they have all the information they need to plot his assailment for the following day. The gang, at their root here, are hobgoblins of the mind, night terrors, harbingers of the unconscious depths; they are frequently obscene, and Matthews believes they 'lie together in promiscuous inter-course and filthy community' while their puppet-shows play in the theatre of his sleeping brain. Those who have had similar experiences in the modern era have frequently described them by analogy with a private and internal cinema – movies flickering on the blank screen of their minds. In lucid states, they express amazement at the skill of the 'director', some part of their brain with which they have no conscious engagement but which somehow sifts the lost archives and stitches what it finds into compelling narratives. The language of psychiatry echoes the same metaphor, describing the process as 'projection'. For Matthews, the obscene content of these shadow dramas, like the putrid effluvia that power the Air Loom, perhaps speaks of the unspeakable reaches of his unconscious, distorted and repellent fragments of his inner life no delusion, however all-encompassing, can fully acknowledge.

The gang may ultimately be malign munchkins in Matthews' head, but they also reflect his real waking life and its adversities. They are, perhaps, all his tormentors conflated: the procession of secret police, political apparatchiks, magistrates, doctors, jailers, keepers and other functionaries of authority who have kept him confined for what has now become the majority of his adult life. Although it would be inappropriately literal-minded to tie them too closely to real people, his story has left some tantalizing clues – for example, the 'atrocious set' who he claimed to Lord Liverpool had been proposed by the Jacobins as his fellow *agents provocateurs*. The pretext for Matthews' confinement has shifted from political crimes to diagnoses of insanity and back again, but the texture has remained constant: the gang members have gradually come into focus as his über-tormentors, the puppet-masters behind the scenes of which the men in revolutionary uniforms or blue coats are merely the projected forms.

Here, again, Matthews' delusions have zeroed in unerringly on a fault-line in the wider culture, given shape and colour to a presentiment that is just beginning to emerge in the world around him. Just as Matthews' breakdown and the Revolutionary Wars reflect each other through a hall of distorting mirrors, so the gang members themselves signify a new force in world affairs: the grand conspiracy of 'hidden hands' and puppet-masters behind the scenes. This is precisely the point in history at which all the now familiar suspects of modern conspiracy theory – the Freemasons, the Illuminati, the Knights Templar and their supporting cast of secret societies, political revolutionaries and revisionists – emerge on to the new political landscape. Once again, against this backdrop, Matthews is playing a solitaire version of world events in the darkness of his cell. Once again, too, he has hit the nail on the head in the most literal manner possible: the meaning of the word conspiracy, 'breathing together', is exactly how the gang and their machine operate.

The French Revolution, like all convulsive world events before and since, was full of individual conspiracies, bred by the speed of events and the paucity of local information. Rumours swept the Paris communes that counter-revolutionaries had entered into a *'pacte de famine'* to starve the urban poor; the counter-revolutionaries in turn were gripped by news of covert plots to kidnap the King. The French army was riven with tales of betrayal from the Paris high command, and the lands they conquered reverberated with reports of republican plots to incite their own peasants to revolt. In Britain, the Traitorous Correspondence Acts were driven through on a wave of panic that subversive forces in France, Ireland and beyond were forming a shadowy international alliance. Burke, in his *Reflections*, claimed that 'already confederacies and correspondencies of the most extraordinary nature are forming in several countries'. But it was only when the Revolution's convulsions began to subside that a new and overarching idea of conspiracy began to evolve: that behind the tumultuous and bloody procession of generals, demagogues and opportunist powermongers lurked an unseen gang pulling the strings.

Matthews, as always, is a shade ahead of his time: he was

already an incurable in Bedlam by the time the first major conspiracy tract was translated into English and had sold its way through edition after edition in the new reactionary climate of the 1800s. *Memoirs of Jacobinism* was a multi-volume work by the French Jesuit Abbé Augustin de Barruel which claimed that the seemingly discordant and random currents of the Revolution had, in fact, all unfolded according to a hidden plan to discredit the Church and make the world safe for atheism. The plan, according to Barruel, had originally been hatched in the Middle Ages by the Manichaean heretics and the Templars, and had been awakened from its slumbers by the cries of liberty and equality from Voltaire and his fellow *philosophes*; it had been set in motion in the decade before the Revolution by the Bavarian Illuminati and other radical tendencies in the Masonic movement. But where had it gone during the blood-drenched years of revolution itself? How could the likes of Robespierre or Danton have been puppet-masters when they had had their own strings so unceremoniously cut? The answer was that the entire Revolution had been carried through by unwitting pawns who had risen and fallen with the guillotine, leaving their hidden masters untouched.

If history is usually written by the victors, conspiracy theory is often written by the losers, and there were few greater losers in the Revolution than the French Church, and especially the Jesuits. But what made Barruel's dense, lurid potboiler of polemic and pseudohistory into a bestseller was the way its sweeping scope overlaid the new left–right divide in politics. Just as the Revolution was more than a local revolt, so Barruel's conspiracy was more than a plot. Events had been almost too complex for anyone to follow, and for the vast majority far too complex to understand; local and national causes and long-buried dynamics had all come into play at once, sparking inexplicable events capable of multiple interpretations. But behind the baffling succession of conflicts,

Barruel posited a concealed pattern: a world for the first time split into two, separated by an ideological ravine. However confusingly the story had played out, it could all be boiled down to an epic struggle between good and evil, a conflict between revolution – atheism and the Manichaean forces of illusion and darkness – and reaction, its standard borne by Church and monarchy, seeking to defend and reassert their divine provenance. This is left and right writ cosmically large, given both a grand ancestry and a defining role in the future of human affairs.

So, just as Matthews was uncovering the secret workings of the gang inside his mind, invisible and diabolical puppet-masters were also beginning to colonize the mass imagination. Others followed in Barruel's wake. The Scottish theorist John Robison's *Proofs of a Conspiracy*, the other founding text of modern conspiracy theory, appeared the next year and chimed even more closely with Matthews' reading. Robison majors on the Illuminati, whom he takes to be occult-working über-Masons who, after they were banned in Bavaria, travelled undercover to Paris to set up the Jacobin Club and spark the Revolution. Their pretext was frequently the intrigues around mesmerism, and their British plots proceeded through covert Illuminatists such as Joseph Priestley, whose Newtonian doctrine of 'the undulations of aetheric fluids' was a Trojan horse for the materialist universe they were attempting to foist on the masses.

Though spun on its head by the politics of the right, much of this is within kissing distance of the Air Loom, to the point where the injustice is striking: Matthews was languishing in Bedlam for his views while the likes of Robison were not only free to walk the streets but to make a decent living from their fantastic theories. Both the popular conspiracies of hidden hands and Matthews' conjuring of the gang represent attempts to answer a question many had asked and few had convinc-ingly answered: how had the Revolution actually happened?

The masses had surely not risen up of their own accord; some force, as yet unexplained, must have compelled them. This same perplexity drives one of Edmund Burke's most famous passages in the *Reflections* where he refers to the French as a 'swinish multitude' – a reference not to their personal hygiene but to the Gadarene swine of the New Testament, possessed by devils and rushing lemming-like to their destruction. 'What incomprehensible spirit of delirium and delusion', he continues, 'has led them astray?'

This is a question to which Matthews, like Barruel and Robison, has a ready answer; one wonders whether, presented otherwise than as the ravings of a lunatic, his theory might have had a similar popular appeal. Certainly the gang, as an international Jacobin conspiracy, has a similar profile to the villains of the popular imagination, and for similar reasons: they were forged in the heat of the Terror, and subsequently presented by politics and media as the enemies of every patriotic Englishman. It's tempting to speculate whether someone like Burke, the spokesman *par excellence* for the reactionary mainstream of British opinion, might actually have believed Matthews' stories had they come to him from a respected source. Burke needed no convincing of a Jacobin conspiracy in Britain, and had welcomed Barruel when he fled to London; he had set himself directly against the hidden agenda of materialist science which he saw behind those progressive voices he termed 'propagators of novelty', of which Priestley and pneumatic chemistry were his predominant symbols. The Air Loom and its gang might have put vivid flesh on the bones of his darkest suspicions.

So we can locate the gang both inside Matthews' head and outside in the wider world, but there is a third and final place to look: within the walls of Bedlam itself. For here, too, there is a complex interplay between the delusional and the real. It's significant that the grand vision of the Air Loom and its world snapped into place only once Matthews entered Bedlam – at which point, of course, it sent its tendrils back in time to rewrite previous events. The occasion of his arrest, for example, is at this point framed by the Air Loom's influence: Erskine's indisposition is plainly ascribed to it, and Matthews' shout of treason has become his Pyrrhic victory. But we hear nothing of the Air Loom in his writings prior to his confinement; it is Bedlam that has crystallized it. The cellar from which the gang operates is next to Bedlam, and another gang plies its trade next to its rival hospital, St Luke's. Their surroundings are dungeon-like, and the power relations within the gang – Charlotte's imprisonment by the others, their pecking-order – suggest a topsy-turvy version of the hospital and its staff, one in which the gang members gloat that Bedlam's true purpose is not to cure the victim but to keep him mad. Haslam's argument is that the mad are not fit to be released; but here, within the details he records, lurks the counter-argument put by Clutterbuck and Birkbeck, that Matthews' most serious problem is the fact that he's locked up. Perhaps, too, the fact that the gang is burrowing around in Matthews' head has resonances with an understandable anxiety that, after his death, Haslam and Crowther are likely to be fighting for the privilege of dissecting his brain.

The most suggestive character in this interpretation, apart perhaps from Charlotte, is one who seems to point the finger of observation directly back at Haslam himself: Jack the Schoolmaster. Jack, like Haslam, is the second in command; like Haslam, too, he is constantly taking notes. He is 'the short-hand-writer to the gang: he styles himself the recorder'. Haslam spent many hours over many months and years in Matthews' cell transcribing the details of these delusions, and there is both plausibility and irony in the idea that this process has fed back into the delusions themselves, that Haslam has been taking notes on himself. There is abundant irony, too, in Haslam's conclusion where he points out that assailment by

Air Loom workings would be no defence for any crimes Matthews might commit; 'nor', he adds with a sarcastic flourish, 'is it at all probable that the accurate records of Jack the Schoolmaster would be admitted as evidence in a court of law'. The irony, of course, is that it's less than a year since Haslam's own accurate records were entirely ignored during the habeas corpus hearing.

There's a further, more nebulous association that plays between the world of the gang and that of Bedlam: the symmetry between mesmerism and psychiatry itself. Is the psychiatrist, in fact, so different from the magnetist? Both claim mysterious influence over their patients – or victims – on the basis of disputed scientific underpinnings; both generate stories of miracle cures and abuse of authority in roughly equal measure. This was a symmetry that had been observed since mesmerism first appeared, and one which had come to public attention during the madness of George III.

The Rev. Dr Willis had made much of his use of 'the eye' in controlling the mad, claiming that there was not a lunatic alive whom he could not stare down and force into submission by the peculiar force of his gaze. During a House of Commons committee hearing into his treatment of the King, none other than Edmund Burke had queried Willis's wisdom in allowing his Majesty to shave with a straight razor. What if 'the Royal patient had become outrageous'? 'Place the candles between us, Mr Burke,' Willis replied ominously, 'and I'll give you an answer. There, sir, by the EYE! I should have looked at him *thus*, sir – *thus*!' Burke cowered before the doctor's 'basiliskian authority', unable to meet his gaze, and the cross-examination was over. Here, mad-doctoring and mesmerism are virtually the same art: doctor and patient are barely distinguishable from the gang and their victim, the former exercising irresistible powers of coercion over the latter. Haslam himself was sceptical of 'the eye', but not of the need for patients to abandon their own will entirely to that of the doctor. The Air Loom's compelling power, the senior functionary taking notes while his minions scurry around in the gloom, poking and prodding at the patient while cracking obscene jokes to one another, surely bears the imprint of Matthews' years under Haslam's care.

And if we were to follow this idea to its limits, might we not conclude that the Air Loom was ultimately not just Matthews' creation, but Haslam's too? Haslam was ambitious to become a specialist mad-doctor, and thus had a profound and personal, if unconscious, need to discover appropriate specimens of madness. Matthews was a peacemaker, always striving to resolve conflicts; but Haslam, by insisting on imposing his will on his patients, made such resolutions impossible. His treatment of Matthews might be said to have helped to force the Air Loom into existence in order to satisfy his unacknowledged needs and desires.

We might be tempted too, by this reckoning, to suggest a reason for Haslam's persistence in banning Mrs Matthews from her husband's company for so many years, surely the cruellest of all the punishments Matthews suffered: perhaps her visits made him less mad rather than more. Certainly his delusions broadened and deepened throughout her absence, and Haslam might have feared that to readmit her would be to rekindle his tiresome early obsessions with his release, and undo his solitary immersion in the world of the Air Loom. The gang members frequently refer to Matthews as their 'talisman', the key to their plan of world domination; but Matthews is equally Haslam's talisman, the doctor's secret weapon in his own grand schemes.

This is the darkest reading of the Air Loom, and also the least mad: it brings the delusion so close to the reality of Matthews' life that there is scarcely a distinction. When it first snapped into place inside his head, it might have brought a temporary functionality, a bandage of fiction over an un-bearable truth, even a screen behind which his mind could quietly begin to repair itself. And if he hadn't found himself in

Bedlam, it might have gradually released its grip, drifted out of focus and left him alone. But whatever relief it might have been when it first manifested itself, Matthews is now paying a terrible price. The Air Loom is all too real; its event-workings are genuinely assailing him. He is not inventing the sensations of vital-tearing, fibre-ripping and bomb-bursting, simply trying to describe what he actually feels. Many of those diagnosed with paranoid schizophrenia complain of agonizing pains, and Matthews' event-workings are still cited in the clinical literature as a classic example. Since they have no discernible cause, these pains are thought to be delusional; but what is the difference between the delusion of pain and the real thing?

Pain and delusion, war and madness, doctor and mesmerist, Bedlam and the Air Loom – all melt into one.

Matthews wrote prodigiously during his confinement, and there must originally have been a mountain of material which would have assisted us in decoding the world of the Air Loom. Sadly, only one other document in his hand survives from this period. The reason we have it, as a marginal note makes clear, is that Haslam saved it to present as evidence in the habeas corpus hearing, though in the event it wasn't required. The reason Haslam chose it is, presumably, similar to the criteria he exercised in compiling the *Illustrations*: because it appears even to the casual observer to be the product of profound and unambiguous madness. It is, in fact, almost a parody of madness, as if deliberately constructed as an insurmountable obstacle to any sanity defence. We might suspect a hoax were it not for the fact that any hoaxer would have to have been mad to pull it off convincingly. As it happens, though, it's clearly the work of our man, its several thousand words packed, impossibly small and impossibly neat, onto a tiny folded scrap of paper.

The form may be miniature, but the same can hardly be said of the content. It is an open letter, the heading of which runs

The 'Omni Imperious' manuscript (actual size)

as follows: 'James, Absolute Sole and Sacred Omni Imperious Arch Grand Arch Sovereign Omni Imperious Arch Grand Arch Proprietor Omni Imperious Arch-Grand-Arch-Emperor Supreme etc., March 20th 1804'.

Grandiose, beyond doubt, but somehow more than that: it's almost as if Matthews is playing up to the cartoonish cliché of madness, or competing to win first prize for the most grandiose title ever. But even if we suspect a glimmer of self-awareness, the tone of the letter that follows offers little room for manoeuvre. It's a long proclamation of rewards offered for the Air Loom Gang, 'Issued for the putting to Death the Infamous Usurping Murderers and their Families & Races'. This is to be accomplished openly and in full public view, hence 'neither Machines of Art, Airlooms, Magnets, Magnet or other Fluid-Effluvias whether of Poisons or otherways are to be made Use of'. Matthews does 'Omni Imperiously and Most Absolutely Command All Persons whomsoever' to pursue this public good, and asks the world to acknowledge 'his Declaration of Allegiance and Duty to Me by so Declaring that I was Born Their Absolute Sovereign, Absolute Proprietor, etc.'.

After this spectacular throat-clearing, the bulk of the letter consists of a list of the rewards being offered to different countries. These have been calculated in proportion to the civil lists of each country, and fastidiously taking into account the local affairs of state: thus 'Holland as for Switzerland Three hundred thousand pounds Sterling Prussia and Brandsburg, &c Six Hundred Thousand Pounds Sterling Poland is Comprized in Austria and Russia, and Prussia America the soi disant State – Five Hundred Thousand Pounds Sterling British East India Company Chief in India and Soi disant directors in England five hundred Thousand Pounds Sterling including the Commander in Chief in India & the Colonels of their Regiments in England . . .'

And on and on and on; we can readily see why Haslam must have felt that here was a document on which he could rest his case. But this is in many ways the opposite of the Air Loom delusions in the *Illustrations*. There, Matthews is a puppet, a cipher, a machine; here, on the flipside, he is emperor of the world. There, he is chained in a dungeon and subjected to 'apoplexy-working with the nutmeg-grater'; here, he demands deference from his global court. This, too, has become a familiar trope in the condition of schizophrenia: subjects alternating between frenzied mental activity and complete blocks of ideas and affect, either gripped by grandiose fantasies or unplugged from the world via passivity phenomena. Haslam, in his evidence at the King's Bench, had stated this clearly enough for any modern psychiatrist to recognize: Matthews is 'sometimes an automaton, moved by the agency of persons, or, at others, the Emperor of the whole world, hurling from their thrones the usurpers of his dominions'. Curiously, the image of Matthews as an emperor inhabiting a palace inside Bedlam would survive him, and indeed take on a life of its own.

As ever, we can recognize here the shadows not just of Matthews' clinical condition but of his real life. The *Omni Imperious* letter is clearly modelled on another document we have already seen: the peace proposal of 1793. There, Matthews set the affairs of nations to rights with broad and confident brushstrokes, and was believed and courted by their leaders; for a while, or maybe just an instant, he held the fate of millions in the palm of his hand. Here, perhaps, is a quasi-magical evocation of that instant of power, a make-believe Matthews himself might not have believed once he had finished writing it. Adopting the Air Loom delusion has not freed his mind from unbearable contradictions, but has magnified them to mythic proportions. He is the ultimate despot and the ultimate victim, hero and zero from one moment to the next.

There is a passage in Matthews' memoir in the *Illustrations* which wraps this riddle strikingly around the real-life emperor of the age, Napoleon. While the gang are event-working the battles of the Napoleonic Wars, they confide to him: 'We told you that you were Buonaparte's talisman, and that we would work him up to as high a pitch of grandeur as we would fix you degraded below the common level of human nature.' Napoleon, crowned emperor in the same year that the *Omni Imperious* letter was written, is now the new measure of man; Matthews, conversely, is the first subhuman automaton of the new machine age.

Yet there is literal truth here, too. Napoleon was forged in the same crucible that destroyed Matthews. It was the defeat of the Girondins which allowed France to turn itself into a war machine, and thence Napoleon into emperor. Matthews is replaying the crucial moment endlessly, from different angles. If the Girondins and the British had concluded peace, Napoleon might have been a general and nothing more. The emperor and the madman, however far apart now, once had passed through the same weave of events: in 1793, one preserved Dunkirk while the other liberated Toulon. Their fates were interwoven from that point on. For the arch-warmonger to become Omni Imperious, the arch-peacemaker had to be destroyed.

Illustrations of Madness was no bestseller, either among the general public or the medical profession. But it's a remarkable work, worthy of the overworked adjectives 'unique' and 'classic', both of which have been attached to it. It's the great showcase for the insight and observation Haslam brought to the mad-doctoring trade, and contains much of his best and most scabrous writing. But it's more than Haslam's work that elevates the book to the extraordinary: Matthews is as much the author as the man whose name appears on the title page, and it is to the fullness of its presentation of the Air Loom that the book owes its reputation.

Though tireless antagonists throughout the years, each ready at any moment to denounce the other as raving lunatic or sadistic fraud, *Illustrations* is a genuine collaboration between the two men. Haslam commissioned the Air Loom sketch from Matthews, and Matthews was happy to oblige – all this, of course, dependent on Haslam's discretionary decision to allow Matthews pen and paper. Matthews read the finished manuscript, which included large sections in his own hand, and effectively signed it off; Haslam takes pains to declare that 'these opinions have been collected from the patient since the termination of legal proceedings . . . where inverted commas are used, the manuscript of Mr. Matthews has been faithfully copied; and that for thus introducing his philosophic opinions to the notice of a discerning public, he feels "contented and grateful" '. There is no reason to believe that Haslam made this up; indeed, it would have been important to his claims of impartial observation that the patient should recognize the account Haslam gave of him. We are left, then, with a final paradox: Matthews being 'contented and grateful' to see the publication of a book that is an extended justification of his confinement and a stern recommendation that he should never be released. Perhaps he decided to overlook Haslam's editorial views, or was happy, in the doctor's own words, to 'leave the reader to exercise his own judgement concerning them'.

But even if we take the book to be a genuine collaboration with Matthews – or take the radical view that it may equally be said that it was Haslam who created the Air Loom and Matthews who faithfully transcribed it – we still need to be cautious about its authenticity. By its very nature, it's two steps removed from the action inside Matthews' head: once by being written down, and again by being written by someone other than its subject. Haslam has captured, diligently and minutely, a snapshot of Matthews' mental world, but it is a world in constant flux. Elements from real life, such as Erskine's tongue-tied indisposition, are retrospectively patched on to it, some becoming enduring motifs and others getting lost in the mix; as we shall see, too, other elements sporadically drop out of the Air Loom matrix and are rediscovered as the mundane objects they always were. In the *Omni Imperious* letter of 1804, the gang members are wanted dead or alive; but there are thirteen or fourteen of them, rather than the seven we find in the *Illustrations*. Haslam has not made up the details, but he has orchestrated them into a fixed and static whole, one which Matthews would of course have recognized when he was shown it, but which could probably never again be precisely recaptured.

Matthews was, in a way, Haslam's great professional romance. His previous case histories, like those of other doctors, had run to a page or two; they would get longer as his career progressed, but the level of attention he lavished on Matthews he would never show to another patient again. Matthews, too, was crucial to the intimations Haslam continued to pursue throughout his career that there was a specific, organic condition lurking in the shadows of the impossible nonsense so tenaciously held as truth by the mad. His description of this condition, and his perception that it typically emerged in young men in their teens and twenties, have led some to claim that he should be credited with the discovery of schizophrenia; had his story turned out differently, we might know the condition today as 'Haslam's Disease', and remember Matthews as its undisputed founding case. The *Illustrations*, though Haslam trod with all the care and circumspection that befitted a man of his scrupulous mental hygiene, was his deepest incursion into madness.

Matthews' response would be to tread the same path in the opposite direction: the doctor's incursion into madness would be answered by his patient's incursion into sanity. It would not be enough, nowhere near enough, for Matthews to be pigeon-holed as an interesting lunatic, a remarkable specimen, a mad-doctor's prize exhibit. He would show that there was a great deal more to him than his lunacy.

7

USEFUL ARCHITECTURE

'It is easy for anyone to say so and so is enough for another;
but trying it on himself would perhaps alter his opinion.'
James Tilly Matthews, *Plans for the New Bethlem*, 1811

WHILE HASLAM AND MATTHEWS WERE COLLABORATING ON THE
unique thought-experiment of constructing the Air Loom, the
all-too-real edifice of Bedlam itself continued to decline. By
1810, surveyors had been brought in several times to assess
the damage, all of them coming to the same conclusion: the
building was literally crumbling to the ground, and to fix it
would be far beyond the governors' financial means. The
survey of 1790 had concluded that 'very extensive repairs are
wanting and necessary', the walls themselves 'decayed and
insecure'; it had recommended five years' minimum restoration work, but the governors were stuck in the permanent
austerity drive occasioned by their accounting black hole,
barely able to afford to run their basic services, and they let
the report ride. It was harder to ignore the fact that, in 1805,
the entire east wing had begun to cave in and had had to be
demolished. The surveyors had returned, this time with an
even more damning verdict. Even though it was plain that the

The Old Bethlem in decline

building had been disastrously neglected – it hadn't been washed, painted, plastered or whitewashed for fifteen years – they were careful to lay the blame on the building itself rather than the governors. It had, they maintained, been defective from the moment it was built in 1676. Lacking any proper foundations, the 'requisite stability' for the building had never existed, and it had long since been 'neither sound, upright nor level'. The governors had hoped that some more of the basements could be converted into cells to make up for the missing wing, but the surveyors insisted that they were too damp. Patching the hospital up was no longer an option. It would be cheaper to build new.

By 1810, Bedlam was running on empty. The number of patients had declined steadily due to lack of money and space: there were now only 119, fewer than half the number when Matthews had been admitted. A special House of Commons committee had been set up in 1801 to recommend a course of action; they had deliberated for years before recommending a move to a new site. The proposal, though, had foundered on the permanent obstacle of money. The governors petitioned the House for funding; committees and subcommittees had pushed the problem back and forth. Bethlem's governors set up a Building Committee that ran a charitable subscription campaign in the newspapers, but the donations that trickled in amounted to a fraction of the ever-growing costs.

Finally, the government bit the bullet. They had their own pressing needs: it was now ten years since the Hadfield case, which had committed them to creating a new institution purpose-built to house the new category of criminal lunatics, and as yet no such institution had appeared. It was agreed that Bethlem would be the obvious site for a criminal asylum, and that economies might be achieved by bundling it in with a new hospital, and contributing part of the cost.

The site of the current hospital at Moorfields had become substantially more valuable over the years. What had in 1676 been a patch of waste ground by London Wall was now in the bustling heart of the City, close to the Bank of England and the Royal Exchange, motors of the booming financial district. The City of London Guild had long been of the view that the extensive grounds were now far too valuable as real estate to be occupied by a decrepit and shrinking pauper asylum. There was more money to be had here, if the governors could find a cheaper site to move to. They considered the new northern suburb of Islington – hilly, airy, ideal for the patients' health – but quickly realized that buying into a desirable neighbour-hood would leave them with too little change to build with. Eventually they settled for a twelve-acre plot south of the river, in Southwark.

Southwark was everything Islington was not. It was low-lying, in the swampy basin below the Thames; it was damp and pestilent; it was overcrowded, most of its residents living in grinding poverty. Also, it was cheap. The vacant lot had

Site of the new Bethlem

been abandoned for several years; one side had been a school for the blind, the other an infamous low-life pub called the Dog and Duck which had fallen derelict years before and was now being used as a makeshift bread-mill. The governors snapped it up.

Finally, plans for a 'third Bethlem', after the medieval original and the current white elephant, were on the move. But there were still many problems ahead, especially for an institution which had been stagnant for so long that it had become arthritic, barely capable of tottering on from day to day. How would the transition be managed? Where would the patients be housed during the years of building? And, most important of all, what sort of building should be built?

This last question encapsulated many of the problems Bedlam faced as it looked towards the future. There was no point in replicating the current building, which had been a disaster from day one. But to consider what a better building might look like demanded some sort of vision for the care of the insane: what it really constituted, how it might be improved, and where current trends might lead it. These were precisely the sort of questions on which the governors dreaded having to express an opinion, and the solution that emerged from the Building Committee was an elegant way of side-stepping them. They would throw the design of the new building open to public competition.

In the summer of 1810, an advertisement appeared in the pages of *The Times*. The Bethlem governors were offering three prizes for the best designs submitted for their new institution by all comers. There would be three judges: James Lewis, the surveyor who had written the most recent report condemning the old building; George Dance, who had been the architect of Bedlam's modern rival, St Luke's, in 1778; and another well-known architect, S. P. Cockerel. The first prize would be £200, the second £100, and the third £50.

Matthews, meanwhile, had been busy. His technical drawings of the Air Loom, and their inclusion in Haslam's book, seem to have inspired him to develop his new-found skills further. Drawing was something for which he turned out to have a remarkable aptitude. His handwriting was always small, neat and calligraphically beautiful, even when writing at high speed and in poor conditions; his prodigious qualities of imagination were peculiarly well suited to constructing complex worlds in his mind's eye. Having mastered the basics, he set his mind to expanding his range.

The first project on which he focused was the design of his Omni Imperious Palace. This seems to have occupied him for the first half of 1810, and apparently swelled to a sumptuous set of blueprints worthy of the grandiosity of its subject. Tragically, it's now lost. Haslam refers to it but didn't bother to save it; unlike the French government, who kept all Matthews' writings on file, Haslam seems only to have saved material that demonstrated the extremes of his patient's madness, and he must have felt that he had this already in abundance. However, the mere fact of the plans' existence would be enough to guarantee the palace a nebulous half-life in the years after Matthews' death, when it would be co-opted into his posthumous legend.

It would take a brave architect, historian or psychiatrist to speculate on what the Omni Imperious Palace actually looked like, but it certainly seems to have inspired those around Matthews to spot the serendipitous confluence of his new hobby with the state of crisis in the building around him. Although his wife was still prohibited from visiting him, the settlement of the habeas corpus hearing seems to have brought him more contact with other members of his family – his daughter Justina, now grown up, and his nephew by marriage Richard Staveley – and both encouraged him to enter the competition to design the new Bethlem. James Lewis, the chief judge, also responded positively to Matthews' enquiries about submitting an entry; as the surveyor of the old building, Lewis had got to know Matthews some years previously. Despite his years in jail and in Bedlam, and despite his madness, Matthews hadn't lost the knack of inspiring sympathy and making and keeping friends. As the project progressed, Matthews asked Lewis many questions of detail, and Lewis remained helpful and encouraging throughout.

On 1 April 1811 the governors of Bethlem received from one of their patients a handsome set of folios containing architectural plans, watercolour impressions and about fifty large pages of notes covered in a tiny, immaculate and by now very familiar hand. Matthews' dossier included not one but four plans, with overlapping alternative details. His covering letter explains that the choice between them is 'a matter requiring the judgements of the faculty as of architects and others', and that he is 'very desirous of being honoured with the opinions of the learned doctors' as to which is the best combination. He wishes to know whether any or all of the plans are 'truly salubrious', a word that recurs frequently throughout the notes and which highlights their most remarkable quality. These are, probably for the first time ever, designs by a lunatic for a lunatic asylum, conceived not from the perspective of the doctors who will manage the hospital but the patients who will live in it. Haslam might have felt confident that his writings on madness were the most insightful and progressive ever to have emerged from Bethlem, but now he had a serious rival.

The drawings are beautiful. Matthews has opted for a neo-classical design along the lines of the current building, but with lightness and elegance and, above all, a functionality the current Bedlam had conspicuously lacked from the beginning. His colouring is fine, tasteful, unobtrusive; as with the Air Loom, the visualizations are accompanied by clean and precisely corresponding schematics which expand the detail. Haslam might have presented his experiences with Matthews under the title *Illustrations of Madness*; Matthews is responding, perhaps consciously, with a work that could well be called *Illustrations of Sanity*.

The plan, in its various alternative forms, has four floors – twice the height of the current building but, as Matthews explains, much more desirable. The patients have no objection to tall storeys: 'on the contrary, the upper ones are most sought by patients, on account of their affording extensive views, and being more salubrious'. Furthermore, extra storeys mean that the basement, currently the least salubrious area, can be dispensed with. The basement in the present Bedlam is more trouble than it's worth: it is three and a half feet underground, 'consequently it is damp, and therefore the Governors have preferred leaving the greater part of it unused, to endangering the patients' health'. Matthews' first move is to elevate the patients literally, and among the patients particularly the women. The female patients will occupy the west wing, 'as being open to the warmest and most salubrious winds, the men being better able to endure the bleaker air'.

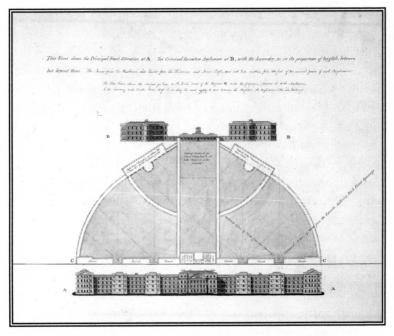

Two views of Matthews' plans for the new Bethlem.

Four floors will accommodate four hundred patients, more than twice the current number, and with a higher standard of comfort and privacy, 'there being not among the whole a two-bedded room; such being improper, as tending oftener to excite than to prevent detestability'. Half of the floors will be for the troublesome patients, who will have extra keepers and restraints where necessary. The other half will be divided equally between 'middling' and 'convalescent': those working towards more privileged status and relaxed treatment, and those who have already earned it. Here, Matthews is breaking with tradition and demonstrating the radical nature of his plans: this is not just architecture, it is therapy in stone. The rule of thumb is, as he well knows, that convalescent patients are a minority, about a quarter of the total. His proportions 'may at first view appear too many for the convalescent class',

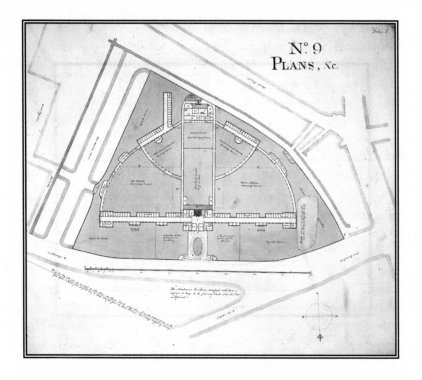

but that is because current regimes are unnecessarily punitive and create more problems than they need to. Incurables, for example, are always held in the tightest security, but there are 'even among those termed the incurables, many who are to the utmost orderly, clean and extremely well-behaved, some exemplarily so, having merely some or other peculiarity'. Here we may perhaps think of the docile Peg Nicholson; more likely, we may be prompted to consider the plight of the author himself.

Another example is the infirmary. In the current Bedlam, it's in a separate block, but 'a detached infirmary is found as far from desirable', Matthews claims, 'as it is advantageous in any other establishment'. Keeping the sick patients far away from the others places a huge strain on the hospital's manpower, which the patients themselves could ease if each gallery had its own sickroom. There are always patients willing and able to look after their fellows: 'patients have a sympathetic compassion for their sick companions which no infirmary keeper can feel'. Once again, the problem can become the solution.

The same is true for the individual cells: by making them a little more comfortable, the governors would ease their own burden substantially. In Matthews' plans, every cell backs on to a flue running up through the walls, 'this flue to be filled with heat, without the smoke entering it'. Warm cells will mean less illness, and less trouble for the doctors. His cells, too, are a few inches longer than the current ones, where 'the want of a trifle more length is often felt by every party'. One of the features of Bedlam life, he points out, is that a trouble-some patient who is chained to his bed can manoeuvre himself to reach his door and 'amuse himself by forcing the door to shut with violence sufficient to produce almost cannon report and spring back for him to repeat it, nearly forcing the door case out of the wall; and standing advanced he can hold at bay and much obstruct the keeper &c. who would enter'. In St Luke's, where the cells are even shorter, the keepers had long resorted in such situations to more draconian restraints: shorter chains or strait-waistcoats. Here, Matthews passes on a fascinating titbit of lunatic lore: these different strategies have led to the common proverb among patients that 'St. Luke's is clean with tyranny; Bedlam's all filth with liberty'. But neither tyranny nor filth would be necessary if there was a little more space. Previous authorities had opined that seven feet by eight was sufficient for a cell's dimensions, but whoever recommended this 'is here disregarded, as he never made the trial upon himself'. 'It is easy for anyone to say so and so is enough for another,' Matthews points out, 'but trying it on himself would perhaps alter his opinion.' The governors, he is gently suggesting, would be unwise to disregard the opin-ions of the mad in this and many other matters. Matthews' status as a patient, which might at first sight seem to be a drawback to his plans, actually confers unique advantages.

All these individual improvements are complemented by the structure of the building as a whole. Its height will not only 'purify the whole building by whatever wind may blow', but will by the same token purify the patients' spirits. It will offer 'the greatest number of varied and open views', which in turn will patch Bedlam somewhat back into the world. 'A view of the public passing and repassing', according to Matthews, 'is highly gratifying to patients in every stage.' Here is one of the few points on which the current Bedlam scores: 'the great consolation in Bethlem, is the busy world moving to and fro in the fine opening of Moorfields'. There may be those, professionals and public, who would like to see the mad shut away, out of sight and out of mind, but the mad themselves enjoy the diversion of the world outside.

By the same token, it's important to consider the face the new Bethlem presents to the outside world. Matthews' plans show a delicate and harmonious classical exterior, which again he presents not simply as decorative but as therapeutic for the patients and thus advantageous to their keepers. One of the most important controlling factors in the patients' state of mind is their sense of the building they are in. Here, the current Bedlam fails disastrously. Its regimented and barred windows 'give to the front of the building next the public that hateful prison look, and as nothing makes a stronger impression on deranged minds than the appearance of the place they are brought to inhabit, the prison application thereof often produces so strong an effect as renders the skilful doctor's efforts useless'. The more forbidding the madhouse, the worse the mad will remain. On the other hand, 'the idea of inhabiting a comfortable or grand place produces content, and that is the best foundation for the faculty to build on'. The treatment of the mad, he is asserting in direct contradiction to Haslam, is more effective if it's a partnership than simply an imposition of the doctor's will on a disempowered patient.

As if to demonstrate the benign nature of this reciprocity, Matthews is at pains to improve the lot not just of the patients but of the apothecary. He has located Haslam's new residence 'in grand front east side of the sole entrance' rather than round the back 'where nothing of the public can be seen, a sure means to force him from home to see how the world goes elsewhere'. It's not only the patients who need contact with the outside world, but the doctors and their families: 'the sight of persons passing and repassing, of St. Paul's, the churches, Monument, great buildings, and from the upper floor the bridges, river, shipping or boats &c., cannot but be as pleasing to families not confined as to patients who are'.

After his years of adversity, we begin to get a sense through these plans of Matthews waking into the world of normality he left behind so long ago. He is clearly on his best behaviour, taking pride in the sanity of his work, perhaps still holding the thought that these plans may some day be dusted off as material evidence in his favour. But, even if this was part of his original motivation, the project has clearly become more than this to him. He is becoming absorbed in it for its own sake, relishing the challenge of mastering new disciplines and perhaps even imposing his visions on a wider world. His notes are full of references to the general progress of the competition; he is clearly hungry for intelligence about the other plans being submitted, and the leanings of the judges towards this or that fashion. His four plans, it turns out, were whittled down from several more which featured curves and diagonal wings, because he has discovered that the 'architect judges do not like any thing but what is right angled'. He has taken note of the House of Commons committee reports on the state of madhouses, and the statutory provisions of the Madhouses Act. His world seems, whether by accident or design, to be opening up from the claustrophobic confines of his own head and the controlling machinations of the Air Loom gang. And, as he turns his attention from the gang, so their power seems to be withering away.

There's a striking example of this in his proposals for the sanitary system in the new hospital, on which he offers a great deal of detail. He's concerned that the cells will be fitted with open pipes for human waste, which is the standard practice pioneered at St Luke's. But 'notwithstanding the loud praises bestowed upon such system at St. Luke's, verbally & by publications', Matthews 'utterly rejects the laying of pipes' and insists that they 'cannot but prove injurious to the patients' health'. They may seem adequate to visitors during the day while the windows are open, but overnight the smell backs up and 'the patient cannot but suffer from the effect during the night when all is shut'. 'The saline particles of the urine encrust them within,' he explains, 'and this always emits a fetid effluvia.'

Here is a phrase we have come across before; Matthews mentions it again, pointing out that even the leaded drawer system at St Luke's is ineffective because 'such drawers yield as fetid an effluvia as the pipes themselves'. Two years ago, the fetid effluvia which assailed him were the Air Loom's gases: putrid human breath, seminal fluids, 'gaz' from the anus of the horse and all the rest. Then, they were signs that the loom was in operation and about to take over his body and mind; now they seem to have become detached from his delusional world and to be reappearing as faults in the plumbing system. He still maintains that he has for many years been doing battle with them, but, in the new architectural context, this battle presents a far more mundane face: he has been plugging the holes in his cell flooring 'by what is called ploughing, tonguing and heading them', which 'prevents wet from penetrating through the joints'.

Here is further confirmation that the Air Loom described by Haslam, an all-powerful and persistent machine, is in fact a system as permeable as the floorboards of Matthews' cell. We have already recognized events, such as Erskine's assailment in the House of Commons, that have been absorbed into it;

now we glimpse the opposite effect of its wheels beginning to drop off as Matthews concentrates his mind elsewhere. This is further evidence, too, that the resemblances between the world of the Air Loom and that of Bedlam are more than co-incidental: the engine of one turns out, looked at from another angle, to be the plumbing of the other.

Does this mean that Matthews is getting better? As we shall see, the evidence continues to point both ways. Perhaps, just as the notion of 'going mad' turns out to be of limited use in understanding his journey, the notion of 'getting better' is less helpful than we may expect. It's certainly of little use to Matthews personally, as he never believed that he was mad to begin with; nor is it of any functional use to a patient who's condemned to Bedlam for life on grounds that, when examined, seem to bear only a tangential relation to his state of mind. But his plans for the new Bethlem surely mark a striking transition from the 'Bedlam-attaining-airloom-warp' Haslam was recording only a year before. Then, Matthews' mission was still his original one: to restore peace between England and France, and to prevent Europe from destroying itself in war. Beleaguered, conspired against, imprisoned and worse, his goal nevertheless remained intact: to save the world.

There can be little doubt by this point that Matthews genuinely believed the world needed him to save it, and that despite all the obstacles and torments in his path he was still its best and only hope. The fact that he had, recently and under duress, refused to recant this belief suggests that he probably still held it while designing the new Bedlam. The temptation to give up his beliefs, to grovel and plead lunacy, must have been immense. In this sense, his persistence in his madness represents a prodigious feat of strength and personal honour: even if the whole world believed him mad, he would not give up. What a shift, then, to accept that he no longer had the power to save the world, and then, rather than collapse in despair or rage in fury, to apply himself calmly and persistently to reforming the mad-business from the inside.

If we look at it this way, which is surely the way Matthews looked at it, this is an act far beyond the capability with which many would credit the mad. It presupposes a powerful compassion for those around him, and at the same time a remarkable wisdom to understand that, while his original mission was as pressing as ever, it was better to try to accomplish something smaller and more attainable. Does such a decision mean that he was no longer mad, or do we simply need to recognize that the mad can be as compassionate and as wise as the best of us?

There were thirty-two other entrants in the competition besides Matthews. As was customary with newspaper competitions, the entrants identified themselves by heading their plans with catchphrases, some descriptive ('Utility without ostentation'), others flippant ('Flippertigibbet of moping and moaning'). Matthews cryptically headed his 'The deuce take it', and signed off as 'James Tilly Matthews, Bethlem Hospital (14 years herein confined)'.

The competition was not, overall, a great success. Matthews' plans failed to make the top three; the first prize was awarded to a pupil of James Lewis, whose motif was the word 'spero' ('I hope') within an anchor. None of the winning entries, though, was adjudged to be suitable for construction. Instead, Lewis was charged with drafting a plan that would incorporate some of the best features of the most promising ones.

But there was, for the first time in many years, a pleasant surprise for Matthews: his designs were awarded an *ex gratia* payment of thirty pounds in recognition of the quality of his work. Matthews passed on the money to Richard Staveley and the plans themselves to 'my daughter Justina to whom I made them a present of, and at whose desire I sent them in competition'. It was a worthwhile fee, perhaps the equivalent of two thousand pounds today, and the first money he had earned in nearly twenty years. Though some have suggested that his reward was engineered by the Bethlem governors in the hope of keeping his friends and family quiet, it was officially proposed out of sympathy for Matthews' plight and in recognition of his 'labour and ability'. Someone, perhaps Lewis, was also struck by its unusual insights into the condition of Bethlem's patients, and suggested that it should be passed on to the College of Physicians. Matthews was excited by this prospect and keen to learn which of the four plans the college most approved, but his opinions were deemed unsuitable for the medical profession. There is a covering note still attached to Matthews' designs: in striking contrast to his immaculately inscribed folio, this is a hastily scribbled and barely legible note from a Mr Roberts, a member of the Bethlem Subcommittee. It reads:

> I am very sorry that the consideration of Mr. Matthews' plans, however ingenious they may be, is not fit to be laid before the College of Physicians, as it would be considered irrelevant to their concerns.

Matthews' claim that his status as a patient gave him unique insights into their problems might, it seems, arouse the interest of architects, but doctors were not prepared to listen. At any rate, not yet.

By the same token, it seems that the architects were not much interested in listening to the doctors. For John Haslam, the new building was the first opportunity he had had in his fifteen years as apothecary to attempt to set up the hospital along more progressive and functional lines, and to correct the institutional failings that had hamstrung him since his arrival. He took a great deal of interest in the designs for the new Bethlem, and began to collect stacks of background material on the form and function of other hospitals which he collated and passed on to the Building Committee. It was crucial, he insisted, that the new building should be 'constructed with all the advantages which modern art and extensive experience could supply'; crucial, too, that it should not duplicate the 'numerous defects of the old building' but should 'incorporate the conveniences and improvements which might be derived from similar institutions both in this country and abroad'. As the most senior staff member resident in the hospital, he might have expected his research to be appreciated and his voice to be listened to. Instead, he was completely ignored. Later, he would describe the new building as 'an ostentatious blazon of national degradation'.

Here, between the lines, we witness a quiet but significant turning-point in the relationship between Matthews and Haslam: for the first time, the lunatic is being taken more seriously than his doctor. This first skirmish takes place on the outlying and neutral territory of architecture, but it presages the change to come, when the same reversal of fortune will occur more publicly, more bitterly, and on the battleground of mad-doctoring itself.

The competition was over, but there was more to come from Matthews. Considering how long he had persevered with his previous mission without the slightest reciprocal kindness or encouragement, it's hardly surprising that the recognition of his new-found architectural talents spurred him on to further efforts. On 6 June the Building Committee received another folio, with a further set of plans and more extensive notes, and the request that they would 'honour him by accepting them'. His original plans had been for four hundred patients; only when he received them back had he learned that the judges had decided to build for only two hundred. He had im-mediately begun a revised set of plans. 'It no longer being a question of prize or premium,' he wasn't expecting them to reverse the decision they had made, but 'remembering with what extreme good nature Mr. Lewis had at all times encouraged anything drawn by me', he begged their indulgence for his further suggestions.

It's clear from this second folio that Matthews was happy to live without the prize, but still troubled by the idea that the new building might not be suitable for the patients. 'I am not attempting to dragoon you into my ways,' he tells them, 'nor to intrude myself upon you or your eminent architect' – but he can't stop himself from reminding them of the importance of their decisions. The new Bethlem 'is to endure probably two centuries, and thousands of helpless beings to feel the effects of its inconveniences, if any there are about it'. A plan may satisfy the governors and the medical profession, but the architects' most pressing duty is to the residents who have no say in the matter.

Where the notes to the first set of plans were fastidiously sane and sober, the second set offer a serious challenge to any assumption that Matthews has 'got better'. Though definitely in a minor key compared to the world of the Air Loom or the Omni Imperious Emperor Supreme, this is a document as odd as any he has written: discursive, inappropriately detailed and filled with familiar – we may have hoped long-forgotten – obsessions. We have seen this pattern before: the pair of letters, the first relatively measured and sane, the second carelessly bursting the banks of reason. Just as the peace proposal of 1793 was followed by the stream-of-consciousness 'Delays are dangerous' letter to Danton, and just as the first entreaty to Lord Liverpool was chased up with wild accusations of conspiracy and treachery, so the new plans find Matthews losing his focus on the intended reader, indulging himself in inappropriate intricacies that expand incontinently into implausibly grand schemes. We may say that he has lost the plot – or, once again, we may say that this is what he really wanted to write all along, and now sees no reason not to.

The first half of the new note is occasioned by Matthews' discovery that 'it is said there is not to be any straw shaft, but the foul straw is to be thrown into heaps, to make manure for the kitchen garden'. This is a matter that clearly excites his attention, as he spends several thousand words discussing the options for used straw disposal. The current building has a shaft, which Matthews insists at length is 'truly dangerous', something the architects seem to have considered since they are planning a new system. Nonetheless, the discarded system is denounced at length: 'it is a wonder and a mercy that the present Bedlam' – Matthews has dispensed with the correct 'Bethlem', which he used scrupulously in the first plans, in favour of the insider slang – 'has never burnt down, so dreadful have the flames from its shaft fires often proved, driving into the very gallery, and more often forcing those feeding the fire to run for their lives, often severely scorched . . .' The 'fetid effluvia' of the used straw makes another extended appearance, taken from the patients' cells soaked in 'sufficient of excrement and urine to cause an intolerable stench'. All this might well have been true, but its relation to the design of the new building is lost in a series of digressions, virtually polemics, on the causes and dangers, uses and abuses of old straw.

The second major preoccupation of the notes is another familiar one, but this time from fifteen years ago: the French cabbage plan. 'There must', Matthews insists, 'be a gardener.' His wages will be thirty pounds a year, his expenses roughly the same again; he will require three hired labourers to assist him, or maybe six or eight of the able-bodied patients, at a cost of fifty pounds over the year; 'seeds, plants, frames, glasses, tools, &c. &c. will as a whole with extras cost £40 per year, wear and tear included'. The entire enterprise is costed down to the last detail, an extended effort to demonstrate that, compared with 'the governors buying in the markets where they might for their money pick the best vegetables for a general supply, they would save £50 a year at least'. But the cumulative effect is a good deal odder than the cabbage plan he presented all those years ago to the French government. Then, he was conscious of the need to hold the Directory's interest, to keep them reading, to work by increments from the no-lose proposal of a trial crop to the grand vistas of a national agricultural plan. Here, he simply seems to be chatting, indulging in detail for the pleasure of it, enumerating the most promising vegetables – 'pot herbs, salads, fruit trees . . . goose-berry, currant and baking apple dwarfs' – and warning of the dangers that 'the curl, seal, dropsy &c. might take the potatoes . . . the blight, caterpillars or so might injure the cabbage crop'.

The whole piece is, in a way, rather a delight to read. Our minds can wander, as Matthews' so clearly does, from his own small plot among Bedlam's ruins into the task of constructing a productive kitchen garden: the neat and labour-saving routines that would make the project easier to manage, the financial outlays and savings, the horticultural hints and tips, the strategies against common perils and pitfalls. Nor are the other patients entirely forgotten: instead of sending them out of the hospital for labouring jobs 'and giving so many patients the continual opportunity of getting drunk', they could be working in the salubrious outdoors within the hospital, rolling the lawn, mowing and sweeping, carrying cuttings out to the compost heap. All this is charming and perhaps even useful, but somewhere along the way Matthews has forgotten that he is writing to 'The Worshipful, the President, Treasurer and Governors of Bethlem Hospital', and that a dozen pages ago he was begging them to heed his advice on the crucial question of the design of the hospital. Even if they were persuaded by Matthews' paean to the virtues of a kitchen garden, surely they would simply hire a gardener rather than listen to one of their patients spelling out his view of a future gardener's duties to them at such length. Although the second plan's content is far from delusional, he has lost his grip on the context: who he's writing to, what's relevant to them, and why they should be interested. In the first plan, Matthews made a revolutionary case for why the architects should be listening to the views of a patient; in this second plan, he is unwittingly reminding them why he's a patient in the first place.

But, as ever, Matthews disappoints our expectations of linear progress from sanity to madness. Just as it seems that his promising but brief foray into architecture is dissolving into disorganized jottings and perennial obsessions, he sharpens up his act again. The second half of 1811 finds him learning the art of engraving from an expert who visited him in his cell and gave him free tuition – perhaps an acquaintance of Lewis, though Haslam later claims to have organized this initiative on Matthews' behalf. In any case, throughout the next year he worked his way systematically through an ambitious new project: a partwork magazine explaining the basics of architecture to a general readership, and offering a range of plans and designs for new houses and municipal buildings. Its title was *Useful Architecture*.

The first issue went to press and was published in October 1812. The whole series, once completed, would constitute an exhaustive primer for anyone considering or involved in a new building, 'from the £50 cott to the £200,000 mansion', in styles 'mostly grounded on the Grecian, Roman, Gothic and plain styles of architecture'. Matthews opens the series with a preface explaining the genesis of the work. 'Many strangers as well as my own friends', he announces, have 'expressed their wishes that I should cause a series of my designs for public and private buildings to be engraved' and 'an eminent architect kindly offered to instruct me in the species of engraving necessary'. Matthews is now 'an etcher of several weeks' progress' and will, over the coming months and years, continue to offer 'designs, wholly etched by myself'. Again, he signs off as a patient in Bethlem Hospital, and requests any interested readers to send comments or suggestions to him at that address.

All but a couple of pages of *Useful Architecture* are now lost, but what survives – a beautifully watercoloured engraving of a Georgian town house with accompanying plans – suggests an orderly work of high technical quality. It seems to have found some favour with the public: a second volume was prepared and published before, in the time-honoured tradition of part-work magazines, it petered out, presumably leaving some but not enough readers asking for more. Ten years after Matthews' death the eminent London architect and collector Sir John Soane was moved to go on a search for a copy, which eventually led him to John Haslam. Haslam replied, perhaps a little tersely, 'Sir, after some search I have found the two numbers of the late Mr. Matthews' publication on architectural subjects.' Matthews the lunatic was beginning to be joined by a new personality, Matthews the architect. Over the coming years, the two would merge and create a third Matthews, largely mythical but destined to be the one who would live on in the public imagination.

With *Useful Architecture* we seem to have moved into territory far removed from madness and sanity, peace and war; but perhaps even here Matthews is modelling and refining his view of himself, his identity and his state of mind. His immediate quest for freedom has long run into a cul-de-sac of Kafkaesque illogic: not only is it impossible for him to prove that he's sane, but the question of his sanity or madness has turned out to be irrelevant to his confinement. He seems increasingly to accept that he's in Bedlam for life, but is nevertheless still striving to be defined as more than simply an incurable lunatic.

Here, perhaps, is the significance in the title of *Useful Architecture*: 'useful' is – apart, obviously, from 'sane' – the one thing the average lunatic is not. There is a shrewdness here, either conscious or instinctive: people who are useful, whatever their quirks of behaviour or political opinions, are rarely locked up, and those who are locked up may equally be understood to be confined for their uselessness as for their loss

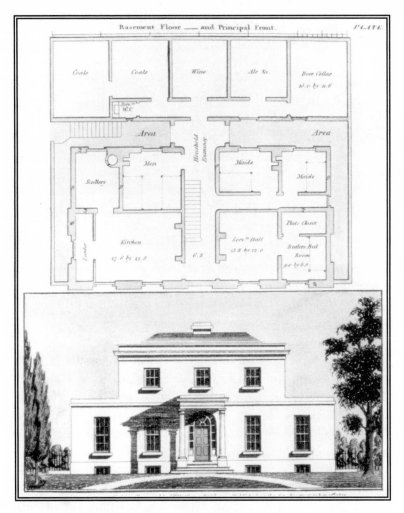

Matthews' illustration for Useful Architecture

of reason. All Matthews ever wanted was to be useful. It was his misguided tenacity in attempting to be useful which landed him in Bedlam in the first place. And if he can never now be sane, at least he can still be useful – first to his unfortunate companions, and now to the world at large.

8

THE FALL OF ENGLAND'S BASTILLE

*'Chains and fetters are fit only for pauper lunatics:
if a gentleman was put in irons, he would not like it.'*
Thomas Monro, *Evidence to the House of Commons*, 1816

JAMES TILLY MATTHEWS MIGHT HAVE BEEN FIRMLY FROZEN INTO HIS Bedlam cocoon, but in the outside world there was another revolution in the air. Despite his isolation, and not for the first time, Matthews seems somehow to have had precise intimations of this new world before it became known to those around him. Within a year or two of finishing his plans for the new Bethlem his precepts and suggestions, which the governors had disdained even to pass on to the College of Physicians, would become the new orthodoxy of the psychiatric profession, and it would be those in authority over him who would be cast aside.

Matthews had joined the last revolution late in the day, and delay had been the curse that had doomed his intervention to failure. This time he was ahead of the game, peering around the curve into the future and forced to wait interminably for the world to catch up. This revolution, too, shuttled across the Channel between England and France; but this time

Matthews would be on the winning side, though he would sadly not live to see his final victory.

The revolution began quietly, in York. In 1777 a new public asylum had been opened there, loosely modelled on Bedlam's more progressive rival St Luke's and other new institutions that had been established along similar lines in Newcastle and Manchester. It had been set up under the charter of offering 'the most humane and disinterested treatment' of the mad but, like so many others, the reality had fallen far short of the mission statement. The sole physician, Dr Hunter, was of the old school: like Crowther in Bedlam, his notions of treatment extended no further than purging and vomiting. He regarded psychiatry as 'an obscure branch of medicine'; he classified patients on admission with loose catch-all terms such as 'flighty', 'wild' or 'furious', and thereafter kept no case notes. Patients were confined as Hunter saw fit, visitors were discouraged and the governors simply rubber-stamped the physician's decisions.

As with Matthews in Bedlam, it was pressure from the only independently interested parties – friends and family – that broke the deadlock. In 1790 a Quaker widow named Hannah Mills was admitted suffering from 'melancholy'. The local chapter of the Quaker Society of Friends attempted to visit her for religious consolation, but were turned away on the grounds that contact with her old society would excite her and make her condition worse. Six weeks later she died, in circumstances that were never properly explained. The Society of Friends investigated the asylum, were appalled by the obstruction they met and the grim conditions they uncovered, and resolved to set up their own asylum offering not medical but pastoral care to the unfortunate and sick in mind of their own community.

The initiative was led by a York Quaker called William Tuke who set himself enthusiastically to fund-raising. Eventually, in 1797, just as Matthews was being admitted to Bedlam, the Retreat at York opened its doors. It was set on an eleven-acre patch outside the city, elevated above the surrounding land to offer better air and to 'command a delightful prospect', and surrounded by gardens and woods criss-crossed with pleasant trails 'to afford an agreeable place for recreation and employment'.

The Retreat itself was a purpose-built hospital, but unlike its predecessors it was deliberately domestic rather than institutional in style. The architect John Bevans, another Quaker, in the first of many precise echoes of Matthews' theories, had decided that it was important that the building itself should be a happy one: 'if the outside appears heavy and prison-like it has a considerable effect upon the imagination'. It is in theory possible that Matthews could have heard of the Retreat and modelled his own plans on it, but it seems unlikely. The York initiative was small and became widely known outside its locale, not to mention within the specialist medical profession, only after 1811. Also, if Matthews had known that his plans had been conceived and executed successfully else-where, he would very likely have told us so, just as he refers to negative examples of poor practice at St Luke's and other institutions. The revolution began slowly and in scattered isolated pockets – none more isolated than Matthews himself.

During their research the Quakers had visited many public asylums, and had been shocked to discover so many patients being kept on straw floors and chained when they became unruly. The Retreat, in contrast, looked like a normal house: wooden furniture, dining tables, glass-paned windows. The galleries looked less like stables and more like large day-rooms that turned into communal dining-rooms at night. The keynote was 'the general comfort of the insane', and security features were incorporated discreetly: the barred gates were hidden, the windows were composed of small glass panes that were impossible to escape through and cheap to replace if bro-ken, and the heavy door-locks were covered in leather to look less threatening.

The York Retreat

The regime was as novel as the surroundings. There were no qualified doctors, for a start; the superintendent was a charismatic local Quaker named George Jepson, whose therapy was modelled on lay community care rather than medicine. Tuke confessed he had 'little occasion for theory', and Jepson was allowed to run the Retreat as if he were caring for any unfortunate or disadvantaged members of the Society. He overlaid the business of management and treatment with a strong religious dimension – patients would recite 'what a blessing it is to possess a sound mind / Lord make me thankful' – but the main daily component of the regime was work. Women polished the furniture, churned the butter, washed the clothes and sat in sewing circles; men laboured in the house and grounds and worked the garden.

Nevertheless, it was impossible for even such a benign and enlightened system to operate without punishment and restraint. The house was divided into lower and upper levels; disobedient patients were relegated to lower galleries, where they had fewer privileges, and compliant ones were promoted to the upper galleries, where they were allowed to participate in some aspects of management. Violent patients were made aware of the 'principle of fear': if they indulged in manic behaviour they were straitjacketed until they understood that they could never win a battle of brute force, but they were never beaten or punished beyond the immediate suppression of their violence. The most unruly were restrained in bed with leather straps. Overall, the carrot was used in preference to the stick, and promises of rewards were fastidiously kept. Case notes show that the staff took pleasure in indulging their patients' whims: 'Mary Evans', we read, 'has also today manifested an inclination for a particular set of tea-cakes. I am not certain whether we understand her meaning but we have sent such as we suppose she wanted.' This was a far cry indeed from Bedlam, and it proved a great deal more successful: at the time when Matthews was drawing up his plans, only four out of the sixty-four patients at the Retreat were restrained in any way. In another precise echo of Matthews' theory, the Quakers insisted that 'whatever tends to promote the happiness of the patient is found to increase his desire to restrain himself'.

The Retreat gained fame suddenly in 1813, two years after Matthews had submitted his plans for reform, when Samuel Tuke, William's grandson, published a book entitled *Description of the Retreat: An Institution near York for Insane Persons of the Society of Friends*. It was the first full-length, detailed account of asylum practice that had ever been published. Like *Illustrations of Madness* it was aimed at both psychiatrists and the general public, but whereas Haslam's effort fell between two stools, the *Description* was an unprecedented and genre-busting success. It crystallized the growing public unease with the old asylum system, and at the same time offered a new template which not just doctors but any lay philanthropists could put into practice. Here was not merely a critique the specialists could not ignore, but a how-to guide for the perplexed which allowed them to take the initiative themselves.

The *Description*'s effects were initially local, but they spread fast. The old York Asylum was most directly in the firing-line. Forced onto the back foot by the Retreat's spectacular results, it conceded to an inquiry into its conditions and practices. The findings were horrific: maltreatment of patients including neglect, filthy conditions and rape; forging documents to conceal patients' deaths; embezzlement on a huge scale. The contrast with its amateur rival on the hill was impossible to ignore. Most of the staff were sacked and replaced, William and Samuel Tuke were elected on to the board of governors, and its practices were rapidly overhauled along Retreat lines. Across the country, asylums quickly began to rechristen themselves 'retreats'. Within a year, the tide of revolution would begin to lap at the door of the great symbol of the *ancien régime*, Bedlam itself.

But the universal embrace the *Description* received had a slightly pious and cloying element. The Retreat came to stand for all that was good, a beacon of humanity in a sea of misery and evil. Few had the courage to question whether it was necessarily so desirable that the treatment of the mad should be entirely stripped of its medical remit and clothed in religious raiment, or whether the system was as suitable for those who were not Quakers as for those who were. Many, notably the radical historian of madness Michel Foucault, have since come to see the Retreat not as a blissful dawn but as the first ratchet in a new machine of coercion which would lead to the dehumanizing mass incarceration of the mad in the Victorian era and beyond. For Foucault, the Retreat patients are not cured but infantilized: 'everything at the Retreat is organised so that the insane are transformed into minors'. The system is bourgeois patriarchy writ large; work is 'imposed as a moral rule', and cure and conformity are inseparable. This is clearly true, but does it mean that the new system is *more* coercive than the old regime of whips and chains? It would not be hard to guess which of the two Matthews would have preferred, had he been given the choice.

What is certainly the case is that the Retreat, as well as a beacon of hope, also became a powerful stick with which to beat the old establishment, and not always fairly. The Retreat was small, privately funded, and chose its clientele from its own social group. Many of its practices, admirable as they might have been, were unsuitable for large, poorly funded public institutions with a duty of care to the entire population. The idealized Retreat was a bright symbol of the first wave of the revolution, but its reproachful shadow would loom oppressively over many well-intentioned failures to come.

The second front of the revolution emerged in Paris, directly out of the French Revolution itself. It drew many of its formative cases from those who, like Matthews, had lost their reason through suffering under the Terror and had been rotting in public asylums ever since. Like the Retreat, it was a revolution of non-restraint: its great practitioner, Philippe Pinel, is forever remembered (with only partial accuracy) for being the first to 'strike the chains from the mad'. But this was more than a revolution of architecture or hospital management. It was a 'medicine of the imagination', a new concept of treatment that had some spectacular successes not merely in terms of containing the mad humanely, but in engaging the patients in their own cures.

Pinel was from the south of France and came to Paris a decade before the Revolution hoping to make his way up the ranks of the medical profession, but he found that his doctor's degree from Toulouse was worth little in the metropolis. He ended up scraping a living as a medical journalist and nurturing, like Haslam, a biting critique of the established medical system, the professional cliques and honorifics that reflected little or no insight or experience. He became interested in

Philippe Pinel

mental illness when one of his friends tipped from 'nervous melancholy' into mania and delusions; Pinel treated him with warm baths and nourishing food and inspired a fitful recovery, but the young man was summoned back to his family where, under the care of doctors, he died.

When the Revolution arrived, Pinel was on the right side. The *ancien régime* of court doctors who had obstructed his progress was swept aside; as a friend of the Republic he was appointed *officier municipal* in his Paris district and began to find work as a physician. He joined the committee set up to investigate the state of madhouses in the capital, and found a regime as backward as Bedlam's. The Bicêtre Hospital, the main public asylum, was filled with patients being either bled and vomited or ignored. 'All the madmen in Bicêtre remain there', Pinel reported, 'until it pleases nature to favour them.' The treatment of madness, he concluded, had fallen into mindless routine and public disrepute and needed, like the state, to be reconceived entirely. In 1793 he was appointed physician-in-chief at Bicêtre; in 1795 he moved on to the Salpetrière, the equivalent institution for female patients.

For Pinel, ignoring received medical opinions on madness by no means implied starting from scratch. Though unaware of the Retreat, he had noted that lay carers were often more effective than doctors; he had also noted that 'charlatans' who played tricks on the mad could often change patients' ideas and behaviours more subtly and effectively than those who attempted to impose an iron will on them. Increasingly he came to believe that madness was produced by the imagination, and it was in the imagination that it could be cured. He read Haslam's *Observations on Insanity* with approval, concurring with the view that insanity was not a disease of the soul but, as Haslam had put it, 'an incorrect association of ideas'. A case that struck him early on was that of a trainee priest who had been told by a horoscope reader that he would die before the age of twenty-five; accordingly the priest became nervous and subject to panics and loss of appetite and, eventually, seriously ill. In this case, the cure came as part and parcel of the prediction: when his twenty-fifth birthday arrived, the condition departed. But such cases led Pinel to conceive a new idea of theatrical intervention, to bring such spontaneous cures under the doctors' control. Instead of ignoring his patients' delusions as Haslam did, Pinel began to think of scenes and performances that would confront his patients with the cause of their condition and allow them to resolve it themselves.

Many of Pinel's early cases run in eerie parallel to Matthews', who, it turns out, was far from alone in developing delusions in response to the Terror and subsequent confinement in a madhouse. One was a famous Paris clock-maker who had lapsed into mania through 'the recurrent terrors incited in him by the storms of the Revolution'; he began to develop an obsession with constructing a perpetual motion machine which grew to occupy all his waking hours, and frequently kept him up for nights on end. As with the Air Loom, the machine turned out to be only the tip of an iceberg of plots and conspiracies. By the time he was admitted into the Bicêtre, he was convinced that he had been guillotined, his head jumbled up with the others in the basket. Somehow the verdict had then been reversed, but he had been given back the wrong head.

When Pinel encountered him in his cell he was unstoppable, drawing diagrams and plans for his perpetual motion machine all over the walls. Instead of trying to control his irrational behaviour, Pinel encouraged it, getting his friends and family to supply him with clockmaking tools and setting aside a workshop for him to attempt to solve his insoluble puzzle. After a while, the clockmaker announced success: the machine was complete, and would now run for ever. When it stopped a few days later, the clockmaker seemed to lose interest, and his obsession with the machine evaporated. He was released, resumed his old trade and never relapsed.

Another famous case was the Guilt-Ridden Tailor. In 1793, at the same time as Matthews' mission to Paris, this man happened to voice his disapproval of the execution of Louis XVI in public. As the Committee of Public Safety came to control public life, he began to be tormented with the idea that someone might have remembered his careless talk, and that he would be denounced as an enemy of the Republic – or indeed that he had already been denounced, and his fate had been sealed behind his back. He became ever more nervous, unable to eat or sleep. Convinced that the committee had the power to read his thoughts, he stopped speaking entirely, frozen in a hunched position and waiting for the guillotine to fall. Pinel's first move was to set him up as a tailor inside the asylum, mending the other patients' clothes; he took to his new public duty zealously and worked out his guilt through the sewing machine. Gradually, his sense of oppression began to lift, but then it fell again and his 'melancholy' returned. Now Pinel decided to move closer to the source, and stage a *coup de théâtre*: he arranged for three of his medical students to dress up in black robes, process to the tailor's cell and hold a mock-session of the committee, at which the patient was tried and acquitted. The shock treatment worked, but again only temporarily: after a brief respite, the tailor's guilt enveloped him once more.

Such tricks were not new, and Pinel wasn't the only person who had begun to use them in post-Revolutionary France, but their implications, once spelled out, were considerable. Here was a model of madness in which the idea of cure, rather than simply management, became a new and potent focus. The old fatalism, the Monro doctrine that psychiatry was 'for ever dark, intricate and uncertain', was relegated to the past. The idea that madness was a punishment from God was also gone: Pinel dismissed the idea of divine or demonic possession, insisting that religious delusion was nothing more than another theatrical set-dressing, and that 'demoniacs of all sorts are to be classed either with maniacs or melancholics'. Madness itself, in Pinel's view, had passed its point of crisis thanks to the 'salutary effects' of the Revolution. The nervous disorders of the previous generation were largely the 'characteristics of a social order ready to expire', and the national mind was now characterized by a new 'vigour and energy'.

Throughout the next decade, Pinel set himself to expanding his theatrical tricks into a rigorous scientific system. He spelled out the theory that treatment should be based on a diagnosis of the origins of the disease, with the physician seeking out the original crisis and allowing the patient to discover a resolution for himself. He kept meticulous statistical records of his cases and their treatments, and reclassified all insanities into five categories. Most importantly, he enumerated the new tools with which the physician now had to work. First, and most famous, was *douceur*, or gentleness: attending to the patients' needs and requests and allowing space for them to frame their own ideas about their condition. This, though, could easily be exploited by recalcitrant patients, and needed to be balanced with an 'appareil of repression', a confront-ational mode that forces the patient towards therapeutic anger and insight. Insights thus gained can be controlled by intro-ducing more powerful affections – friends, families, the idea of release – to allow the patient to begin the process of balancing ideas and making rational decisions. Such are the instruments that can provide the doctor with a systematic process for exposing, combating and uprooting the delirious fixation.

It's fascinating to imagine the effect Pinel's therapies might have had on Matthews. Almost certainly his results would have been far more positive than Haslam's. Matthews' delusions were hammered out of frustration, delay, denial – half a life-time of slammed and locked doors, both metaphorical and literal. For him, Haslam's therapies were merely more of the same, a solid brick wall of professional certainty that to encourage Matthews to express himself was to move not towards the light of sanity but back into the darkness of unreason. Pinel would most likely have started, as he did with the tailor, by giving Matthews a task, setting him to work, making him useful. He might have asked him to grow vege-tables for the hospital kitchen, something we know Matthews dreamed of at Bedlam. He might have encouraged him in his practical designs for the institution, or given him management duties. Under such a regime the Air Loom might never have fully materialized in the first place. If it had, Pinel might have led Matthews further into exploring it, articulating its origins, even seeking it out in the wider world.

Matthews was in many ways Pinel's ideal patient. He had energy and talent to burn, and when we consider how eager Matthews was to please the Bethlem authorities in exchange for so little encouragement, he would surely have responded positively to a physician who made the leap to engage with him.

Pinel's *Treatise on Insanity* was published in English in 1806 and grew in currency over the next decade as the reforming tendency gained ground. Although it was a system that was contradictory in many ways to that of the York Retreat – it sought to reinvent medicine rather than discard it in favour of religion – it was also complementary in others. Both placed a new focus on the needs of the patients: their physical comfort, their emotional dynamics, their preference for encouragement over punishment. Both claimed to be simultaneously more humane and more effective. And, by the same token, both served to indict the established system, and to challenge the competence of the professionals who ran them.

The reform movement in Britain was relatively small in numbers, but well connected and vocal. Some were Evangelists, such as William Wilberforce; others were Benthamite social reformers for whom the conditions in prisons and asylums had become a public disgrace; others were prominent politicians on both sides of the House. In the public debate they engendered, it was no longer acceptable for patients to be cold, or damp, or chained up; physicians were increasingly held accountable for their mortality rates and their failure to take up the new models of non-restraint. Increasingly, the *ancien régime* was becoming guilty until proved innocent.

The reform movement came knocking at Bedlam's door shortly after the publication of the *Description*, in the form of a Quaker philanthropist named Edward Wakefield. Wakefield had been deeply shocked by the scandals at York Asylum and had realized that this was not simply a little local difficulty but a situation that was in all likelihood replicated many times over around the country. He became particularly concerned that London had no alternative to the old-style asylums such as Bedlam and had begun to lobby MPs to set up a committee to investigate them – and, he hoped, recommend their replacement with new charitable institutions like the Retreat. He applied to the Bethlem governors for permission to visit, and turned up at Moorfields for the first time in April 1814.

First impressions were not auspicious. The new building in St George's Fields was now under construction, and all attempts to patch up the old one had been abandoned. Wakefield found a vast, sprawling ruin, most of it deserted or condemned. As he entered the crumbling grandeur of the main façade, he was accosted by John Poynder, the clerk to the governors, who blocked his way, invoking a rule last enforced in the previous century that visitors could only be admitted when accompanied by a governor. When Wakefield asked for a list of governors, Poynder refused to supply one.

Wakefield was back within days, this time accompanied by an MP. He made his way up to the women's gallery, where he found ten patients chained to the wall and clad only in blankets. One of them was particularly lucid, and turned out to be well educated; in fact, in her former life she had been a language teacher. Wakefield would later tell the House of Commons committee that they 'can hardly imagine a human being in a more degraded and brutalising situation'. There was more of the same on the men's gallery. The patients were cold, poorly clothed, some of them chained; Wakefield compared it to a 'dog kennel'. He sat down and talked with the patients, for whom contact with the outside world was a refreshing novelty. In words that could have been Matthews', Wakefield reported that 'they seemed greatly to enjoy the sight [from the window] of people walking, and to derive great pleasure from our visit'.

But when Wakefield moved on to the individual cells, he found a paragon of misery, the patient who would become the *cause célèbre* of England's Bastille. James Norris was an American marine who had been admitted to Bedlam in 1800, certified incurable in 1801 and since 1804 had been pinioned to the wall in an extraordinary custom-built device. Riveted around his neck was an iron ring which was attached to a chain that passed through the wall so that it could be tightened from the next-door cell. Norris had stuffed the ring with straw to ease the choking he suffered when it was pulled. There was a further iron bar around his body, pinning his arms against his sides. Wakefield later brought in an artist to sketch Norris's restraints, an image that would become the most recognizable symbol of the reform campaign.

Wakefield sought no explanation for why Norris was restrained in such an elaborate way. It was the image he wanted; in fact, it was precisely the image he had hoped to find. His interest was not in arguing the pros and cons of the current system, but in shocking the outside world into supporting his calls for an asylum revolution and a new dispensation along the lines to which he was committed. In fact, there were reasons why Norris had been singled out for this extreme treatment. He was, according to keepers and patients alike, the most violent man in the place. He had murderously attacked his keepers on at least two occasions, and had once bitten off a patient's finger. He had unusually slim and perhaps double-jointed wrists that enabled him to slip out of standard-issue manacles with ease. (He also kept a pet cat in his cell, which he fed with his own rations, and spent most of his time reading newspapers and books.) His treatment, though both inhumane and inefficient, was, in truth, a slipshod accretion of responses by an institution without the infrastructure, initiative or motive to do any better. For Wakefield, though, it was far simpler: this was an emblem of a system beyond repair.

James Norris (incorrectly captioned as 'William' in Wakefield's sketch)

There was one other patient Wakefield was particularly keen to see. He had heard – perhaps from previous visitors, perhaps from James Lewis – that there was an unusual inmate who had spent many years in Bedlam as an incurable lunatic, despite several independent medical opinions that he was entirely sane; a man with whom visitors were frequently taken to speak, whose conversation was sparkling and articulate, who was always eager to explain his ingenious ideas and show off his apparently remarkable drawings.

But James Tilly Matthews was no longer there.

Matthews, it transpires, had become quite ill. He had abscesses on his back which refused to heal and became periodically reinfected, leaving him increasingly frail. Richard Staveley had continued to visit him, and had been petitioning the governors to allow him to be transferred to a private asylum with country air where he might stand a better chance of regaining his strength. Staveley had found a suitable location: Dr Samuel Fox's London House to the east of Moorfields, on the borders of Hackney and Hoxton, the district where the private trade in lunacy had flourished since the middle of the previous century. He had solicited Crowther's opinion on Matthews' health, and the surgeon had conceded that a change of scene might do him good. He had petitioned the governors again with Crowther's testimony. Crowther and Haslam were despatched to Dr Fox's, and returned with a statement certifying that it met with their clinical and security standards.

On 26 June 1813 the Bethlem Subcommittee had met and struck a deal. Given that Matthews' 'state of health actually requires a better air for the preservation of his life', and that Crowther and Haslam agreed that Fox's was a 'perfectly proper and safe' alternative, the only question that remained was the fees. They proposed that Matthews' friends and family should pay half the costs – 12/6d a week – and that Bethlem would split the other half with the Home Office, to which Richard Staveley agreed. They stressed, however, that he was not being released from Bedlam. He was being moved for health reasons alone, and would be 'considered in every respect still to remain under the control of the hospital'. The stigma of lunatic, or state prisoner, was not being lifted, but for the first time in nearly sixteen years Matthews was to have a change of scene.

When Matthews arrived in Hackney, Dr Fox took to him immediately. He could not find 'the least trait of insanity' in him; on the contrary, Matthews struck him as a man of 'superior understanding', 'sound judgement' and 'strong intellectual powers' who was extremely eager to make himself useful. It seems, in fact, that he soon made himself indispensable. He took over the management of the accounts, made out all the bills, balanced the books. We have no letters from Matthews himself during this period but it seems that he wrote many: when Fox was busy, Matthews took over most of his correspondence. He also got on very well with Mrs Fox, who valued 'his domestic advice in the running of the establishment'. This, we imagine, included the vegetable patch: Matthews, it seems, finally got to cultivate his garden. Fox's house seems to have been an unexpected and final idyll, if not a release then the next best thing. We can imagine Matthews in the leafy London suburbs, pottering around his cabbage patch just as he had done in his mind's eye throughout the long years in Pleissis and Bedlam.

Edward Wakefield came to Fox's London House to visit Matthews a year after his arrival, during his second summer. He was, he reported, astonished to discover 'a man of considerable accomplishments' and 'great learning'. Of all the patients he had met, Matthews was the one who most clearly should never have been in Bedlam in the first place, a man who 'evidently had never kept such society as that in which he was confined for so many years'. Matthews was probably misunderstood, possibly a genius, but in Wakefield's view not mad, and certainly in no need of confinement. They chatted for some time, and it was during this visit that some documents and letters changed hands. These were among Matthews' last letters. They haven't survived and we don't know their exact contents, but they would soon prove to be the most devastatingly effective he had ever written.

Here was another manifest injustice, a second powerful archetype of institutional inhumanity and unnecessary suffering: the mild-mannered man of learning cruelly and needlessly confined. Not only were the unfortunate victimized and treated like brutes, they included among their number people as sane as the rest of us, even gentlemen. Matthews took his place alongside Norris, the two most egregious and tragic victims of the unreformed Bedlam. But Wakefield's report on Matthews reveals the same selective eye that instinctively interpreted Norris's restraints as gratuitous cruelty. 'Mr. Matthews', he reported, 'was a very unfit person for confinement in Bethlem without pen, ink or paper, the use of knife and fork, any place to which he could retire by himself.' As we well know, this wasn't the case: Matthews had had pen, paper and private cell for the last fifteen years, at Haslam's specific direction. Did Matthews deliberately exaggerate the circumstances of his confinement in Bedlam, or did he just read Wakefield carefully and allow him to jump to the conclusions he knew he was seeking? We don't know, but clearly neither did Wakefield; for him, the image was more important than the detail. Matthews' case would finally be brought to justice, but the defence would be fighting for a new and subtly different Matthews: Matthews the martyr, perhaps even Matthews the myth.

The summer of 1814 at Dr Fox's London House rolled on smoothly and peacefully, but there was a long shadow over this patch of evening sunlight: Matthews' health. His transfer had originally been for three months, but it had been extended on Staveley's representation that the arrangement was working well but that Matthews was still a sick man. In July, Staveley made a last attempt at gaining his uncle's release. Once again he solicited independent testimony from two doctors and presented it to the Home Secretary (now no longer Lord Liverpool but Lord Sidmouth) with his own plea for

Matthews' freedom on the grounds of compassion and ill health.

This final appeal is an echo, with less fanfare and public wrangling, of the habeas corpus hearing of 1809, and with the same outcome. Staveley's case is that Matthews 'is now in a state of health which renders life precarious', that 'he has been reduced to that situation by long confinement', and that Matthews' 'liberation has been so long and still is prevented by your Lordship's office'. The only treatment that remains for Matthews' condition is healthy sea air, and it is for this that Staveley begs 'your Lordship's favourable intervention'.

We learn, too, that Matthews' wife and family, whom he misses as much as they miss him, have now emigrated to Jamaica, from where they continue to 'supplicate his liberation'. Just as their presence in his story has remained ghostly throughout, so now is their disappearance. We can only infer that their long years of penury and their extended prohibition from visiting Matthews have taken their toll. Emigration to Jamaica was, at this time, usually either a very good option or a very bad one: taking charge of a profitable plantation or a last-ditch attempt to scrape a living as household skivvy or colonial servant. For Mrs Matthews, the latter is sadly the more plausible.

As well as Dr Fox's glowing testimony, Staveley also encloses the certificates of two doctors: a local physician named Pett, and the distinguished founder of the Medical Society of London, Dr John Coakley Lettsom. Staveley, it seems, had learned his lesson with Clutterbuck and Birkbeck and decided to wheel out a bigger gun. Dr Pett reports visiting Matthews and finding him in 'an infirm state of health arising principally from considerable abscesses in the back' that are still 'in an open and discharging state'. In his opinion, 'a residence of some continuance by the sea side will probably have a favourable influence on his complaint'. As to Matthews' state of mind, Pett reports that 'his manners were uniformly mild and unembarrassed, that he appeared collected, tranquil and intelligent', and adds the now familiar refrain: 'he betrayed no actual existence of a disordered mind'.

Lettsom is no less positive. On his visit he found that Matthews 'expressed himself with clearness, precision and sense', and, moreover, that Matthews recalled meeting him about thirty years earlier, 'of which he reminded me, as well as mentioned the subjects of curiosity in my house, which had engaged his attention'. Thirty years, of course, takes us back to before the Revolution, making this perhaps our first historical glimpse of Matthews, visiting the famous doctor in his house on the hill above Matthews' own Camberwell residence. Matthews, by this time, seems almost impossibly sane; he has presumably had so much practice at impressing his sanity on medical visitors that he can do all this standing on his head. He even ventures his own diagnosis: his abscesses 'he conceived arose from cold taken in Bethlem Hospital, and the manner he took cold, he explained with clearness of mind, and perspicuity of expression'. Lettsom, too, recommends sea air.

Lord Sidmouth notified Bethlem of Staveley's application, and in August received their response. This, too, was an exact reprise of the habeas corpus deposition: a sweeping but bland contradiction of all the above, buttressed once again by the Commissioners in Lunacy, including two who had pronounced on Matthews five years before. Crowther, Haslam and Monro, according to the governors, were all in agreement, 'entertaining no doubt whatever that [Matthews] continued to be altogether mad, and by no means in a state to be at large'. Three of the commissioners visited Matthews at Fox's on 10 August and concluded without elaboration that he was 'in a deranged state of intellect, and wholly unfit to be at large'. Once again, their honorifics, Doctors of Medicine and Fellows of the Royal College of Physicians all, take up several times more space than their diagnosis.

If Sidmouth, coming fresh to Matthews' case, was surprised to receive this bundle of entirely contradictory medical opinions, he doesn't show it. He evinces no interest in the gulf between them, far less in passing judgement on the matter. Once again, the medical arguments are overridden by the duties of state. 'However respectable I may consider the medical certificates which have been now laid before me by Mr. Staveley,' he decides, 'I do not feel that consistently with what is due to the public I can order the liberation of Mr. Matthews.' He wishes to be informed if the assessment of Matthews' mental or physical state changes, but for the meantime 'I find from the records of this office that Mr. Matthews was originally placed and has since been continued under your care as a dangerous lunatic'. In the absence of consensus the previous decision, however confused or flawed, must stand.

There is more sympathy from Sidmouth than there was from Liverpool, and he leaves the door open for further challenges, but by now it is too late. Matthews' physical health had held out for over a year, but in the autumn of 1814 it began to decline for the last time. On 10 January 1815 he died in Fox's London House.

His condition was almost certainly tubercular, and almost certainly terminal when he was released from Bedlam. Here, probably, is another unstated reason why he was allowed to leave so suddenly: Crowther, Haslam and Monro knew what was coming and didn't want his death on their hands. By any standards, under any system and in any era, this is shoddy and cowardly medical behaviour, a dereliction of the most basic duties of care. They have simply, without releasing Matthews, washed their hands of him. His death is not even mentioned in the Bethlem records. It's more than likely, too, that Matthews knew what was coming: his own diagnosis of his condition displays few illusions. As he spent long hours designing flues and heating systems for the new Bethlem, and petitioning the governors with more suggestions, he probably knew it was already too late for him. It surely casts a different light on the near comical obsession and urgency of his architectural masterplans if we consider that he knew the flaws he was attempting to correct were, even as he wrote, literally killing him.

There's extraordinary poignancy, too, in the timing of his death, just at the point where the tide of revolution was about to sweep away the system that had treated him with such cruelty and neglect for so many years. As it turned out, he had already done enough: he would still get to play his starring role and have his triumphant day in court. There is an odd sense in which death is no obstacle for Matthews. So much of his life was played out in the shadows, locked up in jails and asylums, the musings of his fertile mind carried through the world in letters, drawings and second-hand testimonies rather than in person. In the same way his physical death, when it came, had no effect on the momentum of the events he had already set in motion. Perhaps his strange prescience was such that he knew what was going to happen in any case.

But it's still a terrible shame that he didn't live to see it.

When Wakefield's reports on the state of Bedlam surfaced in the press in the summer of 1814, accompanied by the picture of Norris, the governors were stung into at least the appearance of action. They convened a subcommittee, interviewed Monro and Haslam, and published the results of their investigation. Once again, they employed tactics that had been sufficient to swat away Matthews' accusations: a bland, stonewall rebuttal. 'No foundation whatever exists', they asserted, for 'the general charge of cruelty and mismanagement'. The medical and administrative officers were 'creditable to the governors', and the institution as a whole was 'equal if not superior' to any in the country. Bedlam, they reminded the public, was filled with 'absolutely mischievous and dangerous' lunatics, and it was absurd to expect it to be run like a country house hotel. The next spring Haslam and Monro's reappointments, for the twentieth year in a row, went through on the nod.

But Wakefield was still on the march, and when he returned to Bedlam the next year, he did so with a House of Commons select committee in tow. He had lobbied some influential MPs who had a long-standing interest in asylum reform, and the committee had been appointed early in 1815. Now, he found a regime which had been suspiciously sanitized since his last visit. Some of the staff had been sacked, and replacements hired. The women had proper clothes. No-one was chained up, only one man was ill, and the building no longer smelled of mould and fetid effluvia but 'sweet and clean'. But all this was too little too late; Wakefield had a grander agenda than merely putting the current Bedlam regime on its best behaviour. Just as the fall of the Bastille during the French Revolution had been largely symbolic – when it was liberated, only eight prisoners were found inside – so the institution that had long been known as 'England's Bastille' would be the reform movement's great emblematic prize.

In May, Haslam and Monro were among the dozens of witnesses asked to appear before the committee for cross-examination. But before either of them was called, a lengthy statement was read out by one of the last men they would have wished to be given a platform: Richard Staveley. On 3 May he was invited into the session to give a full account of James Tilly Matthews' sixteen years in Bedlam, and the treatment he had received.

This is the first time Matthews' story is presented by a sympathetic voice from beginning to end, including the missing ten years prior to the habeas corpus hearing. Much of it is familiar, but some is new and very illuminating. Staveley tells us that he knew Matthews for the last eight years of his life, had been introduced to his story by Robert Dunbar (who has since died) and had first met him as the habeas corpus affidavits were being assembled in 1809. He tells the committee of Birkbeck and Clutterbuck's opinion that Matthews was sane, but adds an interesting rider: they, along with everyone who knew Matthews, accepted that 'his mind was certainly affected on one point, but that was more a philosophical point, with regard to an Air-Loom system, as to which he fancied there were certain agents employed by the Hospital to annoy him by different modes'. Birkbeck and Clutterbuck were aware of this, but 'were of opinion that if he was removed from that scene, it would cease'.

This is rather a dramatic revision of the controversy of six years before. Haslam has since devoted a book to expostulating his incredulity that two trained doctors could have missed the Air Loom; now it turns out they were perfectly well aware of it. Why didn't they say so? One explanation is the one Staveley gives, that it was merely a 'philosophical point' – rather like believing in fairies, or in an unconventional religion, or perhaps in Barruel and Robison's conspiracy theories. Another, between the lines of their testimony, is that they judged his delusions to be the product of his confinement, and best treated by his release, which in turn would be best expedited by a clean bill of mental health.

But the next surprise drives right to the point. Matthews, Staveley testifies, was the most gentle and tractable patient imaginable, 'so far from interrupting the peace of the house or giving disturbance', he was 'the man to whom all parties, whether patients or servants of the house, if there were any grievances, made their reference for redress'. The serpent in the grass was Haslam who, for no reason Staveley could understand, conceived a 'violent animosity against this man'. This animosity led to the heart of Staveley's evidence to the committee: Matthews had been gratuitously restrained in chains by Haslam for several years.

This took place before Staveley arrived on the scene, but Matthews told him about it many times and his account was confirmed by independent witnesses. Matthews had been 'disputing the authority by which he had been sent there, or Mr. Haslam's authority to treat him in the manner he did', and Haslam had lost his temper. 'You dispute our authority?' he had replied with an unprintable oath; 'Sir, we will soon let you know what our authority is.' The next day, Matthews was leglocked; later, he was handcuffed, and remained so, by all accounts, for at least two years.

This was a dramatic accusation. Of all the governors and staff at Bedlam, Haslam had by far the best credentials as a harbinger of the new dawn. Not only had he been praised by Pinel for his crisp and progressive psychiatric theory, his writings had frequently been cited by the non-restraint movement as a model of professional practice. His rhetorical cry – 'would any rational practitioner, in the delirium of a fever, order his patient to be scourged?' – had since rung from the lips of many a philanthropist and reformer. Had he not called the punishment of lunatics 'disgraceful and inhumane', and hailed 'gentleness of manner and kindness of treatment' as the only true watchwords of any humane and effective system? If this charge against Matthews was vindicated, everything Haslam stood for would be called into question – not just his practice but his theory, and with it his life's work.

Yet a closer reading of Haslam's work suggests that his stand-off with Matthews could easily have come to this. For Haslam, there was no such thing as a 'philosophical point' that didn't count as true madness. All madness was philosophical – 'an incorrect association of familiar ideas', nothing more nor less. As he made clear in *Illustrations of Madness*, there is no room for differences of opinion: madness is not sanity; the gulf between them is the same as that between black and white. Given this truism, no madness can be connived at or ignored; it must be broken, the lunatic's pride fatally wounded. Thus Matthews' refusal to accept Haslam's authority was an insuperable barrier to his recovery, and no progress could be made until Haslam's agenda prevailed over the patient's. It was a battle of wills, and until Matthews' will was broken, Haslam had no choice but to ratchet up the trappings of his authority with, as he put it in his book, 'severity of discipline'.

So we can imagine how the situation might have arisen, but there are still grounds for the accusation that Haslam violated his own prime directive by restraining Matthews as a punishment. Here, his writing gives little room for manoeuvre. It seems that Matthews didn't have a monopoly on overlapping and multiple personalities: Haslam the author and Haslam the apothecary, if Staveley's testimony is to be believed, seem to have defocused and drifted apart from each other. Matthews might have been the victim of such an internal schism, but perhaps he also had a special power to inflict the same on others, even those who thought their will was unbreakable, their mental defences against lunatics impregnable.

Staveley's testimony rolls on through the habeas corpus hearing, adding several details that didn't emerge at the time. The parish officers of Camberwell had applied pressure to the Bethlem Subcommittee, which virtually amounted to an ultimatum, asking them that 'if we are to be burdened with this expense, admitting that he is a madman, are we not authorised to take him, and put him in our own strong room at the workhouse?' The Commissioners in Lunacy, as their standard-issue certificate suggested, had visited Matthews 'I am not certain whether more than once, but I am certain not more than twice, for a very short period of time'. Dr Monro had given Staveley permission to admit Clutterbuck and Birkbeck to interview Matthews, but 'Mr. Haslam afterwards charged me with surreptitiously bringing medical men to see him without the authority of the Hospital'. Staveley has further complaints about Matthews' discharge to Fox's London House: the staff were simply turning a blind eye to their patient's failing health and, once he had been transferred, never came to visit him, 'which I thought was not at all creditable to the Hospital'. Finally, we return to the disputed story of Dunbar's coffee-house meeting with Haslam, in which the apothecary allegedly admitted Matthews' sanity: when first informed of this 'Mr. Haslam sat perfectly still, and never attempted to refute it'.

The cross-examination was short. The committee wanted to know Staveley's impressions of the weekly Bethlem Sub-committee: Staveley told them that he had attended many times, that often only three or four members were present, and that Monro was rarely among them. He confirmed that there were numerous keepers and servants who would back up his allegations that Matthews had been chained, and that the treatment had been unnecessary: 'the invariable answer I received was, that so far from being the disturber of the house, he was the peacemaker'.

When Haslam was called to give evidence a week later, he had a serious case to answer, not just on Matthews but across the board. He had been apothecary for twenty years, the senior staff member in residence, and was in no position to plead ignorance to the charges that had been assembled. Nor did he go after the sympathy vote. His performance, under lengthy and gruelling cross-examination, was truculent, caustic, often plain rude. He brushed off general enquiries about whether he had visited any of the new model Retreats with a blunt 'No'; when pressed, he added acidly that 'I am not in the habit of listening to those with less experience than myself'. He professed to be uninterested in the ramifications of Norris's case, calling him 'the most mischievous patient perhaps that I ever saw'. But the committee pressed hard on the question of restraints, and Haslam eventually offered that he had originally recommended that Norris should be confined un-restrained in two rooms but was 'over-ruled' by the subcommittee and Dr Monro, who sent for a specialist black-smith to make his customized contraption. When asked whether he approved of the eventual result, he replied dismissively that he 'could not recollect'. He claimed never to have seen the famous picture of Norris's restraints.

As the questioning ground on, he began to spray venom far and wide. Restraints were often used, he admitted, because there were not enough keepers, and the majority were intoxicated most of the time. The most astonishing accusations were made against Bryan Crowther, who had died the month before. For the last ten years, Haslam informed the committee, Crowther had been 'generally insane and mostly drunk'. The committee found it hard to believe that the house surgeon had himself been a lunatic for ten years; Haslam coolly replied that 'he was so insane as to have a strait-waistcoat'. He was 'not the master of his own hands' – an alarming charge against a surgeon, and one certainly confirmed by Crowther's signature on Matthews' discharge certificate in 1813 which suggests an advanced case of delirium tremens or Parkinson's disease. Ultimately, Haslam laid the blame for all this at the hands of the governors, who had left the hospital to its own devices, cash-starved and neglected, ever since he had arrived.

But it was on James Tilly Matthews that Haslam faced the most intense interrogation – questions, Haslam became convinced as they were being fired at him, that had come from Matthews himself. Later, he would state that he was well aware that Matthews had built up a huge dossier of grievances against him. It seems that Matthews had even read most of it to him on several occasions, 'pluming himself on the retaliation he could make for the supposed injuries he had received'. Haslam had failed to rise to the bait: let the madman say what he wished, and let 'those who passed for persons of sound mind' draw their own conclusions. Surely they would be able to 'discriminate the transactions of daylight from the materials of a dream'. But once again Haslam has underestimated Matthews, or overestimated those of sound mind. There is a pattern here: Matthews sneaking in telltale details in *Illustrations of Madness* under Haslam's nose, Matthews' designs for the New Bethlem being rewarded and Haslam's being ignored. Now, the committee was unleashing Matthews' mad dossier on Haslam more or less verbatim. The most plausible inference must be that this was part of what changed hands between Matthews and Wakefield during their genial chat on a summer afternoon in Hackney a year before.

First, Haslam is asked his opinion of Matthews. His reply, as short and dry as he can make it, is, 'that he was insane'. Asked for the umpteenth time to expand, he spells out that 'his mental delusion would have produced mischief, if he could have had the liberty to act according to his delusion'. But did his family not promise to keep him from mischief? Haslam admits they did, but that in his view 'nobody could be security for the conduct of a madman'. Why was he kept forcibly in Bethlem when his friends, family and his parish all wanted him released? Haslam's reply is a verbal shrug. Was Matthews restrained at Bedlam? Haslam is vague: 'I believe he once had a pair of handcuffs on, but for a very little while.' How long was he confined in the gallery before having his own cell? Did he not produce designs and drawings once given his own cell? 'He did begin a plan for the Hospital, if I am not mistaken.' The questions continue, the stabbing thrusts of a dagger. Were Matthews' cell windows glazed? At what time was he shut up for the night? Did he have candles? Were his family convinced of his insanity? ('Not in the least.') Was he ever violent? 'I have seen him violent', Haslam maintains, but 'latterly he was extremely cool'. Haslam, for the first time in his testimony, is no longer scathing but on the run: he can see where all this is heading, and is perhaps trying to calculate who else is going to be called in evidence. In any case, he has suddenly decided to say as little as possible, to hope for the best. The effect is striking: the bluster is gone, replaced by furtiveness and perhaps even a small twinge of guilt.

Haslam is followed into the witness chair, which feels increasingly like the dock, by Thomas Monro, who shows far less resilience than Haslam in standing up to the third degree. He claims to have attended the hospital 'three times a week' since his appointment; confronted with the keepers' testimony that they rarely saw him from one month to the next, he admits that by attending he doesn't mean 'going through the hospital', but simply popping in on the governors. 'Going through', he eventually admits, happens only about twice a month. This admission turns out to be a relief, as thereafter he's able to dump all responsibility for the day-to-day running of Bedlam on Haslam: all medical treatment, he claims, is 'generally left to the discretion of Mr. Haslam'. The revised job description Haslam inherited has become a poison chalice: the apothecary now has no greater authority but much more of the suddenly troublesome responsibility. Monro, when pressed, claims that the hospital's medical treatment is simply an inherited regime, and reverts to his father's fatalism: 'the disease is not cured by medicine'.

When asked about the use of restraints, Monro feigns shock: 'No; I have nothing in the world to do with the irons; I never gave orders for the patients to be put into irons in the whole course of my life.' When questioned on his objections to chains and fetters, he replies that they 'are fit only for pauper lunatics: if a gentleman was put in irons, he would not like it'. He is winking, with nervousness verging on desperation, at the fellow gentlemen around the table: I am a patrician like yourselves, my true world is attending private patients. Bedlam is a world I oversee as a charitable duty but if my apothecary treats the paupers cruelly, he does so behind my back. Of course Monro has been troubled by the accusations of cruelty, but his concerns have been rebuffed: 'I mentioned to Mr. Haslam that I thought there might be a diminution of the restraints, but he always mentioned to me that there would be mischief, and that I should be responsible for any accident.'

Monro is retaliating to Haslam's lack of loyalty in his testimony, though Haslam has far better grounds for feeling no loyalty to an institution that has shown none to him. Haslam's criticisms of Monro, too, are better founded than Monro's of Haslam. Compared to Monro's evidence – craven, feeble, dishonest – Haslam's performance acquires a certain retrospective grandeur. In this his high noon, he is the Wild West gunfighter who knows the new railroad is coming through but sees no reason to abandon his outlaw code of honour. Monro, with his transparently half-hearted stab at reinventing himself as a philanthropist of the new wave, has little honour to abandon.

As it happens, neither strategy will make any difference.

In July, the Committee of Madhouses in England published their first interim report. The vast majority of it comprised transcripts of the testimonies they had so far received; their recommendations at this point filled a mere half dozen pages. The most urgent of these, and the reason they brought its publication forward, concerned the new Bethlem, which was already half-built on its site in St George's Fields, but which the committee felt to be inadequate on some very important points that had emerged thus far in the inquiry.

The first of these was that 'the windows were so high as to prevent the patients looking out': the committee were 'struck with the unfitness' of this design, as 'intelligent persons had stated in the course of the examination, that the greatest advantage might be derived from the patients having opportunities of seeing objects that might amuse them'. Matthews was not alone in suggesting this to architects and experts during the building process, but the committee's term 'intelligent persons' is striking: not architects, not doctors, not specifically patients. Did the documents Matthews passed to Wakefield include his architectural notes and designs which the Bethlem governors had rejected as 'irrelevant'?

Whether he did or not, the remainder of the committee's objections to the building concur almost exactly with

Matthews' own. 'In the sleeping apartments the windows are not glazed', an economy that 'deprives the patients of reasonable comfort, and may in cases be really injurious'. Even more importantly, 'there are no flues constructed for the purpose of conducting warm air through the house'. The architects seem to have decided that unglazed and unheated rooms are the way forward for the nineteenth century and beyond, just at the point when the outside world is expressing its amazement that they have survived since the Middle Ages. This is an objection deserving of 'serious consideration'. It's surely one of the basic functions of any building to keep its inhabitants 'properly warmed'.

There are also not enough toilets, and the sewage system underpinning them is inadequate: 'it seems doubtful whether the drain passing under the beds' will suffice to keep them clean. The fetid effluvia, too, must be dealt with by a modern system, and become a thing of the past. Outside the building, there are four acres of grounds which, under the previous arrangement with the government, Bethlem would sell for profit, but which the committee now strongly urges should be kept. They recommend that it should be 'devoted to the general purposes of the Hospital, from a conviction of the benefits the patients derive from exercise, and in many cases from labour'. The extra land would, it seems, be ideal for a kitchen garden.

We can never prove that Matthews smuggled his plans to Wakefield and that it was these which were incorporated into the committee's recommendations, but it hardly seems to matter: here is Matthews' wish-list virtually in full. True, many of these design features had already been incorporated into the York Retreat and were being duplicated in its successors by the time Matthews drew up his original plans, but only one of these, Nottingham Asylum, is cited in support of the committee's proposals, and the advice of the nebulous 'intelligent persons' looms far larger. Matthews, so persistently ignored throughout the last twenty years of his life, seems one way or another to have exerted an unstoppable influence in the few months after his death. Ultimately, he himself would probably have cared less about the authorship of the new designs than the prospect that no patient in the new building would ever again be condemned to suffer the cold and damp he did, and that many fewer would contract chronic tuberculosis or pneumonia as a result.

There was more to come. For Haslam, Matthews was a hungry ghost. The committee were unsatisfied with the contradictions between his testimony and Staveley's, and decided to dig deeper. In March 1816 they summoned James Simmonds, the head keeper at Bedlam since 1799, to give his account of the way Matthews had been treated.

This turned out to be the killer blow. Instilling loyalty in his staff had never been one of Haslam's great skills; in contrast, Matthews had clearly endeared himself to virtually everyone except Haslam. Neither Haslam nor Monro had sought to protect those working under them, and both had to varying degrees blamed drunk and lazy keepers for the worst excesses of the old regime. Simmonds seems also to have made the calculation that Haslam's days were numbered, and that he could now tell tales with impunity. The floodgates were open, and there was nothing to lose from kicking the apothecary when he was down.

'I cannot think Mr. Matthews was treated properly,' Simmonds told the committee. 'He was a gentleman; he had a genteel education, and I did not think he ought to have had the treatment he had, for he would never offend anybody that did not offend him.' Matthews' madness was limited to some odd ideas: 'he used to talk and run on, that he was the emperor of the whole world, but nothing else'. The committee pressed him for the details of Matthews' treatment; Simmonds confirmed that he was chained by the leg 'because he would not submit to the apothecary'. He himself had 'very reluctantly' hand-cuffed Matthews, who was then chained for 'two or three years'. During this time, 'he never went near a bit of fire'; the abscesses he later developed were very likely the result of his deprivations during this period, 'and I believe they were the occasion of his death'. Simmonds confirmed once more that 'the irons were put on him to punish him for the use of his tongue', and his cross-examination came to an end.

A week later, Haslam was hauled back, Simmonds' testimony repeated to him. There was little he could do but stick to his denials, on the unconvincing grounds that Simmonds had been hired only after Matthews had already been in Bedlam for a year, and 'he could know nothing personally of any coercion which Matthews had undergone' at that time. Simmonds, though, is talking not about Matthews' early months but the missing ten years which followed. Haslam also dismissed the suggestion that Matthews' abscesses were caused by his being held in cold and damp conditions, suggesting instead that they were a result of his gardening: 'he stooped considerably, and dug daily', and 'after such exertion complained of pain in his back, and such is the most probable cause of the abscesses with which he was affected'. Matthews' tiny vegetable plot among the ruins was, we are to believe, not his solace but his murder weapon. This is feeble stuff, un-worthy of Haslam, and a testament to how unerringly Matthews has located his Achilles heel. The committee recog-nized it as such, and didn't even bother with a cross-examination.

The new Bethlem opened its doors on 24 August 1815. The 122 lunatics were transported across London in Hackney carriages into a stern-looking building, a neo-classical barracks that had yet to be customized in accordance with the select committee's instructions. According to concerned observers, they 'must have suffered acute discomforts during

The new Bethlem at St George's Fields

their first winter': the windows were still unglazed and an
eccentric steam heating system that had been selected on the
basis of the cheapest tender failed to heat much of the building apart from the basement in which it was installed. The
building still stands, with more modern sections appended,
and now houses the Imperial War Museum. The old Moorfields
building was demolished, to a chorus of belated senti-
mentality: commentators lamented the destruction of 'the last
building in London that looks like a palace'.

Haslam hated the new building, but his tenure in it was to
be brief. By now the date of the annual governors' meeting for
the reappointment of staff was rolling round again, and
Wakefield had both Haslam and Monro in his sights. He
warned the governors privately that if physician and apothecary
kept their posts, he would persist with his public indictments
of Bedlam in the press. On 17 April 1816 Haslam turned up
to defend himself at the governors' meeting, but this was a
different world from the one in which he had lobbied so
successfully twenty years earlier. The boardroom was no
longer home territory: members of the House of Commons

committee had bought themselves onto it, and backroom deals were out of the question. Haslam protested that the committee's investigation had been tendentious and unclear, leaving him 'without precisely knowing against what charges I am to justify myself'; he reminded them that they had exonerated him from precisely the same charges with a ringing endorsement a year before. But the long knives were out. Haslam and Monro had betrayed the governors in their evidence, and now it was the governors' turn to complete the circle. Both motions for re-election were defeated almost unanimously, and both posts declared vacant.

John Haslam was fifty-two, unemployed and disgraced. His writings were discredited, his claim to a new model of professional practice rubbished; even his application for the humble post of apothecary had been rejected. All revolutions require sacrifices, and he had been sacrificed to the new dispensation as surely as Matthews had been to the old.

9

THE INFLUENCING MACHINE

'We cannot find out the use of steam-engines,
until comes steam-engine time'
Charles Fort, *Lo!*, 1931

HASLAM DIDN'T GIVE UP. INSTEAD, WITH A STUBBORNNESS AND persistence even Matthews would have had to admire, he started a counter-revolution.

His first step was to gamble everything on his long-held dream. He had, over the years, amassed a collection of over a thousand books, many of them medical, but some rarities going back to the fifteenth century. He sold the lot at auction, used the proceeds to buy an MD from Marischal College in Aberdeen, and set himself up in private practice from a small house in Bloomsbury.

Business was slow and money was tight. His name was synonymous with his disgrace in the brave new world of asylums, where the reformers were tightening their grip. In 1817 a new Board of Inspection was set up, its members no longer drawn from the Royal College of Physicians but from lay reformers and magistrates. The whole notion of medical involvement in the care of the mad was increasingly under attack: doctors, it was agreed, had little to offer apart from medieval practices such as bleeding and purging, and cure was far more likely to result from humane management in conditions which were as little tainted with the smell of the hospital as possible. Haslam, with time on his hands, kept up a spate of letters and pamphlets warning of the folly of discarding the doctors. Madness was, he continued to insist, a 'corporeal disease', and should remain 'the peculiar and exclusive practice of the medical practitioner'. Whenever the question of madness was debated in press or public, he was there with a response. He wrote open letters to the Lord Chancellor insisting on the necessity of a proper understanding of terms such as 'unsound mind', 'imbecility' and 'lucid intervals' which were becoming ever vaguer in the new reformed discourse. He attacked the new system of restraints, arguing that straitjackets – the favoured method of the York Retreat – were less humane than chains and handcuffs, as they deprived patients of the ability to feed or even scratch themselves. He became the bulldog for a medical profession that had grave reservations about asylum management but lacked the courage to speak out against the new orthodoxy. In 1824, he was voted a member of the Royal College of Physicians.

The most promising chink in the new armour was in the area of medical jurisprudence around the insanity plea. Public opinion was fickle on this point: one week up in arms about a murderer escaping justice by claiming to be of unsound mind, the next outraged that an unfortunate lunatic had been hanged for want of proper medical opinion. Haslam began to offer himself as an expert witness in trials of criminal lunacy, and to use the witness stand to trumpet the necessity of sound medical opinion. But his usefulness was limited by his arrogance, his lack of compunction about insulting judge and jury alike, and certain new complexities that had crept into his view of madness. The old black and white, light and darkness of the *Illustrations of Madness* had been replaced by a grey scale, a gradation from sane to mad which needed to be finely judged by a medical expert. Now none of us was completely sane, and none of them completely mad either. At the trial of a lady called Miss Bagster in 1832, late in his career, he lectured the court at length on this topic, and was interrupted by the judge who asked where exactly the boundary lay, and what exactly constituted a sound mind. Haslam replied acidly, 'I never saw any human being who was of sound mind.' When pressed, he added, 'I assume the Deity is of sound mind, and He alone.'

In 1827 another select committee was appointed to re-examine the question of madhouses. The reformers were pushing further, criticizing the involvement of the College of Physicians and asking for more freedom for private mad-houses set up by religious denominations. Haslam led the counter-attack. The medical understanding of madness was becoming more robust every year, he asserted, and every year the flaws in the reform ideology were becoming more apparent. 'Religious opiates and demulcents' and other 'ghostly therapeutics' had extremely limited power to 'soothe a raving paroxysm, or compose the distractions of mind that are indicated by delusions, morbid hostilities and a propensity to suicide'. Moreover, the violent mad could never be managed without proper restraints, and those who claimed that they could were either allowing their asylums to degenerate into chaos or using more restraints than they were admitting.

He had a point. Religious consolation for the mad had been around for a long time, with little to show for its efficacy: we remember that John Wesley and his fellow preachers were the first to be banned from visiting Bedlam for doing more harm than good. Some asylum reformers were beginning to admit this; others had retreated to the line that a religious framework in asylums was at least beneficial for the staff. Haslam hit a nerve with his accusation that the woolly-minded humani-tarians had bitten off more than they could chew, and that good intentions were not merely inadequate but positively dangerous.

Haslam continued to rage against the asylums through his long old age. At eighty, he was still blasting out warnings that 'the pretension to effect impossibilities' was turning, however inadvertently, into a monstrous cruelty. All it meant was that more lunatics were being confined for longer, with any hope of a cure receding by the year. The reformers called for more money, more resources, more asylums: now, 'it would seem that the inhabitants of county towns do not consider them sufficiently complete and embellished without the ostensible erection of a lunatic hospital, and such abundant provision can only be paralleled by the pious zeal for building new churches'. Confinement, however well intentioned, 'amounts to incarceration', and of the building of asylums there seemed to be no end.

Haslam finally died of 'debility' – old age – in 1844. The next year, legislation was passed requiring every county in England and Wales to build public asylums for pauper lunatics. At the beginning of the nineteenth century, there had been fewer than three thousand patients confined in mad-houses; by the end of the century there would be well over a hundred thousand, of whom less than 10 per cent were expected ever to recover.

If Haslam's later career was remarkable, so too was Matthews' – especially considering that he was already dead. But, once again, death turned out to be no obstacle. As Bethlem's prize exhibit he had met many people during his confinement, told them of the Air Loom and his Omni Imperious status, and shown them his drawings and plans. His visitors had of course told others – how could they resist? His role in the fall of the old Bedlam had been reported in the newspapers; the various strands of his life had been relayed, embellished, confused, garbled, and attached to other stories. The years after his death saw the birth of his final alias: Matthews the urban legend.

The first written source is in the memoirs of a journalist called Robert Humphreys published shortly after the new Bethlem opened. 'Some years ago', we learn, 'an eminent architect went insane, and was for some time an inmate of Old Bethlem'. When, as newspaper readers will remember, the design of the new building was thrown open to competition, and plans were submitted anonymously by members of the public, 'Lo! It was the production of him who had been confined in the old one' which won first prize. Once his fantasy had become bricks and mortar, the mad architect 'was the first to be confined there'.

It's a neat story, and though it has become detached from Matthews – the mad architect isn't named – it's clearly based on an extrapolation or Chinese-whispers memory of his story. And the story and its subject would intertwine again. A letter written in 1820 by Hester Thrale-Piozzi, the long-time confidante and correspondent of Dr Johnson, gives us a snapshot of the way in which Matthews' story was being propagated among the literary establishment. Tantalizingly, we are picking up the thread in the middle of a conversation, and it opens with some references now impossible to decode. 'I am glad you have been amused by Matthews,' Mrs Thrale-Piozzi writes to her friend Mrs Pennington in Bristol. 'Even I, who naturally hate buffoonery, was much diverted by his story of the yellow soap – which Sir George Gibbs never wearied himself with repeating.' (Yellow soap? Here is something that emerges nowhere else in the Matthews story and yet was evidently regarded as priceless gossip – a reminder, if one were needed, that our written records have probably only scratched the surface of Matthews' fertile inner world.) Mrs Thrale-Piozzi proceeds to tell her friend the rest of Matthews' story as she has received it: 'that he planned the fine new Bethlem Hospital just off Westminster Bridge – and requested a particular apartment for himself'; furthermore, that he still 'resides there much respected, and visited by the great mechanics who do nothing without consulting him'.

Here again is the irresistible element of the myth: that having designed the hospital, Matthews now lives there, in a palace within the prison walls. Here is Matthews the lunatic elided with Matthews the architect – but also, strikingly, with Matthews the Omni Imperious. His most cartoonishly mad manifestation, if it was a quasi-magical act of invocation, has worked: his dream that he was emperor of all the world, ruling from his Bedlam cell, has forced open the door to consensus reality. Whether via his discussions with visitors or via Haslam's testimony of his state of mind, his most grandiose self-image has somehow stuck, propagated itself and outlived him. For everyone passing the story on, Matthews lives still, a mad potentate in his Omni Imperious Palace, the greatest architects in the land venturing humbly through the dungeons of Bedlam to supplicate for his advice.

The proliferation of this image is an intimation of the arrival of that great Romantic archetype, the Mad Genius. Matthews was always recognized as an exceptional madman, and as such the question of his madness was problematic and disputed, but there was little sense during his lifetime that his madness was a trivial by-product of his prodigious creative gifts. Now, though, the equation seems almost automatic: if he was mad and talented, then of course he was a genius; we cannot expect our geniuses not to be mad. Like a benign version of Hannibal Lecter, Matthews might need bars to protect the world from his passions, but locked within his mind are treasures we still need to seek out for our own illumination.

In the following decades Matthews' story cut loose again. Writing a year after Haslam's death, the biographer of the architect James Gandon tells the story that his subject worked on the designs for the New Bethlem. To prepare for his work, he made many visits to the old hospital (by now a byword for gothic depravity). He was progressively tormented by nightmares, and by waking visions; gradually, he began to fear that he was going insane. In his frenzy he scribbled out the plans for the new building, in the course of which he developed 'brain fever' and nearly died, before eventually recovering. There is no record of James Gandon actually submitting any designs for Bedlam: this is surely Matthews the mad genius incognito, replaying the image of the plans for the new building spilling frantically from an unhinged mind.

Both Haslam and Matthews set out to be remembered, and both have been, though neither of them very accurately or in ways they would have expected. Haslam, fairly or otherwise, has survived largely as a notorious footnote to medical history, a symbol of the disgraced Bedlam and the dark days before the dawn of humane treatment of the mad. Matthews would surely, given the choice, have sacrificed his nebulous afterglow of misunderstood genius for better treatment during his lifetime, but of the two he would have been by far the happier with his posthumous destiny.

But the great survivor of the story is undoubtedly the Air Loom. At the point when it presented itself to Matthews, the notion of human minds being covertly controlled by machines was an outlandishly novel concept – the talisman of his madness, and the hallmark of his isolation from consensus reality. Today, in the brave new world of electricity and chemistry of which Matthews had such vivid intimations, the notion is no longer novel, and barely even requires explanation: it's familiar to every twelve-year-old who has read comics and watched *The X-Files* or any number of Hollywood movies that turn on the possibility of brainwashing or mind-control devices operated by anyone from aliens to the CIA. What requires explanation today is not the notion itself, but the fact that this now free-floating concept originated in the first place in narratives on psychiatry and madness. The Air Loom and its spectral-cum-mechanical progeny seem destined to survive at least as long as, and maybe longer than, many of the famously defining shifts of its era. We now hear and read frequently, for example, that the old left–right politics, begun during the French Revolution, is on its last legs; in contrast, the Air Loom represents the birth of a modern myth that increasingly permeates our culture.

The Air Loom began its long march into the collective consciousness with the growth of nineteenth-century psychiatry. As the asylum population swelled, and new technologies proliferated from Matthews' shards of prevision into an unmissable dynamic in the culture, psychiatrists became increasingly familiar with the claim that their patients' minds were being manipulated by hidden machines. In 1886 the doctor William Ireland could write that 'the insane are quick to catch at new scientific notions to explain their delusions. Complaints of being electrified and being magnetised against their will have long been common; and since the invention of the telephone, they have said that there are telephones in their rooms, or that people use this instrument to torment them.'

The Air Loom resonates powerfully through the overheated psychiatric literature of the nineteenth century's *fin-de-siècle*. The playwright August Strindberg, during his baroque nervous breakdown, became convinced that there was a concealed electrical machine under his bed which influenced his dreams while he slept. The eccentric London bookseller William Nathan Stedman fixated on the Prime Minister William Gladstone as the incarnation of the Antichrist who 'could see and hear all round the world' and who had covertly commanded the Ripper murders through his 'infernal mesmerism'. One of the most celebrated patients in psychiatric history, Daniel Paul Schreber – on whose case Freud based his diagnosis of paranoia – was assailed by cosmic rays that constantly effected 'miracles' closely parallel to Matthews' 'event-workings': they controlled the minds of those around him and perpetrated terrifying physical tortures on his body (including, in Schreber's case, transforming him into a woman). By the beginning of the twentieth century such fantastical devices had become common enough to merit their own technical term: psychiatrists began referring to them as 'influencing machines'.

The first man to make a systematic investigation of what influencing machines really were, where they came from and what purpose they served was the psychoanalyst Victor Tausk, whose own story is hardly less strange than those he assembled in the course of his researches. Tausk was a highly respected lawyer who had become a judge while still in his twenties before, in 1909, becoming a member of Sigmund Freud's inner circle in Vienna and retraining as a doctor to qualify himself for a new career in psychoanalysis.

From the beginning, the relationship between Tausk and Freud was volatile. Freud had famously rigid expectations of his disciples: they were collaborators on his project, expected to work to his agenda rather than to challenge it. He liked to play with his ideas, often for several years, before publishing them in their definitive form, at which point there should be no dispute about their provenance. Tausk, in contrast, had what Freud regarded as an 'impetuous urge for investigation': he delighted in pushing the envelope, anticipating future developments and leaping into publication with sketches of bold new horizons. He quickly lost patience with Freud's dogged focus on dreams and infantile sexuality and began to pioneer original researches on the psychology of the artist and the philosophical implications of psychoanalysis. For Freud, this was attempting to run before the infant science had yet proved to the world that it could walk. The unstable dynamics of their relationship were exacerbated by the arrival of Lou Andreas-Salome, intellectual dynamo and former love object of Friedrich Nietzsche and Rainer Maria Rilke, who joined the Viennese circle in 1912. Though she was powerfully drawn to

An early 'influencing machine', drawn by a mental patient around 1910

Freud, there was no chance of an intimate relationship: Freud had an ordered married life, and hated emotional complications. Instead, she began a passionate affair with Tausk.

While Freud and his disciples tended to focus on neuroses and personality disorders, Tausk was far more interested in the psychoses, which he saw as the big game of the disordered mind. These categories were still fluid and confusing: Eugen Bleuler's term 'schizophrenia', meaning 'split mind', was still used alongside the older term favoured by his collaborator Emil Kraepelin, 'dementia praecox', or precocious dementia. Generally, too, the condition was classified as a neurosis rather than a psychosis: in Freud's view, it was a 'narcissistic disorder' caused by an infantile obsession with the self. Paranoia, however, was a psychosis: Freud had diagnosed Schreber (at second hand) as the classic case of such subjects, whose minds had begun to manufacture their own realities, in his view through repressed homosexual longing. But he regarded neither paranoids nor schizophrenics as suitable subjects for analysis. They were *unheimlich* – 'uncanny' – and, like delinquents, addicts and perverts, 'unworthy' of psychoanalytic treatment as they rarely responded to its insights. They were also problematic patients: confronting them with the underlying dynamics of their condition often made them worse, and they were a high suicide risk.

Tausk had a different view of what was going on in paranoia and schizophrenia. These people, in his view, were not narcissists, but lacked some vital component of the ego which was required to organize their perceptions and make sense of life in the way everyone else did. This is why psychoanalysis was ineffective: the subject's ego was weak to begin with, and the effect of analysis was usually to make it withdraw further. Such cases became his professional obsession, and the fact that it was peripheral to Freud's project is probably the reason why Tausk, despite his heretical views, managed to stay in the circle for so long. The main source of friction between the two

Victor Tausk

men was by now Tausk's bid for the ultimate accolade within
the circle: to be analysed by Freud himself. He petitioned the
great man in 1913 but was refused, Freud fearing that it
would bring tensions to a head and disrupt the entire project.
Instead, he allocated Tausk to Helene Deutsch, who was herself under analysis with Freud at the time. Deutsch and
Tausk's sessions, unsurprisingly, revolved almost exclusively

around one subject. Tausk's endless ruminations on Freud were reportedly characterized not by anger or frustration, but by a deep sense of grieving and loss.

The watchspring of tension was broken by the Great War, which scattered Freud's circle; Tausk spent much of it in mental hospitals in Belgrade where, among other things, he collected an unprecedentedly large number of influencing machine delusions. He returned to Vienna in 1917 to find the world of psychoanalysis fissured by crises. Many had come to believe that the Vienna Society's dynamics were terminally warped by Freud's own contradictory expectations of his disciples: he demanded obedience of them, but once they had submitted to this intellectual castration he lost respect for them. Pierre Janet, Alfred Adler and Carl Jung had all split from the circle, but Tausk, committed to psychoanalysis but without a body of work that could earn him his freedom, remained. Within months, he delivered his greatest, and last, scientific paper to the Society, on 6 January 1918. It was entitled *On the Origin of the 'Influencing Machine' in Schizophrenia*.

The influencing machine, he announced, is 'a machine of mystical nature'. It is perceived as a machine, but this perception is always hazy at the edges. It has all the trappings of a machine – 'boxes, cranks, levers, wheels, buttons, wires, batteries and the like' – but its functioning always transcends the subject's technical understanding. Just as the Air Loom plans included a vague superstructure of sails and other appendages, and a door to a hidden chamber into which Matthews could never see, so every subsequent influencing machine extends beyond its palpable nuts and bolts into mechanics that remain unknowable. But, for the subject, this is not evidence that the machine is not real: on the contrary, 'all the discoveries of mankind are regarded as inadequate to explain the marvellous powers of this machine, by which the patients feel themselves persecuted'.

The reason subjects believe the machine is real is that it works. It produces a set of effects – Matthews' 'event-workings', Schreber's 'miracles' – they can see, hear and feel, whether they wish to or not. It presents pictures to them, often two-dimensional ones rather than the 3D of typical hallucinations; in 1918, patients typically interpolated a modern machine operation, 'generally a magic lantern or a cinematograph', but we recognize Matthews' pre-cinematic notion of puppet-shows projected into his dreams. The machine forces thoughts and feelings into the brain, and is thus often described as a 'sensation-apparatus'. It even produces physical effects: skin conditions, erections and – a detail particularly suggestive in Matthews' case – abscesses. These effects are often ascribed by the subject to 'air-currents, electricity, magnetism or X-rays', but such rationales are in truth gauzy screens for unconscious processes that can only be understood in this way because they are independent of the conscious mind, 'strange to the patient himself'.

The function of the machine is to persecute the subject, and it is 'operated by enemies': for every Air Loom, there is a gang. Tausk declares that 'to the best of my knowledge, these are exclusively of the male sex' (the Glove Woman, Augusta and Charlotte could have enlightened him). The way in which the machine is operated is, like its internal workings, usually shadowy – 'buttons are pushed, levers set in motion, cranks turned' – and the operators, like their machine, are shrouded in an obscurity that prevents the whole picture from being laid bare.

Tausk's view is essentially that the influencing machine is a projection the subject produces, without volition, to satisfy 'the need for causality inherent in man'. These things are happening; I am unaware of how they are happening; my brain provides a ready explanation from the materials it has to hand. For some, the frame is God and cosmic conflict, for others, it is technology – not real technology, but often a canny reading of where technology seems, or perhaps wishes, to be heading. Other patients, though, dispense with any explanation, suffering the same effects 'of emotional changes and strange apparitions within the physical and psychic personality, without the intervention of any foreign or hostile power'. Thus the influencing machine doesn't reveal a special type of disorder, but rather conceals underlying similarities with other disorders which lack the machine apparatus.

Ultimately, the influencing machine points to an underlying confusion between real events that are taking place in the outside world and internal events that live only in the subject's mind. For Tausk, as a psychoanalyst (even if a renegade one), this confusion is rooted in early childhood. The infant gradually discovers a world beyond breast and parents, a world in which these things are not constructed entirely for his or her benefit but have an independent existence in an outer realm. The healthy infant comes to integrate these perceptions by making a distinction between the outside world and its internal thoughts. But the paranoid schizophrenic, as this category of disorder would come to be known, doesn't fully learn this distinction. Consensus reality and mental projections never entirely separate, the boundaries between the internal and external worlds remain porous, and external causes are inserted to make sense of mental events. What the influencing machine finally stands for is the subject's own body, a mechanical (and thus phallic) projection of their internal mechanisms into the outer world.

Tausk's paper was felt by some to be remarkable, but for Freud it was at best a glittering and seductive sideshow, a distraction from the main prize. Tausk soon realized that he too must leave the circle, but he agonized over the necessity to murder the father. He ended his analysis, fell in love, and made the painful decision to marry and, at the age of forty, start a new life. But, ultimately, he couldn't find the strength to do so. On 2 July 1919 he committed suicide with clinical firmness, shooting and hanging himself simultaneously. His suicide note was, of course, written to Freud, and presented an entirely rational act. 'I have no melancholy,' he wrote. 'My suicide is the healthiest, most decent deed of my unsuccessful life . . . I am only dying somewhat earlier than I would have died naturally.' He left instructions that all his papers should be destroyed. It took a full day to burn them.

Freud's obituary for Tausk, published just as he was beginning to formulate his theory of the death instinct, was the longest he ever wrote; but the truth was that Tausk's end was a relief, and Freud rarely spoke of him again. Most of the second generation of Freudians, in England and America, lived and died without ever hearing Tausk's name. Nor was his work destined to live on in the broader world of psychiatry. As evidence began to accumulate that schizophrenia was a condition with physical underpinnings, attention shifted towards attempts to explain it through organic causes rather than psychodynamic processes. In a sense, the professional discourse moved not into uncharted waters but back into something much closer to what Haslam had proposed: since we are talking about a physical disease, there is nothing to be learned from the fevered sufferers' ramblings. As the biological basis of some mental disorders became more clearly understood, there followed abundant examples of the cruelty of blaming personality and upbringing for physical conditions such as autism or insanities brought on by illnesses such as thyroid problems, brain tumours or George III's probable porphyria. Childhood trauma and arrested emotional development seemed to have limited explanatory powers for the psychoses: Matthews is perhaps a case in point, since we know nothing of his early life but can locate much of the world of the Air Loom in his adult crises. As the new paradigm took hold, the study of schizophrenia moved away from Tausk's insights and into a new world dominated by neuroanatomy and medication.

*

But the new world produced ever more influencing machines, and their origin and meaning became no clearer. Diagnostic categories sharpened up, new drugs appeared, new treatments such as electro-convulsive therapy, insulin coma and pre-frontal lobotomy came and went. Many subjects' conditions were relieved, many more found their febrile inner worlds traded for the blankness of a chemical or surgical cosh, but their mystical machines refused to come into clinical focus. Even today, few expect that neurochemistry and genetics will ever be able to tell us why some subjects frame their delusions in terms of imaginary machines: this is a question not about the forms of madness but their content, and thus subject to environmental factors rather than organic ones. Given the relentless flood of psychotic disorders twentieth-century psychiatrists had to treat and manage, it's hardly surprising that they felt they had more important priorities than to sit around speculating on the meaning of influencing machine delusions.

Nevertheless, a new window of understanding was being opened up – not by the doctors, but by the patients. As people diagnosed with schizophrenia began to tell their own stories, the template of the Air Loom became more and more familiar. Remarkable among the wave of first-person narratives of delusional psychoses was the pseudonymous Barbara O'Brien's book *Operators and Things*, published in 1958. O'Brien, like Matthews, seems to have been driven mad by politics – in her case, office politics. A successful corporate manager, she became increasingly horrified by the ways in which her male colleagues manipulated one another, jostling for promotions with dirty tricks and cruel mind-games, while she was expected to spend every day watching grown men surreptitiously tearing each other to pieces and pretend it wasn't happening. One morning she awoke to find three ghostly figures standing at the foot of her bed and announcing that they were 'operators', controlling beings who manipulated human minds ('things') without their hosts' knowledge. They began to take over her life, directing her to hop on a Greyhound bus and travel across the States while various gangs of operators fought internecine feuds inside her head for control of their 'experiment'. The gangs, as we may expect, had their Air Looms: 'stroboscopes', which enabled them to influence her mind from a distance.

The experience was terrifying, but also shot through with almost inexplicable flashes of prescience. Not previously a spontaneous person, she began to have 'hunches' of unerring accuracy, the operators seemingly steering her on a charmed course over obstacles she would normally have found insurmountable. O'Brien recovered spontaneously: after six months, the operators dumped her in a psychoanalyst's office and left her in peace. As the dust settled, she came to believe that the world of operators and things had been analogous to a movie directed and screened by one part of her unconscious mind to keep her occupied while another part quietly set about repairing the trauma that, unknown to her, was poised to tear her apart irreparably.

Simultaneously, too, such narratives began to spill out into popular culture in contexts far removed from psychiatry. Many of the earliest stories from flying saucer contactees, the founding myths of the mass-market UFO phenomenon, revolve around alien influencing machines, the Air Loom now in orbit. We hear of brainwashing, reprogramming of minds via cosmic rays, alien wires hooked into subjects' heads to capture their thoughts, magnetic implants identical to the one Matthews located in his own brain shortly after his admission to Bedlam. Richard Shaver, whose tales caused a sensation when first published as fact in the sci-fi magazine *Amazing Stories*, told of subterranean humanoid gangs who had been influencing his mind by 'electronic surveillance, through mind-contacting and mind-influencing machinery'. Approaching these tales from our perspective invites the rather worrying conclusion that

The Air Loom in orbit

many are neither alien encounters nor colourful hoaxes but psychotic episodes – but also, by the same token, the rather heart-warming realization that some who are visited with such conditions can process them effectively, if bizarrely, without needing to be medicated, locked up or lobotomized.

Parallel to these Air Loom Gangs in sci-fi drag,

neurophysiology was producing a suggestive trickle of results that seemed to point to the possible reality of mind control. During the 1940s Dr Grey Walter developed EEG brain topography, and attempted to map the images and structures he found onto machine automata; around the same time, Wilder Penfield discovered that electrodes implanted in the brain could stimulate specific memories and sensations. Within the new paradigm of cybernetics, the brain might be conceived as a circuit-board that could be rewired, a computer that could be reprogrammed or a radio that could be tuned to distant signals. But although these experiments are still cited by true believers as harbingers of real-life Air Looms, they serve if anything to underline how far away we are from being able to transmit thoughts or compulsions from a distance. Penfield himself believed that his work entirely eliminated the possibility of mind control: even with the most intrusive technique imaginable – electric needles stuck directly into the cortex – sensations could at best be prompted haphazardly rather than transmitted or compelled. Even today's blue-sky researchers such as Michael Persinger, a professor at Laurentian University in Canada who has demonstrated the remarkable potential of strong magnetic fields across the temporal lobes to elicit complex hallucinations, provide no framework for the targeted communication of thoughts or commands from a distance.

But the science of mind control received a defining boost from the CIA during the Cold War. Alarmed at press reports that American soldiers had been 'brainwashed' by obscure black arts of Korean military science, the agency funded a long-running series of covert projects intended to produce techniques for disorientating, rendering amnesiac and repro-gramming animal and human subjects either against their will or without their knowledge. Many of these projects were shockingly cruel, little more than torture, and the results were kept silent for decades until forced into the open by the

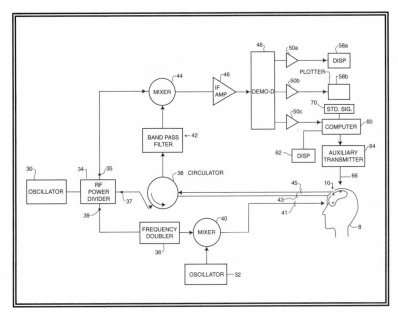

Blueprint for a mind-control device, available on the internet

statutory declassification of documents. These revealed little we didn't already know. Drugs and electric shocks can scramble brains and produce amnesia and irreparable cerebral damage, but are poor at forcing unwilling subjects to tell the truth, and at implanting specific false memories and subconscious commands. Hypnosis can confuse people, but it can't coerce them. The paradigm drawn from contemporary technologies – that the brain might be programmable like a computer, tunable like a radio or rewirable like a junction box – seemed to be a metaphor with limits. Neurochemistry was by now proposing that the brain was less like a machine than a gland, messily organic, obscurely self-regulating within a hormonal soup.

The CIA research was above top secret, but notions of brainwashing and covert military operations were humming through the culture around it, and providing potent ammunition for fictions of conspiracy and control. The most enduring was *The Manchurian Candidate*, a story that, in the novel by Richard Condon and subsequent film, revived James Tilly Matthews' messy collision of mesmerism and politics. The story turns on the possibility that a hypnotized or brain-washed subject may be unconsciously implanted with an instruction – say, to assassinate a political leader – which can be triggered by a signal of which the subject himself is un-aware. Thus a military power may have at its disposal human time-bombs, innocent citizens incapable of giving them-selves away yet primed to respond to their puppet-masters' signal: kiteing and brainsaying for the Cold War age.

The Manchurian Candidate was well-judged satire, pitched into a liminal space where few could confidently deny its premise, and it still informs a disputed territory of fiction and belief. Theories based on its truth proliferate in conspiracy literature and on the internet, and the historically minded among their proponents have repeatedly pointed to James Tilly Matthews as mind control's first victim. Given the assumption that the CIA's mind-control experiments worked (and are still working), Matthews' case fits like a glove. He was exposed to an experimental mesmeric programme during the French Revolution while it was also being used to direct the Paris mobs; the hidden hands were intending to brainwash the British people in the same way. But he escaped the cage, and was locked up as insane by a British government that was, as Matthews himself always insisted, complicit in the secret war. The Air Loom was the mind-control prototype, Matthews the first in a long line of voices to speak out against the covert hijacking of power by a technocratic elite, and to be brutally silenced.

In the years after *The Manchurian Candidate*, the influenc-ing machine became a vehicle for other distinctive fictions, the most influential author of which was Philip K. Dick. Dick combined the profession of prolific hack writing with an intense and hypochondriacal fascination with psychotic dis-orders: he diagnosed himself both paranoid and schizophrenic at various times, included schizophrenic characters in his novels, and late in life was visited by a series of visionary episodes which he struggled with courage and insight to incorporate into his understanding of the world at large. His science fiction novels and short stories, now familiar from endless Hollywood adaptations and borrowings, play out dogged iterations of the notion that consensus reality is in fact the construction of some form of influencing machine: a covert military simulation designed to test our behaviour, a set of memories generated artificially to force our conformity to a hidden agenda, a consumer fantasy sold to us by megacorporations or mind-reading extraterrestrials. Dick himself eventually came to believe that the universe was a giant projection of an über-influencing machine, equally imaginable as computer, alien intelligence or God. For him, as for the eighteenth-century satirists, the world was a great Bedlam, but it was also the event-workings of an infinitely huge Air Loom.

From this point on, it would be a massive undertaking to follow the routes the notion of the influencing machine has followed, criss-crossing through conspiracy subculture, mass entertainment, tabloid rumour, delusional confession, artful fiction and urban legend. But it would also be unnecessary. The reason why the machine that controls the mind has emerged from the far shores of madness to become a new myth for our times is neither the real-life science of mind control nor the genius of fiction-writers nor the endless amplification and recycling of such ideas through the mass media and the Hollywood dream machine. All these are symptoms, not causes; the idea resonates because we ourselves are finally ready for the Air Loom. Its world is now ours, filled with rays, ethers, beams, particles and gases we barely understand, powering inscrutable machines that project shadow worlds into our minds from unseen basements and cellars. Television, radio, phone, computer: all act from a distance, transmit images and messages, stimulate our senses and minds with precision, intelligence and cool persistence. We live cocooned in an invisible magnetic web; like Tausk's subjects, we all experience a third level of reality intermediate between the outside world and the inside of our heads. Two-dimensional realities assail us constantly, blurring the line between what we have actually experienced and what we have simply imagined. No wonder we respond to stories that attempt to negotiate this new dispensation for us, and offer myths and metaphors, trivial or profound, to teach us how to contemplate the loom and become acquainted with the gang.

James Tilly Matthews was not a prophet. He was a gifted, perhaps fragile individual who suffered intensely, and for little if any reward. If any group were to claim him as a posthumous hero, it should really be the peace movement, or those campaigning for the humane treatment of the mentally ill, rather than any postmodern cultural theorist. It's impossible to hear his story without feeling sympathy for him, and if we sympathize with him we must also find it tragic that he was ever forced to the point where the Air Loom manifested itself. It took many years of betrayal, injustice, neglect and cruelty, compacting him with almost unimaginable pressure, to turn his burning coals of anger, confusion and frustration into a diamond of madness, whose facets he cut with great skill to reflect scenes that still mesmerize, yet still burn almost too fiercely for us to gaze upon. But to turn this diamond under the light is not to collude in his suffering: he would have wished us to look at it, not to look away. Etched into it is not only the story of his own life and convulsive times, but a faint image of something more. It's almost as if he, or some part of his mind, had been opened up to the dream of the machine itself, and its crazy hunch about its own evolution.

You used to have to be mad to see it, but now, finally, the Air Loom is starting to come into focus for the rest of us.

BIBLIOGRAPHY

Alleridge, Patricia, *Bethlem Hospital 1247–1997 A Pictorial Record* (Phillimore and Co. 1997)

Andrews, Jonathan; Briggs, Asa; Porter, Roy; Tucker, Penny and Waddington, Keir, *The History of Bethlem* (Routledge 1997)

Archives des Affaires Etrangères, Paris: *Correspondences Politiques – Angleterre, Volumes 586–589 (1793–6)*

Bethlem Royal Hospital Archives: *James Tilly Matthews (Box 61 [8], Box D23)*

——*James Tilly Matthews' Plans for the New Bethlem Hospital: The Deuce Take It (1811)*

——*Minutes of Bethlem Building Subcommittee, etc.*

——*Minutes of Bethlem Governors' Subcommittee 1797–1815*

Burke, Edmund, *Reflections on the Revolution in France* (Penguin 1968)

Byrd, Max, *Visits to Bedlam: Madness and Literature in the Eighteenth Century* (University of South Carolina Press 1974)

Carpenter, Peter K., 'Descriptions of Schizophrenia in the Psychiatry of Georgian Britain: John Haslam and James Tilly Matthews', in *Comprehensive Psychiatry*, vol. 30, no. 4, 1989

Coyle, Mike, 'The Influencing Machine' in *MindNet Journal*, Vol. 1, #90, 1996

Crosland, Maurice, 'The Image of Science as a Threat: Burke vs. Priestley and the "Philosophic Revolution"', in *British Journal for the History of Science*, 1987, 20, 277–307

Crowther, Bryan, *Practical Remarks on Insanity, to which is added a Commentary on the Dissections of the Brains of Maniacs, with some account of Diseases Incident to the Insane* (London 1811)

Cruden, Alexander, *The London Citizen Exceedingly Injured . . .* (T. Cooper, London 1739)

Darnton, Robert, *Mesmerism and the End of the Enlightenment in France* (Harvard University Press 1968)

Digby, Anne, *Madness, Morality and Medicine: A Study of the York Retreat* (Cambridge University Press 1985)

Doyle, William, *The Oxford History of the French Revolution* (Oxford University Press 1989)

Dybikowski, J., *On Burning Ground: An examination of the ideas, projects and life of David Williams* (The Voltaire Foundation at the Taylor Institution, University of Oxford 1993)

Edwardes, Michael, *The Dark Side of History: Subversive Magic and the Occult Underground* (Corgi 1980)

Fara, Patricia, *An Entertainment for Angels: Electricity in the Enlightenment* (Icon Books 2002)

Forrest, Denys, *Tea for the British* (Chatto & Windus 1973)

Forrest, Derek, *Hypnotism: A History* (Penguin 1999)

Foucault, Michel, *Madness and Civilisation* (Routledge 1989)

Friedman, Barton R., *Fabricating History: English Writers on the French Revolution* (Collins 1988)

Goldstein, Jan, *Console and Classify: The French Psychiatric Profession in the Nineteenth Century* (University of Chicago Press 1987)

Hampson, Norman, *The Enlightenment: An Evaluation of its Assumptions, Attitudes and Values* (Pelican Books 1968)

Hansard: *Parliamentary Debates*, Vol. XXXII (27/5/1795–2/3/1797)

Haslam, John, *Illustrations of Madness* (1810, repr. Routledge 1988, with an introduction by Roy Porter)

——*Observations on Insanity: with Practical Remarks on the Disease, and an Account of the Morbid Appearances on Dissection* (F. & C. Rivington, London 1798)

——*Observations on Madness and Melancholy* (J. Callow, London 1809)

Hibbert, Christopher, *The French Revolution* (Penguin 1982)

Horrobin, David, *The Madness of Adam and Eve: How Schizophrenia Shaped Humanity* (Bantam Press 2001)

House of Commons: *Report from the Committee of Madhouses in England* (11 July 1815)

Howard, Robert, 'James Tilly Matthews in London and Paris 1793: His First Peace Mission in His Own Words', in *History of Psychiatry*, vol. 2, 1991

——'Useful or Useless Architecture? A Dimension of the Relationship between the Georgian Schizophrenic James Tilly Matthews and his Doctor, John Haslam', in *Psychiatric Bulletin*, 1990, 14, 620–622

——'A Lesson from the History of Psychiatry: Competitive Tendering for Services and Defective Central Heating Systems in Georgian New Bethlem', in *Psychiatric Bulletin*, 1991, 15, 566–568

Howells, John G. (ed.), *The Concept of Schizophrenia: Historical Perspectives* (American Psychiatric Press Inc. 1991)

Ingram, Allan, *Voices of Madness: Four Pamphlets 1683–1796* (Sutton Publishing 1997)

Jamison, Kay Redfield, *An Unquiet Mind: A Memoir of Moods and Madness* (Picador 1995)

Jennings, Humphrey, *Pandaemonium: The Coming of the Machine as Seen by Contemporary Observers* (Andre Deutsch 1985)

Kottmeyer, Martin S., 'Alienating Fancies: The Influencing Machine Fantasy in Ufology', in *Magonia*, #49 & 50, 1994

Landis, Carney (ed.), *Varieties of Psychopathological Experience* (Holt, Rinehart & Winston 1964)

Mander, Jerry, *Four Arguments for the Elimination of Television* (Morrow Quill 1978)

Maniquis, Robert M., 'Holy Savagery and Wild Justice: English Romanticism and the Terror' in *Studies in Romanticism*, Fall 1989, 28, 3, 365–395

Marks, John, *The Search for the 'Manchurian Candidate': The CIA and Mind Control* (W. W. Norton 1981)

Masters, Anthony, *Bedlam* (Michael Joseph 1977)

Matthews, James Tilly, *Useful Architecture* (S. Bass, London 1812)

Melechi, Antonio, *Fugitive Minds: On Madness, Sleep and Other Twilight Afflictions* (Heinemann 2003)

Moffett, Cleveland, *The Reign of Terror in the French Revolution* (Ballantine Books 1962)

O'Brien, Barbara, *Operators and Things: The Inner Life of a Schizophrenic* (Elek Books 1960)

O'Donoghue, E.G., *The Story of Bethlehem Hospital from its Foundation in 1247* (T. Fisher Unwin 1914)

Parry-Jones, William, *The Trade in Lunacy: A Study of Private Madhouses in England in the Eighteenth and Nineteenth Centuries* (Routledge & Kegan Paul 1972)

Pinel, Philippe, *Treatise on Insanity* (tr. D.D. Davis, Sheffield 1806)

Porter, Bernard, *Plots and Paranoia: A History of Political Espionage in Britain 1790–1988* (Unwin Hyman 1989)

Porter, Roy, *English Society in the Eighteenth Century* (Penguin 1982)

——*Mind-Forg'd Manacles* (Athlone Press 1987)

——*A Social History of Madness: Stories of the Insane* (Phoenix Giant Press 1987)

Prickett, Stephen (ed.), *England and the French Revolution* (Macmillan 1989)

Roazen, Paul, *Brother Animal: The Story of Freud and Tausk* (Allen Lane/Penguin Press 1969)

Roberts, J.M., *The Mythology of the Secret Societies* (Secker & Warburg 1972)

Robison, John, *Proofs of a Conspiracy* (1798, reprinted Western Islands 1967)

Royle, Edward, *Revolutionary Britannia? Reflections on the Threat of Revolution in Britain 1789–1848* (Manchester University Press 2000)

Russell, David, *Scenes from Bedlam: A History of Caring for the Mentally Disordered at the Bethlem Royal Hospital and the Maudsley* (Baillière Tindall 1997)

Schama, Simon, *Citizens: A Chronicle of the French Revolution* (Penguin 1989)

Scull, Andrew, *The Most Solitary of Afflictions: Madness and Society in Britain 1700–1900* (Yale University Press 1993)

——with MacKenzie, Charlotte and Hervey, Nicholas, *Masters of Bedlam: The Transformation of the Mad-Doctoring Trade* (Princeton University Press 1996)

Siegel, Ronald K., *Whispers: Voices of Paranoia* (Crown Publishers, New York 1994)

Tausk, Victor, 'On the Origin of the Influencing Machine in Schizophrenia', in *Psychoanalytic Quarterly*, vol. 2, 1933

Tench, Watkin, *Letters from Revolutionary France* (1796, reprinted University of Wales Press 2001)

Thomas, P.D.G., *The House of Commons in the Eighteenth Century* (Clarendon Press 1971)

Thompson, E.P., *The Making of the English Working Class* (Penguin 1963/1991)

Thorne, R.G., *The House of Commons 1790–1820* (History of Parliament Trust/Secker & Warburg 1986)

Tuke, Samuel, *Description of the Retreat: An Institution near York for Insane Persons of the Society of Friends* (1813, reprinted Process Press 1964)

Turner, T.H., 'Schizophrenia as a Permanent Problem: Some aspects of the historical evidence in the recency (new disease) hypothesis', in *History of Psychiatry*, vol. 3, part 4, no.12, 1992

Williams, David, *Autobiography: Incidents in my own Life which have been considered of Some Importance* (1810, reprinted University of Sussex 1980, ed. Peter France)

Williams, David, 'The Missions of David Williams and James Tilly Matthews to England (1793)', in *English Historical Review*, vol. 53, 1938

——'Un Document Inedit Sur La Gironde', in *Annales Historiques de la Révolution Française*, vol. 15, 1938

INDEX

Air Loom: construction, 10–11; effects, 11–14, 17–19, 173–4, 178–9, 284–5; 'event-workings', 173–4, 178, 204, 207, 278, 284; gang, 18, 174–6, 182–3, 201–3, 206, 207–8, 210, 222, 284; Haslam's description, 74–5, 169, 172–7, 178–9, 258; idea of, 277–8; illustration, 170–1; motive force, 11, 145, 172–3; origins, 200–1; as paranoid delusion, 24, 203–4; plans, 170–1, 274, 283; as reality, 27, 203–4; testimonies on, 74–5, 258

Andreas-Salome, Lou, 279, 281

Augusta, 175, 284

Aulard, Alphonse, 115

Aust (Under-Secretary of State), 110

Baldwin, Richard, 77

Barruel, Augustin de, 198–9, 200, 258

Battie, William, 39, 49

Belcher, William, 65

Bentham, Jeremy, 91, 246

Bergasse, Nicholas, 151–2

Bethlem Hospital (Bedlam): admission policy, 22–3; criticisms of, 39; designs for, 215–25, 227–31, 255–6, 265–7; Governors Subcommittee, 57–8, 260, 261; history, 28–32; magnetic influences, 155; Moorfields building, 32–4, 39, 211–13, 269, 274; new building, 213–15, 247, 265–6, 268–9; number of patients, 40, 212; public spectacle, 35–8, 39; records, 255; regime, 34–5, 39–41, 247–8, 257, 274; staff, 34, 267; Wakefield's investigation, 247–50, 256–7, 269

Bevans, John, 236

Bicêtre Hospital, 241–2

Bill the King, 18, 175, 194